Martha

8 40

W9-BFG-022

A Soul's Journey

Reincarnation, Karma, and Past Life Memories of the Holocaust

A Healing Guide for Your Spiritual Self

A SOUL'S JOURNEY

Empowering the Present

Through Past Life

Regression

JEANNE AVERY

BORU BOOKS

Austin, Texas

A Soul's Journey: Empowering the Present Through Past Life Regression © 1996 by Boru Publishing with Jeanne Avery

All rights reserved. No part of this publication may be used, reproduced or transmitted in any form or by any means, electronic or mechanical, including photocopy, recording, or any information storage and retrieval system now known or to be invented, without permission in writing from the publisher, except by a reviewer who wishes to quote brief passages in connection with a review written for inclusion in a magazine, newspaper, or broadcast.

Library of Congress Catalog Card Number: 96-85199

ISBN 1-887161-12-0

Published in the United States by
Boru Publishing, Inc.
12004-B Commonwealth Way
Austin, TX 78759

Distributed to the trade by
National Book Network, Inc.
4720 Boston Way
Lanham, MD 20706

Boru Books are available in quantity for promotional or premium use. For information on discounts and terms, please write to Director of Special Sales, Boru Publishing, Inc., 12004-B Commonwealth Way, Austin, Texas 78759.

Designed by Marysarah Quinn

Manufactured in the United States of America

98   97   96   5   4   3   2   1

Dedication

To my two Pisces mothers, now in spirit form; my angelic birth mother, Lucy, and my adored Missy, known to my children as "Granny," both strong and extraordinary southern women. My two "steel magnolias" insisted on intellectual accomplishments and encouraged creative expression, especially in my music. Most of all, they stressed the importance of expansion of the heart and growth of the mind.

To my dear friend, Peter Cooper, who has recently departed from the earth plane—a fellow traveler and heart-connected friend forever and to his beautiful wife, Mary, who holds an equally huge space in my heart.

To the gracious gentleman, Adam Jung, who made it possible for me to write amidst the serenity and beauty of his marble villa in Ibiza, Spain. And to a newly refound friend (no doubt my past life associate in riotous, good fun), Adrienne Papp, who facilitated my being in that special environment with the Mediterranean at my feet and just down the cliffs from my computer.

To my editor, Nan Gatewood, who has guided me and held my hand through all five books, and to her baby who will be born at the same time as *A Soul's Journey*. To Ann Weems, Sally Arteseros, and Cindy Clark who added special editorial support—my deepest thanks.

To the most wonderful and loyal secretary/associate one could hope to have—Linda Wendover.

To Uttara McGhee.

To my Ibiza friends who gave aid and comfort in so many ways throughout the gestation of this book—an emotional and heartwrenching time. To my Ibiza "families" Mac and Trudy Adams, Sally and Bartolo Noguera, and my adopted "kids," the Noguera children—Carlos, Carolina, and Elena; the Von Ryckevorsels, and my "family" in Spain, Juan de Aguirre and Magdalena.

My gratitude goes back in years to friends who have helped me in many ways and throughout difficult times—especially Marilyn Rothkopf, a friend and sister from our early twenties. Among many others, special mention goes to Casey, Marsha and Walter Arnheim; Kay and Ken Chapin; Sicily Williams; Clark Johnson; Sam Green; Gerda and Stan Cooke. To all my extended family— the Truaxs, the Normans, the Henesys, the Millers; and the Strasbergs, Susan and Jennifer. To many wonderful friends.

To the healers who have energized me when the spirit was overloaded—Dr. Richard Blasband, Sigmund Bereday, Karen Bolander, Dr. Byron Gentry, my darling Swami Chakradhari, and most recently Nicolai Levashov, physicist and master healer whose book, *The Final Appeal to Mankind* will be published in early 1997.

And always to my adored children—Sharon, Diane, and David—and my fabulously gifted grandchildren—Charles and Stephanie Andrews, and Lucas and Charlotte Jane Henesy. To Lori and Lee.

We have all walked together throughout many lives. For that I'm grateful.

Jeanne Avery
June 1996

TELL YE YOUR CHILDREN OF IT,

AND LET YOUR CHILDREN TELL THEIR CHILDREN,

AND THEIR CHILDREN ANOTHER GENERATION

Joel 1:3

Contents

Foreword

A Soul's Journey is an important book. I am not surprised because Jeanne Avery has written important books before this one. To do so again, at this critical point in human history as the twentieth century is ending, has to be as gratifying and pleasing to Jeanne as it is to us, her readers.

The book's message unfolds on at least three levels. The first is the level of the individual, his or her personal understanding, health and evolution. I have been using regression therapy in my psychiatric practice for the past fifteen years. I use hypnosis, although Jeanne's method, where the patient remains more conscious, is every bit as acceptable. More than thirteen hundred patients of mine have remembered vivid childhood, in utero, or past life scenes. Others have had intense spiritual experiences. Many have witnessed their psychological and physical symptoms resolve as the childhood or past life roots of their current problems have been identified. As the past life recall is integrated into their current life understanding, patients feel more peaceful and experience more joy in their lives.

In addition, many of my patients have recognized present day loved ones while scanning the vistas of their past lives. Reconnecting with such soulmates or soul companions, and we all have more than one, can be a powerful learning experience. In our physical bodies we learn primarily through our relationships. Reunions with soulmates can be very dramatic, and I have described these meetings in detail in my books.

The second level is that of the community, whether small or large. Our individual karma must intersect and influence the individual karmas of others in our groups, our communities, our nations. We are all rowing the same boat. We are all connected; we are all mutually interdependent. What we do affects everyone and everything.

The Holocaust was one of the worst nightmares in our history. Jeanne skillfully documents its lasting effects on various individuals, groups, and cultures—whether Jewish, German, or Other. Yet we see, as I have similarly seen in my regression work, Jews returning as Germans, Nazis coming back as Jews, and other permutations. We are here to learn, and to do that we must learn from all sides. We come back to experience directly the fruits of our actions.

I frequently point out to people that we cannot shrug off the global consequences of thermal warming, of ozone layer depletion, of the elimination of whole species and the resulting chaos in the balance of nature, of over-fishing and over-farming as the world's population increases, or of widespread pollution. It is not only our children and grandchildren who will be born into such a noxious environment. We are coming back, too.

The third level is that of human consciousness. As the soul progresses it must shed negative thoughts and emotions. We have incorporated the fears and prejudices of others as we have traveled through lifetimes. These must be unlearned. Qualities such as fear, hatred, violence, greed, anger, and worry need to be released. Underneath these negative traits are the positive ones: love, hope, faith, harmony, compassion, understanding, patience, and balance.

This raising of consciousness is happening, although slowly. It is the best hope for mankind. Teachers such as Jeanne Avery help to hasten the process, and I hope that she continues to write, encouraging spiritual transformation.

Brian L. Weiss, M.D.
Miami, Florida
July 1, 1996

Introduction

I HAVE BEEN doing regression sessions with my clients since 1967, but it is only since 1987 that people have come forth with information about a life lived in Nazi Germany. Of all the myriad of memories that have emerged from the consciousness of my clients from the beginning of my experience with past life regression, I chose to connect a book about a search for the soul and its journey to past life memories of Nazi Germany. I had two good reasons before beginning the book, but a deeper reason became clear while I was writing the manuscript.

I have long wanted to share some of what I have discovered over the years about the evolutionary process of the soul. My own investigation has taken place over three and a half decades; information has been gleaned little by little. When I thought about thousands of regression sessions that I have conducted during my life, it seemed to me that if I wanted to demonstrate the resiliency of the soul, the most profound and moving way to do so would be to discuss some of the events that took place when the Nazis controlled Germany. If I could share information that came forth from the very people who died so needlessly, who could survive the Holocaust *after* dying, and quickly return to tell the tale, how could anyone ever doubt the amazing continuation of life and the survival of the soul?

My purpose is not to leave the reader with a sense of horror or of sadness, but with a new perspective. I would earnestly hope that the retelling of these past life memories can be healing, because many of the victims of those brutalities are on earth once more. They have survived and emerged through rebirth to express life once again. "They" can kill us, torture us, ridicule us, and here we are again.

That was the first reason that occurred to me. Second, and even more important is the conviction that as thinking, caring humans we cannot allow such evil to flourish again. Awareness is a first step. Fifty years after the end of World War II, we are reviving memories of the Holocaust through photographs, books, films, and museums. In all the times in history where acts of brutality have occurred, there has never been such an example and stimulus to force mankind toward positive, preventive action. It is imperative that we stop this kind of inhumanity by learning about it, confronting it, and taking action to prevent its reoccurrence. As it has been said over and over, but never too often: *never again.*

I began to ask inner questions at a very early age. Why did certain things happen to me and my family that were not what one would consider part of a normal course of events? My life was changed when I was only two years old because of my father's tragic death. In retrospect, the sad events of that time forced an early search for the meaning of life. At some point, it dawned on me that many people also had some early hardships that they, like I, took great pains to conceal. I suddenly knew I was not alone.

My search brought some answers, but mostly it brought more questions. Since World War II began when I was very small, a lot of those questions were stimulated by what was going on around me. I began to ask why? As all parents know, young children always ask that endless question. My questions were not about why the sky was blue, however, but about why people should die. And why they should fight with each other to bring about more death and sadness.

Some of those questions remain unanswered to this day. Why were Nazi atrocities allowed to escalate? Why didn't people in war-torn countries know about the catastrophic treatment of Jews? Why was such evil allowed to flourish right under the noses of fellow countrymen? Since my early search coincided with what was happening in Nazi Germany, it seems fitting that I should use examples of regression sessions related to that time frame in this book.

I have been privileged to peer into many thousands of people's lives through their venture inward. The information that has emerged has never ceased to cause me wonder, as the logic that arises from the revelation of patterns is both consistent and amazing. From the beginning of our soul experiences, we create attitudes and behaviors that continue throughout each life. We may put on a new suit of clothes or a new body each time around on the earth plane, but we don't change inside. When a person can achieve an understanding of his or her deeply entrenched patterns in the short space of three hours of regression therapy, the new perspective he has on himself or herself and his or her existence is life-changing. It goes beyond the mere words and understanding of reincarnation, for the person reaches an eons-deep experience of himself.

I began doing regression therapy because of the profound change my only formal regression session had on my own life. Some very sad things emerged and were aired during that process. I recalled details of my father's death, and saw precisely what occurred from the moment my mother learned of his demise. I had always said, "I didn't know my father," but

I discovered that within the short space of two years I had established a very strong bond with him. I realized that my own reaction to his death took the form of anger rather than sadness, and could then understand much about my later reactions to many things. I was able to verify my visions by reading a newspaper account of the events. The story was written in a narrative style, even giving details about neighbors' reactions. That story dovetailed exactly with the film that ran through my mind during the regression. (Journalism in the South, when I was two years old, was somewhat lurid and certainly less cut and dried than what we might expect to read today.)

What I had observed in my regression was my mother's reaction to the loss of my father. As we walked toward our house, returning from an errand—my mother protectively holding my hand—we saw a large group of people gathered on our porch. These well-meaning people took me away from my mother, down a hall to a kitchen, and gave me a biscuit to eat. I wanted to be with my mother so I cried. As I was nibbling on that biscuit, the tears were running down my cheeks and the biscuit became quite wet. The well-meaning people finally took me back down a hallway to the room where my mother was slumped in a chair. Then the real significance of that moment hit me—in her grief my mother didn't turn to me for comfort. In fact, as I was placed in a child's rocking chair nearby, she didn't seem to know I was even there. I was quite angry at my father for causing her unhappiness. I could hear myself saying to her in my mind, "Who needs him anyway? I'm here, Mother. You can depend on me." A major part of my loss was that of my mother's attention. Throughout my life, until she died, I never felt that she needed me.

Those memories were deeply buried. I had no conscious recollection of my father's death. When I was older, my mother had explained to me why I didn't have a father, and I cried for him. Still, my heart went out to her because I finally understood why she had an underlying sadness, even though she laughed and smiled most of the time. But the regression session revealed my decision to protect my mother by leaving her alone! Although that may seem simplistic, to me it was a deeply profound realization that explained much about my later life.

Few of the people who came to me for regression sessions had any clue that they might have lived in Germany as recently as the late 1930s or 1940s. The three examples of people who saw themselves on the Nazi side of the war certainly did not expect anything so shocking to come to light. Yet in spite of the shock, all of the individuals, no matter what their role in the terrible drama, achieved a new understanding of their current lives and experienced deeply felt healing.

Since the purpose of a regression session is to untangle knots on the thread of consciouness it is my belief that everyone can release a special quality of joy by untying those knots—knots that have tangled and accumulated over many lifetimes.

Thought of in another way, the individual undergoing a regression must reach what I call a "dropped stitch" in the fabric of his or her life and be able to see the stitch weaving itself right again before I can end a session. When that dropped stitch is reached, I don't have to offer very much to help the person see his or her own patterns and begin to release joyous energy.

The Tibetan Lamas that I have been acquainted with have been exiled from their own country by the invading Chinese and they own nothing except perhaps some shoes, the pieces of cloth they wear, and a few items they need for special ceremonies. Yet they have a particular kind of humor and joy. They laugh and laugh. I think it is called "Cosmic Joy." Their joyousness comes from an inner sense of peace.

I earnestly hope that reading *A Soul's Journey* will help you in the discovery of your own karmic knots and the eventual unraveling of them, and the realization of cosmic joy.

A Soul's Journey

1
Awareness

In the most popular spy novels there are always intricate plots with powerful figures using fiendish machinations to exploit situations to their own ends. People are murdered, disappearing so that they are never found again; enormous amounts of money change hands; morality is nonexistent; international power dealings remain concealed; spies, Interpol, the Mafia, and secret agents go about their terrifying missions. Usually in these novels, the hero wins out—good over evil.

But none of these plots can compare with what happened in real life, under the Nazi regime in Germany, before and during World War II. We stretch our imaginations as we read popular novels, but we put aside our practical belief system. After all, these are only plots born from the vivid fantasies of writers. It couldn't happen in real life.

But it did.

How could such wide-scale atrocity have happened in a civilized world? And why do we continue to ignore mass murders, terrorism, and gruesome tortures around the world? Why would some people deliberately choose evil over good?

Psychology and psychiatry make an attempt toward some kind of explanation of mankind's actions by pinpointing early moments when events occur that might warp the mind and set a person on a downward spiral. It is obvious that a traumatic situation can produce one result in the behavior of one person, whereas the same situation may cause a different reaction in another. But no psychological examination can begin to explain the degree of evil that existed in the minds of the Nazis, or the fiendishly warped plots that were conceived to torture Jews.

Persecution policies against the Jews had been brewing in Germany since 1933. By September 15, 1934, The Nuremberg Laws, enacted by the Nazi Party Congress, deprived Jews of German citizenship and made intermarriage between Aryans and Jews punishable by death.

At the same time, SS (Schutzstaffel) leader Heinrich Himmler started a program called "Lebensborn," or "life source." Young women of pure Aryan blood were encouraged to volunteer their services for the welfare of Germany and mate with SS officers to produce blond, blue-eyed babies. These children were to carry on the "thousand-year Reich." The women were housed in comparative luxury, almost as if they were staying at a country club or resort, with plenty of food, leisure, and companionship. Since Germany had just emerged from a depression with 5.6 million people unemployed and in a bankrupt state according to capitalist standards, this deal with the SS must have seemed attractive to some women. At least it was a way of having security for nine months. After that the women would leave their children to be brought up by the Nazi regime as part of the state breeding program. More than likely these women were caught up in idealistic messages concerning duty to the new Germany. However, nothing may ever quite explain to their now-grown children how their mothers would agree to such an offer, for they were orphans, martyred to the cause of Naziism. Hitler also offered cash incentives to Germans who would marry, and cash awards for each new child born of the union. Jews were not entitled to these benefits, as they no longer had German citizenship.

The campaign against Jews progressed rapidly as Hitler in 1935 promised a new order for Germany based on "racial purity." How could the majority of German Jews ignore the writing on the wall? Why didn't other countries come to their aid? Did everyone think the situation would simply go away?

On May 13, 1939, The *SS St. Louis* of the Hamburg-Amerika Line left Hamburg, Germany carrying 937 Jewish refugees fleeing Nazi oppression. It was the last major shipload of people to leave before the war began. The passengers all held apparently valid Cuban visas, and had been approved for exit from Germany by Joseph Goebbels. But Cuba refused them entry. The ship applied to the United States for asylum, but the U.S. quota of 25,957 German immigrants had been filled. The ship was turned away from American shores as well. At the last minute, as the ship was heading back to Germany, four countries—Britain, France, Belgium, and Holland—agreed to accept the refugees. A conference was then organized by U.S. President Franklin Roosevelt to develop facilities for Jewish emigration. Although delegates from thirty nations attended, nothing was accomplished.

After the war's start, years passed before Hitler found a solution to mass extermination. The rest of the world gave him plenty of time to experiment with methods of death, however. Before the gas chambers, there were many types of clumsy attempts to rid whole towns of Jewish inhabitants.

Eventually, German civilians were organized into squads called "Einsatzgruppen." These were special action units of ordinary citizens who had but one mission—they were traveling murderers who had unwritten orders to kill Jews without regard for age or sex. These groups were made up of doctors, lawyers, and businessmen who for some reason were unable to serve in the regular army. Some were university graduates, even theologians. They were substantial, law-abiding citizens, not criminals. How could the world stand by and allow this to happen?

To even attempt to understand how these people were able to commit cold-blooded murder, we need to look at the subtle but effective campaign by the Nazis to convince the populace that the Jews had been the cause of the past German economic difficulties. Throughout centuries, persecution of Jews had been linked to economic depression. Confiscation of Jewish goods and property was a sure way to increase revenue. Sometimes the Nazis used haranguing and the instilling of fear to influence the populace to carry out orders to kill the Jews. Since a prime German virtue was to carry out orders from authority figures without question, the Nazis could use this sense of duty to further their ends. But, Daniel Jonah Goldhagen, in his book, *Hitler's Willing Executioners, Ordinary Germans and the Holocaust,* says that the citizens acted as they did because of a widespread virulent regard of the Jews as a demonic enemy. Certainly there were many non-Jewish Germans living in fear, as well as their Jewish compatriots.

Other nations were aware of some of these atrocities, but humanity chose to look the other way. Even after the war, when concrete evidence of concentration camps was made public, many people either refused to believe that they existed or simply didn't want to know. Even now, many people would prefer to live in a state of unawareness, even denying the existence of persecution and death camps. Any denial may be an unconscious way to avoid heeding a call for action. As long as one can stay safe in one's cocoon, he or she can avoid taking personal responsibility for group injustice.

Many people may acknowledge what happened in Nazi Germany, but naively believe that nothing so evil could happen again in a more enlightened world. Many survivors of camps just want to forget the past and get on with their lives. This is an understandable reaction, but lack of confrontation on the part of the general public is dangerous. This attitude may stem from a lack of information about, a lack of caring, or a desire to hide one's head in the sand.

These terrible acts of violence will continue unless something occurs to get the attention of the people at large. The public must be convinced that evil can only flourish if nothing is done to stop it. As of today, more than fifty years after the end of World War II, there have been six major wars in which untold numbers of people have been killed. And there have been instances of the same kinds of atrocities that occurred in Nazi Germany in each of these subsequent wars.

Reports of discoveries of mass graves, torture, and the slaughter of innocent men, women, and children can, to this day, fall on slightly deaf ears. And some of the injustices of World War II still stand, even though they could be corrected this half-century later.

For example, Elie Wiesel, Nobel Peace Prize recipient in 1986, points out in an opinion piece for the *New York Times* on January 20, 1996, that the legendary anti-Nazi German journalist, Wili Carl Ossietzky, was jailed in 1933 after opposing the country's rearmament. He was awarded the Nobel Peace Prize in 1935 and subsequently offered freedom by Hermann Goering if he would reject that honor, thereby rescinding his anti-Nazi statements; but he refused to compromise his principles. Ossietzky died in a concentration camp hospital in 1938 at the age of 48. In 1992, a group of German intellectuals asked the judiciary to annul his conviction, but their petition was refused. By such a refusal, the judges confirmed the former verdict that Ossietzky's protest of Hitler's heinous political ideology was still a crime. So, as Mr. Wiesel points out, the hero has once again been repudiated and humiliated. Although this conviction remains, there are, thankfully, eloquent individuals such as Mr. Wiesel who courageously take a stand on principle to help mankind awaken to the horror of man's inhumanity to man.

After the defeat of the Third Reich, the same judges who swore allegiance to Hitler switched sides and continued to preside over German tribunals. The whitewashing, and the subsequent reward to people who somehow managed to change sides and get away with their evil deeds, is shocking. In letting these injustices slide by without confrontation, evil is allowed to flourish, and can spread with surprising speed. Many people automatically tend to copy what they see around them. Others feel helpless and don't know what to do to stop the horror from accelerating.

The term "hundredth monkey" phenomenon was coined in connection with the evolution of animal behavior, but this phenomenon can apply to the transmission of human habits and trends, as well. The "hundredth monkey" phenomenon was observed and named when behavioral scientists discovered that monkeys on a remote island in Southeast Asia suddenly began washing their sweet potatoes before eating them. Someone observed one of the young monkeys trotting to a nearby river, potatoes in hand. This youngster taught its mother to wash her potatoes, too, and eventually a few more monkeys on the island began washing their potatoes as well. Six years passed, during which time all of the young monkeys started washing their potatoes, but not all of the adults. Then an amazing thing happened: one morning critical mass was reached. Although there had been many monkeys still eating dirty potatoes that morning, by nightfall, almost every single member of the tribe had learned to wash its potatoes. An even more amazing event then occurred as, out of the blue, monkeys on *other* islands gained the awareness that potatoes taste better when clean; they started washing their potatoes, too. How did they know to do this? Trends, thoughts, habits, apathy, and even evil can be contagious on a very subtle level when critical mass is reached. We *can* influence other people by thought directed positively toward the higher consciousness, as well as by overt action and confrontation.

A little-known fact, at least in the United States, is that concentrated efforts have been and are still being made to inform German children about what happened in their country before they were born. Children in European schools are taught about the Second World War in mind-grabbing ways. Certainly in Holland, and in present day Germany, steps are taken to make sure that young people will learn from what transpired. *The Diary of Anne Frank* is required reading in Dutch schools. German children are given examples of Naziism in every subject across the board. Sadly, U.S. schools have not followed suit.

One young German woman—we will call her Helena— currently living in a major German city told me how she learned about the horrors of the war in school. A lot of guilt about the German atrocities was instilled in the minds of the young people of her generation. I was touched when she worked up her courage to inquire, "If I visit the United States will people hate me because I'm German?" When I assured

Helena that she would not be blamed for another generation's evil-doing, she was not really convinced.

Helena told me that in her school they were inundated with examples of Hitler's evil. In every subject, whether it was English, German, history, or science, examples of Nazi crimes were introduced. The teachers stressed the Germans' inability to look and to see what was happening. With all the reports that have emerged, it is now an acknowledged fact that the Nazis were masters at contriving devious ways to fool the Jews into cooperation and enlisting the aid of the German populace. Special classes in Helena's school were dedicated to Jews and their martyrdom.

One of Helena's teachers devised an interesting way of showing how the Nazis were able to reach the minds of the German people. The class was first asked to pick a sign that might compare to a swastika. Next they were told to choose a special hand signal that might be similar to the Nazi salute. Then they were to choose a code word that might relate to "Heil Hitler." As time went on and the project developed further, the whole class began to feel especially close to each other. They began to help each other, and eventually started to leave other people out of their activities. This exercise finally spread throughout the whole school. Evidently the combination of hand signals, words, and emblems made an impression on the subconscious mind that created a feeling of exclusivity. Ultimately, the children were shown how those feelings related to Naziism and were told how dangerous they could become. Much of mankind's inhumanity to its fellow man boils down to an "I'm okay, you're not okay" attitude. With new methods of technology bringing about global communication, it is hoped that this insular position will give way to a more humanitarian approach. But fighting evil can be a tough task. There is a fine line between allowing freedom of the press, free will, and freedom for each country to devise its own politics, and the urgent need to devise ways to protect the innocent.

But can we change the world without interfering with free will? Can we change ourselves when we feel justified in expressing anger, or wanting to get even, over a real injustice? How can the people who remember dying during the Holocaust let go of the horror? And why would they have been born into such conditions in the first place?

Surfacing Past Life Memories of Nazi Germany

There is another way that people are becoming aware of what really happened. That is through the incoming souls who experienced degradation, torture, terror, and death, and who have come back to tell their stories to the world. Perhaps the world is ready to listen.

At the time of the Harmonic Convergence in 1987, the theory of reincarnation gained more acceptance in the minds of many people. The Harmonic Convergence was the end of a cycle within the Mayan calendar that began in the year 1519 and marked the beginning of the Mayan Messianic Age. The cycle of high energy and spiritual growth described by that special date in the Mayan calendar inaugurated many significant events. For example, Alexander Arkhipov of Moscow's Radio Astronomy Institute identified nine out of 4,500 "sunlike" stars that may be the scene for intelligent life. It was also a time when the calendar year was shortened by one second to adjust to the

Gregorian calendar, and the largest supernova since 1604 was detected and observed in the Large Magellanic Galaxy. Groups around the world got together to pray, meditate, and ask the universe for more enlightenment. Books and articles began to appear in the western world that explained the theory and concept of rebirth from lifetime to lifetime. That belief system was already part of much of Asian thought and religion. Practitioners who could conduct regression sessions into past lives emerged in all cities. These sessions ranged from individual psychic readings that recounted past lives, to helping an individual awaken his or her own memories through acupuncture or hypnosis.

I had been conducting regression sessions, without the use of hypnosis, for clients of mine since 1967. The method I used was very nearly 100 percent successful. When I read an astrological chart and saw a particular configuration that suggested the need for such a session, I would always tell the person about the process.

I deliberately chose September 1987, the time of the Harmonic Convergence, for the publication of my book, *Astrology and Your Past Lives*. In that book, I explained the theory of reincarnation and the process of going through a regression session. I wrote primarily to people who could relate to the astrological system of looking at cycles. When I set up an astrological chart, I can see patterns that exist in the present lifetime, but I may also be able to determine why these patterns exist in the first place. I try to clarify whether these patterns are part of a parent's mandates, influences from peers or society, or whether they are there from birth, innately built in on a soul consciousness level. The structure of an astrological chart can also indicate to me the specific type of condition from a past life that might lead to these continued patterns in the present lifetime. In the book I was able to cite many case histories of people who had already had the experience of a regression session and discovered for themselves the reasons about conditions in the present time. Requests for regression sessions began to match the number of requests for astrological readings.

But an interesting phenomena began to occur among the large numbers of people who came to me for these sessions after reading the book. Quite an amazing number of people revealed lifetimes that were lived in Nazi Germany. I had included in the book only one story of a man who recalled his life as a Nazi, because up until that time, his was one of a few such recollections among my clients. But in 1987, some forty years after the war's end, it appeared that many people had been reborn from that time and had reached an age where a review of a past life seemed important to them. Obviously there had to be a rapid turnaround in order to be back on the earth plane once again so soon.

But why? Why would a soul want to come right back to this sphere of existence without having proper time for review and healing in the spiritual realms, especially if death had been brutal? Why had so few people come forth with memories of having been a Nazi? Perhaps there had been fewer Nazis who had died and had been reborn in this country and were of an age to undergo a regression session. Perhaps the Nazis who had been killed and reborn were unwilling to face the kinds of subconscious memories that might haunt them. I could only conclude that some of the souls who were reincarnating rapidly, and were impelled to bring memories to the surface through regression sessions, have, indeed, come back to tell the truth of what had really happened. Many Jews who were killed in concentration camps came back as non-Jews in this life. Many returned to be born into the same faith.

Another possibility for the rapid return could involve the unexpectedness of the death, coupled with the cruel method of dying. If some of these people had been killed without warning, they may have been literally unaware of being dead. If that were the case, and they were not very far off the earth plane, they may have been pulled, like a magnet, into an awaiting pregnancy, hardly aware on a conscious level of what was happening. However, if the shock was severe, some of those souls may have come back very quickly just to seek immediate comfort, fully aware—at least at the moment of fetal entry—of what they were doing. It became obvious to me that whole groups of people were born into families who were like strangers, where they felt little or no familiarity. Often that was a strong reason for a person to come to me in the first place. So many people revealed feeling like a stranger in a strange land during childhood that it led me to start asking everyone undergoing the regression process an important question during the review of the birth process. I would ask, "Do you know your mother, or is she a stranger?" Quite a few people answer that question by saying, "She is a stranger."

An opposite situation also became clear during these regression sessions. Sometimes it seemed that people had reincarnated to find the families who had died with them, adopting different relationships in the new life. One strong theory in the belief system of reincarnation is that "birds of a feather flock together."

In either instance—of attraction or non-attraction to immediate families—the person undergoing the experience can identify people from other lives. In some instances, groups of people have come together again to re-live the same patterns. They may or may not have the same relationship to each other in the new life, but the core structure of their former association is *exactly* the same. In going through the regression sessions, people can fully understand why they may feel like an alien in their family or why they feel especially close to one or another member of that family.

Healing the Present

In regression sessions, it is very important to me that the individual realize the purpose of taking a look at the past. It is much less essential to know *who* one was, than to learn *what patterns* have been carried over. I would have a hard time taking an individual back through a time of horror only to expose him or her to more nightmares in the present life. *The purpose of going back is to heal the present.* Sometimes it takes very little discussion about those patterns for an individual to recognize the need for change. If one has been a victim over and over again, it is not difficult to say, "I'm tired of that role." The individual can see what happened in the past to create such a situation and what is necessary in the present to change that altogether. Simple awareness seems to bring its own healing.

There is a thread of consciousness that continues through all spheres and throughout all time. If we have tied a knot on that thread of consciousness, it is inevitable that the knot continues to be retied over and over again. When the pattern that relates to that knot in our consciousness becomes unbearable, we seem to take the time to untie it. That is what can be accomplished by awareness, and a regression session is one method of pursuing more awareness. When an individual can become more consciously aware of why a situation occurred and what his responsibility was, *without guilt,* in creating a condition or event that was ultimately disastrous or dangerous, he can take steps to avoid doing that again.

It is my opinion that there can be one moment in time when a different choice would have made a big difference in later experiences. The outer circumstances may have remained exactly the same, but the trauma connected with the experience would have been different—perhaps less severe—with a more careful choice at a critical moment. Sometimes I suggest that a person engage in private sessions with him- or herself after our time together, in order to completely forgive the self and others. Like wiping a blackboard clean, the process may be easy or it may take several attempts to wash away images from the past. But it can be done. I cannot tell a person who has been a victim of death in a concentration camp how to forgive Hitler and the Nazis, but I can help point out what happened in a previous life, before Nazi Germany, that set up such a tragic experience as a victim. I always stress that blame of self will not reconcile anything. That can be difficult when one has committed an act of brutality toward others, because on a soul consciousness level, we *do* have a conscience. Acknowledgement of responsibility is important but awareness is different than self blame or guilt. What usually happens in such an instance is that the latent guilt causes one to set up unbearable conditions in the present as unconscious self-punishment. Even if an individual had been victimized, a small inner voice may say, "I should have prevented it." That solves nothing. It is with recognition and acknowledgment of what really happened that one can clean the slate and create a new life script. The balance comes from making a contribution in an area where one has formerly committed a negative act.

Many times an individual can recognize physical health patterns that have their roots in a past life. If one had been killed by being stabbed in the heart a weakness can still exist in the etheric patterns of the physical heart. It can be life-saving to understand where and why physical weaknesses exist.

To my way of thinking, it is only in the light of reincarnation that some present day events and conditions make sense. But it is not important to believe in reincarnation in order to reveal important or useful information to oneself. Before beginning a session, I always stress that even if what emerges in the regression session is only imagination, that imagination is a creation from within. In any case, it is my observation that if an individual can reveal a lifetime to himself without the aid of hypnosis and with the concrete, judgmental mind firmly in gear, he is less likely to doubt what he sees or senses. In general, I find that less skepticism exists about the whole subject of reincarnation as time goes on. But whether one believes is not the real issue. The process of going back in time works successfully either way.

It is always interesting to do a regression session with a person whose memories include a description of a relationship in the present life that seems to come from a past association. If the identified person chooses to do his or her own regression and can corroborate information that had already been revealed, without knowing any data beforehand, it seems to give even more confirmation that such an association really existed. There have been many cases where that has happened. (See chapter 8.) I have also attempted to corroborate regression session memories with factual accounts by people who lived through similar experiences and have either written about them or related them to writers. I check for historical confirmation, as well, and try to discern whether the people who have done regression sessions with me have read the accounts that give confirmation to their stories.

A belief in reincarnation does not give one the excuse to get away with whatever he can in this lifetime. If anything, it encourages each person to believe in the innate ability to change, *once we know what it is that needs changing.* Clearing out the debris in the unconscious mind helps to release a creative potential to project onto the mirror of life what one chooses, instead of falling into an all-too-familiar trap over and over again.

2
Reincarnation, the Wheel of Karma, and Regression

I‌T MAY BE just as important to describe what reincarnation is *not* as to describe what it *is*. In the introduction to *Edgar Cayce's Story of Karma*, compiled and written by Mary Ann Woodward and Hugh Lynn Cayce, Edgar Cayce's son, cites a prime example of common misconceptions about reincarnation. He says, [Many people think that] "Reincarnation is a foolish belief of ignorant masses that man is reborn as an insect or animal."

It has been my experience that people resist the idea of reincarnation because they think it is ego boosting, or boasting, and that it absolves people of taking responsibility for their actions. Some of the comments I've heard are, "Everyone remembers being a king or a queen!" or "It's my karma. There's nothing I can do about it." I've done many thousands of regression sessions since 1967 and relatively few people undergoing those sessions remember a lifestyle of royalty. There have been, more often, examples of people who saw hardships in past lives.

Understanding about the particular karma we have created in the past gives clarity about what we must do to balance the scales in the present and create better conditions in the here and now. Reincarnation does not give one permission to be passive or fatalistic. It can enable an individual to have more understanding and acceptance of things as they are, but as *active* awareness, not as a passive shrug of the shoulders. It is said that true wisdom is the ability to change what you can and accept what you cannot.

Edgar Cayce:
The Sleeping Prophet

When I read *There Is a River,* by Thomas Sugrue, a wonderful book relating the story of the life and work of Edgar Cayce, I discovered the theory of reincarnation. The book changed my life. Reincarnation was the first theory that made sense to me, and that satisfactorily answered a number of questions that had nagged at me since childhood. In the early '60s I went to Virginia Beach, Virginia, with friends several times to see for myself where this phenomenal man, Edgar Cayce, had lived. We were able to walk into his former home and have access to the thousands of readings he had given throughout his adult life. I spent time poring over these readings, long before the elaborate library was built to house and protect the treasures that had been carefully recorded throughout his life.

Edgar Cayce was called the sleeping prophet. After an incident that impaired his eyesight and threatened his means of livelihood as a photographer, he began to discover a hidden ability within himself that actually scared him in the beginning: he was able to put himself in a trance and diagnose people's illnesses. It didn't seem to matter if the person was present in the room with him or hundreds of miles away. He seemed able to see into the body of the person requesting the reading, tuning into any inner imbalance. He could then recommend effective treatment where more traditional techniques hadn't worked. Records were carefully kept so that he could follow up on his subjects' well-being. A very religious man, Cayce continued to teach Sunday school and attend the Methodist Church every week as long as he lived. He was a man of conscience and was extremely fearful of doing something that might harm people and be "the work of the devil." Since his prescribed treatments seemed to help people, he felt he could safely continue this strange work.

Cayce was put to the test, however, when he had to help his own family. His wife was seriously ill with tuberculosis and his son had a near-fatal accident. His readings for them and the resultant prescribed treatments, fearfully given though they were, saved both their lives. He was also told about his own impaired eyesight. The reason for the condition was explained to him, and he was given precise instructions about what to do to correct it. His restored eyesight enabled him to resume his work as a photographer in order to earn a living (he never charged money for a reading). By the time of Cayce's death, more than 16,000 readings and case histories had been recorded by his faithful secretary, Gladys.

One case history stands out in my mind. A two-year-old girl was thought to be mentally retarded. She had seemed to be especially intelligent until a certain age, when she began to lose the ability to do the things a normal toddler was expected to do. Her panicked family took her to many specialists, but no one gave them much hope. In desperation, the mother wrote to Cayce to ask for a reading. Cayce tuned in to a time when the child had fallen out of her pram as a baby and had injured a part of her spine. The incident had been forgotten. It had not seemed terribly traumatic or dangerous at the time, but energy going into her brain had evidently been blocked by the fall. Cayce gave simple instructions for correcting the spinal injury manually, thereby releasing the flow of energy into the brain. Within a short period of time she was able to perform the functions of a normal two-year-old.

Cayce made all of his diagnoses in an unconscious state and was unable to remember anything he had said while in the trance state. The language of the readings was very different from Cayce's normal speech patterns, and the voice that emerged was lower and more commanding. Cayce's recommended treatments described techniques and used terminology that were totally foreign to Cayce in his normal state. Since people responded to his suggestions and wrote long, glowing letters of thanks, Cayce could accept his strange gift. But he always questioned the source of the information. He gradually accepted that the information seemed to come from a universal consciousness.

Eventually, Cayce's reputation spread to an intellectually elevated group of people and caught the attention of some professors of philosophy at Harvard University. The professors contacted Cayce, hoping for permission to visit him at his home in Virginia Beach in order to ask him some special questions. Cayce had no idea what they might ask. He was a simple man, with no guile, and could only trust that whatever came forth from his own subconscious might help him understand the gift.

He went through his usual procedure, taking off his shoes and loosening his tie, and lay down to sleep. When he awakened, feeling refreshed as if he had merely taken a nap, he saw very strange looks on the faces of the people in the room. The professors seemed quite excited. Cayce's secretary and wife, who had been in the room during the question and answer period, appeared startled and confused. It seemed that Cayce had confirmed the theory of reincarnation and had explained a great deal about the soul's journey through an earthly existence. To the Cayce family and friends who were raised according to strict Southern Methodist doctrine, this was terribly upsetting information. Yet they saw the positive results of his readings for people all over the world and could hardly expect that false information would suddenly come through this simple and dedicated man.

In the session with the professors, Cayce had discussed very profound issues relating to reincarnation, using vocabulary that he could not have understood in his waking state and explaining with great clarity all the subtleties of a complex theory.

Cayce's education had been scattered, and he was not considered to be very intellectually advanced. Without the aid of his "unseen helpers," he might not have gotten through school at all. One night his exasperated father laid down the law. He told young Cayce that he was going to learn his lessons for school the next day if they had to stay up all night long. After many hours of drilling by his father, Cayce asked to be able to take a little nap. Before he went to sleep he was told by a lady, who appeared before him, that if he would merely sleep with his head on his books he would know everything in them. When Cayce awakened after his short nap, he knew his lessons backward and forward. He was promptly given a beating for playing games with a devoted father who had worked with him for so many long hours!

So for Cayce to discuss advanced philosophical theory with intellectual giants, conveying information that was hitherto unknown to some of them, seemed especially amazing. One of the bits of information that came from Cayce's unconscious was that all thoughts and deeds of every person on earth are recorded in the ethers in something called the Akashic Records. At the time I read about the Akashic Records, in the early '60s, it was a bit difficult to conceive of where those records might be, or how it was possible to get so much information into some space in that higher strata. My best imagined scenario was that the records were like a huge, dusty library where you could go to the stacks and read about a particular time or place from a massive, heavy book. Now that we understand about computers and microchips, the possibility of a record of every thought and deed of every individual who ever lived residing in space doesn't seem so farfetched at all.

Over the remaining years of Cayce's life, the group of people dedicated to working with him began to ask their own questions. The sessions extended beyond health readings to include information about past lives. Many of the readings began to incorporate information confirming that some health patterns had beginnings that were rooted in other incarnations. All of the thousands of readings given by Cayce over the years now exist in a library at the Association For Research and Enlightenment (ARE) in Virginia Beach, a hugely valuable resource that is open to all.

How Did It All Begin?

Edgar Cayce was asked an essential question in his readings for the Harvard professors. How did it all begin? What was the fall of man? Evidently at the very beginning of time itself, according to Cayce, souls first felt the need for new experiences and began to cut away from the one force or God consciousness. The comfort and security of oneness gave way to a need for expression of individualization. (During a regression session, one young lady described the sense of joy of oneness on a spiritual plane. She said, "I can see myself as a little squiggly in a sea of bliss. But there is no sense of individualization. So I have an urge to cut myself off from the rest and come into earth again.")

Some souls began to hover around the bodies of animals to satisfy their curiosity about activities they could observe. The spirits were especially curious about the physical sensations among the animals, such as sexual pleasure and the pleasure of consuming food, reported Cayce, and they discovered they could enter the bodies of animals at moments of sexual activity, share the animals' sensations, and then leave at will. As that entry became more and more frequent, the sparks of spiritual consciousness began to be trapped in the animals' bodies and couldn't get out again. Then came a need for a better physical form to house the spirits as they began the painful ascent from the trapped condition back to total spiritual consciousness and the sense of oneness with God. This concept of original sin is quite different from that held by traditional religion. It is interesting that the Spanish word *sin* [pronounced *seen*] means "without." (This is certainly not to say that sexual activity as an expression of love and harmony prevents one from having spiritual connections as well, but the physical pleasure always ends and leaves one feeling alone again. There are certain practices of sexual activity, such as the Indian practice of Tantra Yoga, that incorporate rituals especially for the purpose of attaining a higher spiritual connection with a partner. But these are always conducted after methods of purification and with the intent of evoking higher consciousness. Sexual activity that is brutal, injurious, or hurtful to another keeps an individual on the gross physical side of life; we will see how the Nazis used these practices for the evil enslavery of the Jews.)

With the conscience of the soul as a dividing line between man and animal, God gave mankind the gift of free will. So it is that concept of free will, *conscious choice*, that enables man to evolve back to the oneness of the elevated spiritual life. It may take centuries for the souls that are trapped in purely earthly pleasures to realize that they are also missing the divine comfort and perfect harmony they once knew. That realization may come about as a result of tremendous suffering, which eventually awakens the soul and brings the consciousness to the awareness of the need for connection with God and fellow souls again.

As more and more people are accepting the concept of reincarnation, many psychologists and psychiatrists are beginning to understand how past life memories can be utilized in solving their patients' present day problems. An individual may approach the review of his or her past lives as a matter of simple curiosity, but the true benefit of such a review is the healing that comes as a result. Patterns, both in matters of health and psychology, seem to continue throughout existence. When an individual finds the beginning of the pattern, the solution is there as well. Amazingly, the birth process, itself, relates precisely to the way we make changes all through life. When we understand that "formula," which we enscribe as we enter the earth plane, we can go back to rewrite the birth survival script and release new energy in daily activity.

Reincarnation in Culture and Religion

Belief in reincarnation is central to Eastern religion, culture, and heritage. It is accepted as a fact, a truth, and a philosophy. As an example, Tibet had a monarchy established solely on the basis of reincarnation. Perhaps a lesser known fact is that belief in reincarnation has also been a part of Jewish heritage. Historians of religion have discerned belief about reincarnation and an afterlife in Jewish tradition from biblical times through the Middle Ages. In his book *Beyond the Ashes,* Rabbi Yonassan Gershom relates, "Isaac Luria, a sixteenth-century rabbi who is regarded as one of the greatest Jewish mystics of all time, not only taught reincarnation but was reputed to be an accurate past life reader. The same has been said of Israel ben Eliezer, known as the Baal Shem Tov, founder of the Hasidic movement in the eighteenth century. Reincarnation stories from both of these teachers and their disciples abound in written and oral form."

Belief in reincarnation is part of everyday life in India and in all countries where Buddhism is the religion. Many stories are told about finding lost friends, families, and loved ones after their death and rebirth. But perhaps the most profound example of the practical application of this belief in reincarnation is the method of determining the rulership of the country of Tibet.

The choice of His Holiness, the Dalai Lama, is based solely on reincarnation. It is believed that, having reached a supreme level of consciousness, the same soul comes into life again and again to be embodied as the Dalai Lama. It is also believed that if a soul has attained the level of consciousness as a "High" Lama, that soul is always a high Lama. The method of finding and recognizing the new incarnation of a High Lama is the same as finding and recognizing the new incarnation of the Dalai Lama. (Eventually it may become common practice to use similar techniques to recognize new incarnations of people we have loved and have seemingly lost through death from other lifetimes!)

The Dalai Lama represents in his person the return to earth of Chenrezi, the god of grace, one of the thousand living Buddhas who have renounced Nirvana in order to help mankind. Chenrezi was the patron god of Tibet, and his reincarnations were always the kings of Tibet. The people of Tibet pray to the Dalai Lama as a Living Buddha rather than as a king, yet he is the ruler of the land.

An ancient prophecy foretold that the fourteenth Dalai Lama would not rule in Tibet. The current Dalai Lama, the fourteenth, came to the throne when he was only fifteen, with the threat of invasion by China imminent; indeed, his coronation in November 1950 was too late to prevent the takeover of Tibet by the Chinese. He was allowed to rule until March 1959, when he was forced to flee for his life in disguise. Since that time he has been in exile, traveling around the world to further the cause of world Buddhism and thereby fulfilling the prophecy. If the Chinese had not taken over Tibet, forcing him to flee, the likelihood of seeing a Tibetan Lama, much less the Dalai Lama himself, in the Western world would have been very slim indeed.

While I was writing my second and third books I lived in Ibiza, Spain, one of the Balearic islands in the Mediterranean. During the writing of *Astrology and Your Past Lives,* I had the rare gift of sharing my five-hundred-year-old *finca* (farm house), with a Tibetan Lama for short periods of time. Lama Tsultrim would come to Ibiza from Barcelona, where he lived in a Buddhist Center, to give courses to his devotees on that island.

Ibiza is known as one of the high energy spots of the world and is especially acknowledged to have very high healing energy emanating from the land. There are many stories of European physicians who recommend that their patients move to that island in order to have a healthier life. My home had been a center for Tibetan Lamas' visits before I had come to the island, and I was delighted to be able to continue the tradition and actually meet a Lama born in Tibet. I felt greatly honored to give my home for these teachings and for his shelter. One of my friends who had studied in India said, "Jeannie, until you have actually met an enlightened master, you cannot imagine what ecstasy really is." I recount many of the experiences with Lama Tsultrim in my book, *Astrology and Your Past Lives.*

I prepared for Lama's visit by making my home as comfortable as possible for the small entourage that accompanied him. Other people prepared the food he enjoyed and changed my decor from anything Hindu to Tibetan. I was told by one Russian artist that the tradition was to hand Lama a white silk scarf upon meeting him and accept it back after he blessed it. We had little access to silk in those days in Ibiza, so we used a length of cheesecloth instead. I was quite excited but very calm as the time approached for his arrival. As Lama walked around the corner of the house I handed him the scarf for his blessing. As he handed it back to me, I burst into tears and could not stop crying for three days. The energy from his mere presence was so strong my body could not contain it all. The tears were a release for the overload to my system. Lama understood, and we laughed and talked in spite of the frequent discharge of water from my eyes.

One of the most interesting times would come when Lama and I would walk in the garden. Although Lama did not speak

English and I did not speak Tibetan, we could communicate very well through gestures, a strong psychic connection, and a small amount of translation. We would take walks in the garden where he told me reincarnation stories that I understood perfectly well. Being in the presence of an enlightened one makes negative thought, anger, or nonproductive activity almost impossible. The level of energy is so strong that it instantly helps an individual in his own efforts to resolve karmic situations and relationships.

Lama told me about a time when he was visiting Paris. A boy of about twelve came up to him on the street, grinning from ear to ear, and said, "Don't you recognize me? I'm..." and he gave his former Tibetan name. It seemed that Lama Tsultrim had a very close friend when he was a young child and had missed him after the boy had suddenly died. After all those years, he re-met his friend in Paris, once again in a young man's body, but this time with a great disparity in their ages.

He also told me a story about a group of his friends, Lamas, who had visited Canada. Suddenly a small boy of about six raced up to them on the street, blocking their way. He tugged on their sashes and robes and said, "Lama Sera, Lama Sera." In this way, he told them that he had known them and recognized them from the particular monastery (named Sera) in Tibet where they had all lived together in a previous life. There are stories in my book *Astrology and Your Past Lives* of young children who recognized Tibetan Lamas traveling in their respective countries, and greeted them by saying "Lama Sera, Lama Sera." These children could not possibility have known what a Lama was, much less the name of the monastery where they had lived without having a past life memory of those Lamas. The children remembered being young monks and living in the monastery. They even used their former Tibetan names.

Finding the New Incarnation
of the Dalai Lama

The discovery of the correct incarnation of the fourteenth, current, Dalai Lama constitutes quite a story. Heinrich Harrer, who eventually attained a position as the tutor of the Dalai Lama, was fortunate to hear a firsthand account of the discovery from the Commander in Chief of the Tibetan Army, Dzasa Kunsangtse, one of the few living eyewitnesses to the event. Harrer recounts Dzasa Kunsangtse's story in his fascinating book, *Seven Years in Tibet*.

"Some time before his death in 1933, the thirteenth Dalai Lama had given intimations regarding the manner of his rebirth. After his death, the body sat in state in the Potala in traditional Buddha posture, looking toward the south. One morning it was noticed that his head was turned to the east. The State Oracle was straight-way consulted, and while in his trance the monk oracle threw a white scarf in the direction of the rising sun, that is, toward the east. For two years nothing more definite was indicated. Then the regent went on a pilgrimage to a famous lake to ask for counsel. When the regent, after long prayers, came to the water and looked in its mirror, he had a vision of a three-storied monastery with golden roofs, near which stood a little Chinese peasant house with carved gables....(with us it is generally, but mistakenly, believed that each rebirth takes place at the moment of the predecessor's death...Buddhist philosophy declares that years may pass before the god once more leaves the fields of heaven and resumes the form of a man.) Search groups set out to explore in the year 1937...Following the signs, they journeyed eastward in quest of the Holy Child. The members of these groups were monks and in each group...they carried with them objects that had belonged to the thirteenth Dalai Lama.

"The group to which my informant belonged journeyed...until they reached the district of Amdo in the Chinese province of Chingnai. In this region there are many monasteries, as the great reformer, Tsong Kapa, was born here...They began to fear that they would fail in their mission. At last after long wanderings they encountered a three-storied monastery with golden roofs. With a flash of enlightenment, they remembered the regent's vision, and then their eyes fell on the cottage with carved gables. Full of excitement, they dressed themselves in the clothes of their servants. This maneuver is customary during these searches, for persons dressed as high officials attract too much attention and find it hard to get in touch with the people. The servants, dressed in the garments of their masters, were taken to the best room, while the disguised monks went into the kitchen, where it was likely they would find the children of the house.

"As soon as they entered the house, they felt sure that they would find the Holy Child in it, and they waited tensely to see what would happen. And, sure enough, a two-year-old boy came running to meet them and seized the skirts of the Lama, who wore around his neck the rosary of the thirteenth Dalai Lama. Not at all shy, the child cried, 'Sera Lama, Sera Lama!' It was already a matter of wonder that the infant recognized a Lama in the garb of a servant and that he said he came from the Cloister of Sera, which was the case. Then the boy grasped the rosary and tugged at it till the lama gave it to him; thereupon he hung it around his own neck. The noble searchers found it hard not to throw themselves to the ground before the child, as they had no longer any doubt. They had found the Incarnation. But they had to proceed in the prescribed manner.

"They bade farewell to the peasant family, and again returned a few days later—this time not disguised. They first negotiated with the parents, who had already given one of their sons as an Incarnation to the church, and then the little boy was awakened from his sleep, and the four delegates withdrew with him to the altar room. Here the child was subjected to the prescribed examination. He was shown four different rosaries, one of which—the most worn—had belonged to the thirteenth Dalai Lama. The boy, who was quite unconstrained and not the least bit shy, chose the right one without hesitation and danced around the room with it. He also selected out of several drums one which the last Incarnation had used to call his servants. Then he took an old walking stick, which had also belonged to him, not deigning to bestow a glance on one which had a handle of ivory and silver. When they examined his body they found all the marks which an Incarnation of Chenrezi ought to bear: large, outstanding ears, and moles on the trunk which are supposed to be traces of the four-armed god's second pair of arms.

"As soon as they crossed the border between China and Tibet...the little Dalai Lama distributed blessings as naturally as if he had never done anything else. He has still a clear recollection of being borne into Lhasa in his golden palanquin. He had never seen so many people. The whole town was there to greet the new embodiment of Chenrezi, who at last after so many years returned to the Potala and his orphaned people. Six years had passed since the death of the 'Previous Body' and of these, nearly two had elapsed before the god re-entered a human body. Everyone was astonished at the unbelievable dignity of the child and the gravity with which he followed ceremonies which lasted for hours. With his predecessor's servants, who had charge of him, he was as trusting and affectionate as if he had always known them...I knew how much the young king desired to lead his people one day out of the fog of gloomy superstition. We dreamed and talked endlessly about enlightenment and future reforms.

"It was not easy for the young king to satisfy the demands made on him. He knew that he was expected to give divine judgments and that what he ordered and what he did were regarded as infallible and would become a part of historical tradition. He was already striving by means of week-long meditation and profound religious study to prepare himself for the heavy duties of his office. He was much less self-assured than the thirteenth Incarnation. Tsarong once gave me a typical example showing the dominating character of the late ruler. He wished to enact new laws but met with bitter opposition from his conservative entourage, who quoted the utterances of the fifth Dalai Lama on the same context. To which the thirteenth Dalai Lama replied, 'And who was the fifth former body?' The monks, thereupon, prostrated themselves before him, for his answer had left them speechless. As an Incarnation he was, of course, not only the thirteenth but also the fifth and all the other Dalai Lamas as well."

Lifetime to Lifetime

Obviously not everyone can incarnate on such a high level of awareness as the Dalai Lama, because, like yesterday to today, we pick up exactly where we left off. If we have developed a high level of consciousness and awareness before death, we continue to exist on that plane in the "in between" state, or on the spiritual planes. If we have persisted in spiritual blindness, and remain asleep in life, we awaken in that same state. We may have a new personality, new physical characteristics, and different life circumstances, but the knots on the thread of consciousness that weave throughout lifetimes are still there. The beautiful golden stitches are there, too. Decisions we've made in past lives, even the unconscious ones, precondition the specific circumstances in the present life. Therefore it is possible to plan ahead as well as to look backward! But first we have to know what those knots represent.

Death, like sleep, can bring a much-needed rest. There is usually blessed forgetfulness and time for healing, until the individual is ready to resume the weaving and stitching. If there have been severe traumas from previous incarnations, this is the time and place for recovery.

The spiritual planes also provide a kind of schoolroom. The soul reviews former lives before coming back in physical form to rectify imbalances, or resolve karma. This review enables a soul to choose the experiences to be incorporated into the next life, for *the working out and reconciliation of karma can only take place on the physical plane.* Envisioned another way, the spiritual planes might be thought of as summer vacation after having failed algebra. You can study up over the summer, but you still have to go back and take the exam over again to get the credit and to be sure you have it right. Karmic conditions can only be healed on an experiential level in a physical body, so there is a good reason for having a regression session to review past lives and the karmic knots while still on the earth plane.

Past life regression therapy is a way of speeding up the evolutionary progress. If karmic conditions are reviewed through a process of confrontation, acceptance of responsibility, and forgiveness, a cleansing and healing can take place. Productive new choices can be made consciously, because we can allow those good conditions to happen. Progress on the spiritual plane is facilitated as awakening occurs and levels of consciousness are upgraded.

Reincarnation and
the Catholic Church

If reincarnation is a belief system accepted by Eastern religions and even in certain sects of Judaism, why is it omitted from the teachings of most Western religions? A decision was made in 325 A.D. at the Council of Nicaea, summoned by the Roman Emperor Constantine, that mankind was not ready to handle the responsibility of knowing about reincarnation and karma, and it was then banned from the teachings of the Catholic Church. This council was the first ecumenical council of the church. It supported the doctrine that God and Christ are of the same substance. It was as recently as 313 A.D. that the Emperor Constantine had established tolerance of Christianity and the persecution of Christians in Rome was ended.

I used to wonder if priests, especially those trained in the intellectual Jesuit tradition, were taught the doctrine of reincarnation. As early as 1960 I began searching for a Jesuit priest who would discuss this with me. It took about twenty-five more years before I discovered that this knowledge was kept from them, as well. I have conducted regression sessions with two priests—one was a Jesuit, and both have become very close friends. To their own amazement, both priests saw themselves as priests in several past lives and knew why they were led inexorably into the same role again.

Knowledge of reincarnation and karma implies responsibility. But it is always possible to put off dealing with one's responsibilities and say, to paraphrase Scarlett O'Hara, "I'll think about that in the next life!" Therein lies the danger. The karmic load can become quite burdensome if a buildup of debt occurs; that would be like neglecting to pay one's bills once too often. The decision to postpone learning one's karmic lessons is of course an option, for mankind has free will, but delaying the payment of karmic debts brings a high interest rate in the next life. The universal laws may not be so lenient as bankruptcy laws on earth. The price of suffering in the next life may be too high. In fact, if the soul has chosen specific experiences to be resolved in the present life, it is even wise, when one is strong enough, to ask the universe to give one even more to take on in the present time.

It appears that a lot of people get away with a lot of things, but on a cosmic level, every single act must be reconciled, even to the smallest detrimental thought. The fear of the Emperor Constantine and the churchmen, who decided that fourth-century mankind was not ready to know the truth about reincarnation, may have been well-founded. If the knowledge of reincarnation is used as an excuse for negative actions ("I can't help myself; it's my karma"), the soul level damage is even greater than if negative actions are undertaken in ignorance. The cycle of rebirth does not provide an excuse for misdeeds. Just as we might use deferred payment on credit cards, when our large expenditures catch up with us, it can be quite upsetting. Once this has happened and a lesson has been learned, if we continue to repeat the cycle with awareness of the consequences, the damage becomes even more insidious and progressively more difficult to correct the situation.

What Is Karma?

In the book, *Ponder On This*, based on the writings of Alice Bailey, who channeled information from the Tibetan Master Djwhal Khul, a discussion of karma goes deeply into eons of time. "The law of karma is the most stupendous law of the system and one which is impossible for the average man in any way to comprehend, for, if traced back along its central root and its many ramifications, one eventually reaches the position where causes antedating the solar system have to be dealt with....This law really concerns, or is based on causes which are inherent in the constitution of matter itself and on the interaction between atomic units, whether we use this expression in connection with an atom of substance, a human being, a planetary atom, or a solar atom."

In an attempt to simplify a very complex subject, imagine being on a ferris wheel, fated to go up and around, over and over again, for eternity. Eventually you may begin to get motion sickness, hate and detest every moment of that cycle, and want to get off! If you have a fight with the person in the seat next to you, fixate on the creaking of the machinery, or take out your frustration on someone else, each revolution only gets worse. The next time around, you're in no mood to see the birds flying in the sky or hear the music of the calliope in the distance. If you sink into the depths of despair, your perceptions become warped.

Or, each time around, you could observe new joys in the ever-changing skies and feel rapture over the beauty of the sunrises and sunsets.

If, on one of your go-rounds, you succumb to anger and rage, perhaps shoving someone out of a seat, or even pushing him over the edge to die, you can sink lower and lower into more darkness and despair. It becomes very difficult to reverse the patterns and change your actions when such depths are plumbed. With each revolution of the wheel, you are also faced with antagonism from the people you have harmed, and you again return it in kind. This might be likened to guilt of commission. The penalty for this kind of behavior, karmically, is more difficult than the penalty for the guilt of omission.

Apathy and fear produce guilt of omission. Even if an individual has achieved harmony within himself, to feel superior to or ignore the plight and suffering of those around him puts him in danger of creating karma as a result of that apathy.

There is a connection between each human being; on a soul consciousness level, we are all one. It's not too hard to see that each individual has a responsibility for his or her own growth, and a need to keep his or her spiritual balance. But what can we do to help others who have fallen into unhappiness or evil? Each person has free will and must make his own choices. He cannot be forced or coerced into change, *nor can anyone else effect change for him.* But there are ways to help someone help himself.

Fortunately there are many enlightened beings on earth and in spiritual realms to guide and help those who seek them out by asking for help. These enlightened beings have passed their own tests and have evolved to the point where their presence can help others heal their own consciousness. A biblical verse says, "Ask and ye shall receive." To find a source of true guidance one need only ask with all sincerity. When the student is ready, the teacher really does appear.

Love and Forgiveness

Each man must find, for himself, the way to walk the fine line between good and evil, responsibility and self-containment. Painful examination of every thought and deed, with the immediate decision to transmute any negativity to the positive side, can help balance the pairs of polar opposites. And those poles must be balanced before the wheel of karma is left behind. Every jot of the law must be fulfilled before the soul is free. As an example, if we catch ourselves being revengeful, angry, and unforgiving, it is important to stop—immediately—and change the attitude. If we commit even the smallest act that will lie on our conscience—even if we get away with it in the eyes of man or the law—we will have to rectify that act sometime in a future experience.

The process of balancing the scales may demand more concrete action than just forgiving one's enemies, and a Pollyanna attitude may actually be dangerous, for it may not be safe to actually physically embrace an antagonist. But since balancing the scales can take place primarily in the mind, the act of deliberately changing one's thoughts, and then doing something positive to rectify a situation, can be a way to clean the slate. There is a stratum of consciousness where thoughts are transmuted faster than the speed of light. It is possible to effect a healing with someone by having an "astral" conversation with that person. He or she will get the message, sometimes better than if it were communicated in written or oral form. It is important to know, however, that an individual cannot carry on that conversation, astrally, unless he is clear as to what to say. If the astral thoughts are still tinged with anger, that anger will be communicated. Sincerity is an important part of the process.

Pride is a big danger as one eliminates overt wrongdoings (sometimes moving on to more subtle ones). Transactional Analysis (TA) calls it an attitude of "I'm OK, You're not OK" (as opposed to "I'm OK, You're OK"). TA also describes a "rescue triangle" in which the rescuer rescues the victim, and the victim becomes the persecutor, who ends up persecuting the rescuer! In truth, most rescuers have an attitude, even unconsciously, of "I'm OK, and you're not." Nobody really wants to be rescued. It is resented, eventually. But how do we help our fellow man? Helping a person to help himself works every time. Sending the person healing, loving energy on that astral level encourages and energizes one to find the solution to a problem or a situation by themselves.

Development of love on a universal level is the most powerful healing agent of all. On a personal level, we may not like the actions of another person, but if we can acknowledge and see even a dim, faintly flickering light of spirit inside, it can help the person heal him- or herself. This is impersonal love, not passion or personal, possessive love.

But how is it possible to love the Nazis, to forgive Hitler, and to find any spark of humanity within the people who tortured and killed millions of Jews with sadistic pleasure and no mercy?

Group Karma

As I began this book, I wondered why I happened to be writing about the Holocaust as opposed to another subject. Of course, I wanted to share the information that was coming forth from regression sessions, and my deepest, most heartfelt desire is to do anything I can to help stamp out man's inhumanity to man (or animal or plant).

More than that, however, I believe there are no accidents in life, and there is a reason for everything. So I questioned the reasons behind the obvious motivation. I was not in Germany during the war; I had no relatives who suffered there; and I am not Jewish. The book is partly due to someone else (who shall remain unidentified)—a man, a Catholic, who was an impetus for my writing it. This is not just an interested friend who encouraged me, but someone who shares an equal responsibility for the book. He is part of an astounding story that emerged from one regression session in particular, but I felt there must be even more of a reason lurking behind the obvious fact that he was acting under his own inner universal guidance in facilitating this book.

When Elie Wiesel finally found someone who would publish his terrifyingly moving document, *Night,* few people wanted to read about the Holocaust. "Such depressing subject matter," they said. Elie Wiesel had an important reason for writing his book. He is Jewish. He lived through the nightmare of the camps. He has written thirty books so far, all devoted to the same cause. He cannot let people forget what happened when "a cultured people turned to genocide and the rest of the world, also composed of cultured people, remained silent in the face of genocide."

So why me and why my Catholic facilitator?

I was born in the South, a Protestant, and I had little contact with Jews until I attended school in Washington, DC, and then, primarily, because I was a baby-sitter for a wonderful little girl in a warm Jewish family. But as my own lifetimes began to come to the surface, and continued to emerge much later on, I found that I had had two very important lifetimes, both as a Jewish mystic. Many years before I discovered reincarnation, however, an interesting thing happened. I was married, had three small children, and lived in Shrewsbury, NJ. I attended the Presbyterian Church, and my children attended Sunday school. Since I was trained as a musician from the age of four, studying classical piano, and I was also a singer, it was natural to be part of the church choir. Music, but singing in particular, was my passion.

Imagine how delighted I was to be hired for a special weekly singing assignment after singing a solo in church. I was asked to be the soprano soloist for a Reformed Jewish Synagogue that rented our church auditorium on Friday nights. I was also expected to sing at the high holy days services, Rosh Hashana and Yom Kippur. I was twenty-four years old.

The organist taught me to read Hebrew phonetically, and I had a wonderful year singing with the Cantor. The second year was a tough one for the temple, as they ran low on funds. I was upgraded to the position of Cantor for that year, singing his music as well as my own solos. On high holy days, the services lasted all day long for several days, and included extensive and difficult music. I loved every minute of it, and the minor harmonics of Jewish music fit my voice perfectly. Even the phonetic Hebrew was easy for me to learn. Was that just an accident, or were the vibrations from two lives as a Jewish mystic still operating in my aura, unbeknownst to me? I recalled these two lives much later on. In fact, one of the former lifetimes came to the surface as I was writing this book.

It is my contention, especially after conducting thousands of regression sessions over twenty-eight years, that a soul on the wheel of karma needs the experience of all races, colors, and creeds. (Be careful, therefore, of prejudice against a person, group of people, or religion. You may have to experience the very thing you criticize in others.)

My understanding of my lives as a Jewish mystic answered my questions about my own part in relating past life memories of suffering at the hands of the Nazis. But what about my "co-responsible" person? Ours is a continuing working relationship, but our coming together could have been for one or two sessions only, as is true with some of my clients. I now consider him a very dear friend and a very special person, but when I first met this man, I was quite afraid of him. I was scheduled to do a regression session with him at our first meeting, so I had to overcome any personal feelings and simply relate to him on a professional level. After many working sessions, we gradually developed a closer, if guarded, professional association. I was actually never particularly curious as to what our past association might have been, if any.

One morning as I awakened, I suddenly knew what our past connection had been. I saw, in a very quick flash, like electronic ticker tape at the stock exchange, a scene in Spain. It was a dungeon and a man was standing over me in a very threatening manner. I recognized my new friend as a priest-judge-inquisitor during the Spanish Inquisition. He was Catholic then and is a Catholic now. It was 1492, and he interrogated and may have tortured and killed many members of a mystical Jewish sect called Marranos (the word originally meant pigs). The Marranos were Jews in Spain who converted to Christianity under coercion, but were thought to secretly continue to practice Judaism. Their counterparts were Jews who had converted to

Christianity, called Conversos, and were above suspicion. I was one of those people who was held in a dungeon for further examination about my beliefs. For some reason, even though his manner was extremely frightening and he interrogated me extensively, he didn't hurt me and he spared my life. I don't know why he was kinder to me than to others, because it was questionable as to whether I would be tortured and killed or allowed to live. I was heavily interrogated by him, and I'm sure I was due to die like the others. But something swung his decision, and he let me live.

I don't know if my "co-worker" has the same memory that I have. But in my mind, we have come together to heal our personal karmic wounds, easily done and already accomplished I believe, perhaps for the more important purpose of revealing information about healing even more difficult karmic wounds on a wider scale.

I know of two other of my lifetimes that related to the Catholic Church, both of them very emotionally painful and both closely associated with my being beheaded! In this lifetime it was almost impossible for me to go to a Catholic Church with my Catholic husband because of the anguish I felt inside my body. I could not begin to explain it to him, nor do I think he knew what I was feeling. That intense mixture of emotion was something I couldn't understand myself. I didn't know why I cried bitter tears every time I tried to attend Mass. Fortunately, that reaction has since been healed.

I know that I was persecuted as a witch in Salem in my last lifetime. Once again I might have been put to death, but after a trial, I was allowed to live. As a punishment and a warning, I was dunked in and out of a body of water for an eternity, it seems. I died as a result of pneumonia. Was that life a carryover from the mysticism of the Spanish Inquisition? Was that lifetime a

precursor to my questioning of organized religions as the ultimate authority when I was a very young child? Did it have anything to do with my being a female Cantor in a Reform Jewish
Synagogue? Is all of that a precursor to my writing this book?

The Essenes

The other lifetime I most identify with as a foundation for
my spiritual quests was as an Essene. The Essenes were a
monastic Jewish sect, some of whom lived near the caves of
Qumran, near the Dead Sea in what is now Israel. The Dead
Sea Scrolls, discovered in a cave at Qumran in this century,
were the records and teachings of the Essenes and were a major
archaeological find. Some of them have been translated and
published, but a tug of war still exists between the Jewish religious authorities and the Catholic Church as to who has the
ultimate claim to these important records, for the scrolls were
translated into modern language by a Catholic priest in the
Vatican. This issue has reached the courts but is not yet decided. Until a decision has been made, much of the information
remains hidden and unpublished.

It is thought, and it is my memory, that the group of Essenes
who wrote the Dead Sea Scrolls had an important mission: that
of invoking the spirit of the great soul who would come into
physical life and show the world, by example, how to love one's
enemies, forgive injustices, and walk in the pure light of the
God spirit. By going through his life in such a way that he publicly passed all the initiations on earth, and by constantly teaching those around him that they could follow his example, he
performed a great service to mankind. For it was a great sacri-

fice and a great expression of love for humanity to return to the darkness of the earth plane instead of remaining in the lightness of spirit. We know that soul by the name Jesus, who became Christed through his own initiation of torture on earth. In addition to invoking this soul, it was also the sacred duty of the Essenes to choose and prepare the mother who would bear the child for this great sacrifice.

I had the rare privilege of meeting a woman who had been intimately involved with the Dead Sea Scrolls during her whole twentieth century life. She was a client and became a friend. Her father, now deceased, devised the code and method for a computer system that would allow this gigantic and important body of work to be preserved after its translation. For most of the years of her adolescence, her father collaborated with the priest at the Vatican in Rome who was the prime translator of the scrolls. Naomi was born Jewish, but spent more of her life attending Catholic ceremonies at the Vatican than going to a synagogue. Working on such information as had emerged from the Essenes in Qumran gave Naomi's father and her whole family a broad concept of religion.

According to my friend, there is good reason why two of the major religions of the world should be concerned about the release of information contained within the scrolls. Some of what will be revealed, eventually, may blow apart some of the most sacred beliefs of both Judaism and Christianity. Perhaps when it is time for all this information to be revealed, and in the "New Age," the dawning of true awareness, there will be but one religion or spiritual awareness.

Naomi and her husband were among a group of friends who drove to my house in the country one winter day. I had prepared lunch for the seven people who were there, but I was unprepared for the discussion around my long pine table. The people were friends of mine who had not known each other previously. They had come to my house for a variety of reasons. Three came to do some work with me and had been staying there for a few days. One client was from Canada, another from Georgia, and another from California. Four people were from New York City. I had not specifically invited them to meet each other, although I was delighted that they would do so. It all happened quite by accident. As we began talking about Naomi's father and his important life's work, Naomi told us some of the information that is contained in the disputed parts of the manuscripts, then added that there was much more to emerge from the translations. What she shared was quite staggering. As a stunned quiet settled over the table, each person eventually volunteered that he or she had already remembered a lifetime as an Essene! I will never forget that day. How was it arranged that we should meet again so unexpectedly? Who worked out all the details?

When I first discovered my lifetime as an Essene, I was with two therapists who were friends. We were not in a regression session, but simply talking, when something that was said triggered a memory within my mind. I closed my eyes almost involuntarily, and saw myself in a group of people that I knew were the Essenes. The feeling of harmony and joy in my heart and body was utterly beautiful. My friends said that my face took on a whole new look and that I shone with light as I described what I was seeing. I know that was my happiest lifetime on earth and I can recall that image at will when I need to feel a sense of oneness and high purpose again. The man Jesus, for he was human in the time of the Essenes, has always seemed like a very personal friend to me, not some remote figure to be worshipped at a distance. Jesus had been a great teacher in all of his former times on earth, but it was in this lifetime of great sac-

rifice and love that he showed the world, by his own resurrec-
tion, or return after death, the potential for oneness with God
for each and every person.

Everyone whom I have regressed to a lifetime as an Essene,
whether Jewish or non-Jewish in the present time, has had the
same feeling. I seem to know in my heart, as well as in my mind,
that this profound teacher gave us the example of what each and
every person must achieve: that the expression of universal love
is the ultimate way to get off the wheel of karma and reunite
with the God force. It is distressing to me to hear that so much
of what he said is misinterpreted by the variety of churches that
profess to believe in his teachings. How do I have the audacity
to say that? I, who have not studied theology, nor attained a
position as an authority on the subject? I, who as a person living on the earth plane, am obviously not yet free of my own
karmic anchors?

The Essenes were dedicated to working in complete harmony toward something that would, hopefully, bring healing and
enlightenment to the world. We shared the essence of pure love
and joy in our glorious experience. Those with the same memory have all described the wonderful sense of joy that permeated that life. They have also shared with me dreadful and
mournful feelings of intense grief knowing what that special
Master, friend, and teacher would have to endure. Although we
knew it had to happen that way, we suffered terribly to watch
him die, aware of his very human suffering in a very human
body. One young woman, who was especially close to him,
described in her regression session, her presence at Golgotha.
Upon seeing the agony of his death, an experience so painful
she couldn't bear it, she remembered running away and feeling
that she had abandoned him at the time of his greatest need
because her own pain was too great. Her latent guilt was very

heavy until she regressed to that time. *Self*-forgiveness was the hard part for her, because she knew she had already been forgiven by him. This woman again works within a spiritual community, dedicated to bringing truth and light to humanity. She is now able to do her work with greater fullness of heart. Her present contribution balances the scales within herself, for self-punishment or guilt only creates schism and splits.

Are the reincarnating group of souls who were Jews dying in concentration camps back again so soon to teach us about survival of the soul? Are they group souls who volunteered for the mission, martyring themselves in order for humanity to learn? Are they here to heal us in their own special way?

Regression Therapy

It is possible to tap past life experiences without the use of drugs, hypnosis, or any other artificial means. The information locked inside the human brain is staggering, and we have easier access to our unconscious than we may imagine. Like learning to use a computer, there are certain keys to punch and commands to give that will open up huge files of data.

The thread of consciousness permeates every life. Everything that is woven or strung on that thread is still there. It's a matter of unraveling the threads, much like unraveling a row of knitting. My instruction before a session begins are that the concrete, judgmental mind must be put aside for a time, and trust be allowed free reign. If one is doubtful about what may be "only an intuition," the doors of that part of the mind remain locked forever. Skepticism has to take a vacation. The purpose of the session is to learn how to access stored information and bring it to the surface. If one can do this with my guidance, one can also continue to access information later, at home alone, without any help.

In fact, one regression session may be all it takes to open up the storeroom of data on many lives. Many people who have been through intensive therapy, even psychoanalysis, have expressed amazement at the information from the present life alone that emerges during a regression session. Some memories come to the surface that have never come to light even with years of therapy.

After the review of the present life, with some discussion about the patterns we created even at the moment of birth, past life information seems to come to consciousness very easily.

There are some basic questions that I have developed to help unravel the threads. The purpose of these questions—which may seem unimportant, even inconsequential—is to keep the left brain busy while the right brain has a chance to open up. When the regression session is finished, the patterns of this present life, including crucial birth survival decisions, are crystal clear. It also becomes obvious that these patterns are *exactly* the same as they were many centuries ago, for we do not change until, by conscious thought and awareness, we decide to change. We may have changed clothes and put on different cultural habits, but inside we see quite clearly that we are the same as always.

It doesn't seem important to believe in reincarnation for memories to come forth. One southern gentleman courteously went through the whole session because it was a gift from someone else. He saw himself as a congressman from a particular district in Virginia in the 1800s. Before our session, this gentleman had no knowledge of reincarnation, and certainly had no belief in rebirth. He was quite stunned by the images that came to mind during the session. He was wide awake, not under any form of hypnosis. He wasn't at all sure he wasn't just making things up. Evidently, he went to the Library of Congress and investigated the historical accuracy of the information that emerged during his session. He not only confirmed his name and found himself in the list of congressman from that exact Virginia district, but he verified some of the details of his life at that time. Details had emerged during the session that he couldn't possibly have known about, since he didn't know that congressman had existed before his session with me. He is still convinced that the donor of the session and I went to great lengths to create a hoax! Of course that would be an impossibility. And even if the gentleman never accepts what came forth from his own subconscious, I'm sure a healing of sorts took place on some level. If he did make it all up, this gentleman has an astounding ability to tune into historical facts, psychically, of which he had been previously unaware.

Sessions last about three hours. Usually the person is not tired afterward and has no sense of how much time has passed. In fact, the usual feeling at the end is a sense of lightness of being. For after all, a lot of nonproductive energy gets released. Most of the time, strong emotions, even tears, accompany the details that come forth. That is usually a strong confirmation to the person that the memory is accurate.

There are many instances where two people, who have no chance to compare notes, have seen each other in their individual regression sessions. These past life memories can help heal troubled relationships, whether those relationships are familial, platonic, or passionate. We seem to come back, over and over again, attracting the same people into our lives. Sometimes we change roles and even sex, but the emotional ties that existed in the past are the same in the present. Awareness of this fact can help us accept the proposition that we better get it right in the present so we don't have to continue having the same painful associations in the future. On the positive side, wonderful relationships can be valued even more when we realize that we *have* flocked together before.

Even if past life memories are as painful as remembering a life in Nazi Germany, bringing them into daylight relieves the subconscious of the dark decisions that may have been made at times of pain and tragedy.

Thankfully, every night is followed by dawn and a new day, which bring with them a renewed chance to heal the soul.

3

Awakening

UNTIL I LEARNED about rein-
carnation, I had a hard time understanding the inequalities of
life. As a child, I worried over the condition of people in general. In the South, the circumstances of my life were such that
I was exposed to all economic levels. I knew people who had
beautiful homes, shiny cars, and beautiful clothes; and I also
knew people who were so poor they hardly had enough to eat.
It hurt me to see people who struggled with extreme physical
disabilities, and I questioned many things that didn't seem fair.
I became aware that some people with hardships seemed
cheerful and happy, and also knew that others, who seemingly
had everything, could be sad or discontented. I marveled at
the resiliency of one elderly blind woman I loved who was
always laughing at small things and making jokes. This wonderful woman crocheted gorgeous, museum-quality bed-
spreads and table cloths, even though she was blind. Since I
observed so much, I asked a lot of questions. But no one could
seem to tell me why some people were born into privileged

situations, whereas others had real struggles just to make it through each day.

I watched Irene, our black cook, work hard every day without complaint. I loved her enormously and still do. (I hope she hears me, wherever she is now.) Each summer when I returned home after being away at school, I raced in to reach my arms around her enormous waist to give her the biggest hug I could. And one day I heard my aunt say that she always treated her Negro help with courtesy and helped them whenever she could, but she wouldn't want to have lunch with them or any Negro person. I don't think she realized how bigoted she was, but I was devastated by her remark and never trusted that aunt again. Eventually I learned that racial bigotry was not confined to the South nor to the color of one's skin. My aunt meant no harm. She felt she was being kind. She was merely repeating what she had observed and was taught in the tradition of her upbringing. But it would seem that she was still asleep on a soul consciousness level.

In the light of reincarnation, a soul may have to experience all races and cultures if that is what is needed for the remedy, growth, or balance of the soul qualities. Allowing oneself to have prejudice or to scoff at minority groups may set up a future lifetime where the scoffer comes back as a member of the race or group in question. If an individual is critical or feels superior, he or she creates the basis for a boomerang situation. He may have to walk in the shoes of the person he criticized to know what it is like, for all the scales eventually have to be balanced.

As a child, I saw many examples of tragedy and man's inhumanity to man, but I never saw evil. I didn't know it existed.

Past Life Psychic Connections

When World War II was declared, I was a very small child. But I glued myself to the big radio that sat on the floor of our sunroom, my ear as close to the speakers as possible, until I was told to do something else. I was terrified to think of what it must be like to live through the nightmares I was hearing about on the radio. The RKO Pathe Movie-Tone news, at the Saturday afternoon matinee, was even more vividly graphic.

I can still see that little girl sitting on the floor by the big radio with tears flowing freely down her cheeks. I was so grateful to be born in America. I had no relatives or ties to European countries, but, having a strong religious background, I thanked God for keeping me and the people I loved away from the terror of bombs, with all that shattered glass and rubble that had formerly been buildings or homes. My heart hurt for all the children, adults, and animals who lived in fear. I couldn't imagine the terror of hearing the scream of a plummeting bomb, not knowing who or what it might destroy in the next second. I felt a terrible, sympathetic physical pain if I saw a soldier who had lost a limb. I rolled bandages for the Red Cross and frantically collected tinfoil to mold into huge balls for the war effort.

But I didn't know what Hitler was doing to the Jews.

For some reason, I didn't like food as a child. I ate next to nothing and my family worried because I was very thin. Little did I know, then, that someone very close to me in a previous existence was suffering what I was so thankful to be protected from. My friend Bettina, whom I had to wait some thirty years to meet, was two years younger than I when Poland was invaded. Her family enjoyed a comfortable, even luxurious, lifestyle. Bettina's father raised Arabian horses. The Germans confiscated their home, and in spite of the fact that Bettina's family was not Jewish, put the entire family in a concentration camp.

One of Bettina's unerasable memories of childhood was of terrible hunger. She told me of a time when her mother was quite sick and the German guards gave her mother a tiny bit of extra chicken. Her mother began to share that measly extra portion with Bettina, who was only two years old and incomprehensibly hungry.

The older children said, "No, Mother, you need that food yourself so that you can get well." Bettina remembers the anguish of her hunger pains and the guilt she felt as she accepted that extra tiny bite of chicken, thus depriving her mother of some small amount of nourishment. She remembers being very angry at her brothers and sisters for putting her in the position of making such a choice.

As I write this story, having told it many times, my eyes fill with tears to think that my darling friend should ever have wanted for anything in her life. I cried as she told me this in her regression session, and I'm crying still. This touches me so deeply that I know, and could never be convinced otherwise, that I was not able to eat as a child because Bettina had no food. We discovered in her regression session that we were sisters-in-law in a Greek life. The closeness that existed then still exists today. But that is another story in another book. Bettina and her family were, fortunately, released from the camp but were never to return to their beautiful home.

Bettina told me that when her mother would point out very beautiful objects and would comment that they had owned things more beautiful than those before the war, Bettina thought her mother was just being snobbish. Years later, someone went back to Poland and was able to photograph her former house and some of its contents; Bettina then knew her mother was being truthful. My friend spends no time indulging in thoughts of what might have been, nor is she self-pitying. But there are still wounds that go deep within, and the direction of her life was changed forever at a very early age.

Beginnings of a Search

My family took me to Sunday school and church every single week. I happily curled up next to my mother, enjoying the music and sometimes taking a little nap if the sermon was too long. But as I reached the age of five or six and started to listen to what was being said, I began to ask philosophical questions. The ministers stressed that salvation of the soul depended on, among other things, regular attendance in church. I asked my mother, "What if someone lives very far away from a church and has no way of getting there? If he or she has God in his or her heart, and reads the Bible every day, will that person still be condemned to Hell?" I persisted in asking other rather simplistic and naive questions, but no one seemed to have any answers. At age eight, I hesitated to confront the minister directly, but I began to irritate some members of my family by finding many discrepancies in the logic of his sermons. So as soon as I was old enough, I began to investigate a variety of religious theories, going off to churches of different denominations on my own. I listened to a variety of ministers in the hope of finding answers to my questions, and although I continued my religious search into adulthood, all of the ministers could ultimately only convey the message that God was just and that suffering was part of the human condition.

But how could a just and loving God allow some of his children to suffer so horribly? I could not shake the questions, even though my faith in God remained eternally strong.

Understanding Universal Laws

After I read *There Is a River,* about the life of Edgar Cayce, and learned about reincarnation and karma, many things that were puzzling to me began to make sense. Evidently the main purpose of reincarnation, coming back into a physical body on earth over and over again, is for the soul to have a chance to work out the karma, or debt, that has been accumulating, and balance the scales for past mistakes. As we have said, it is necessary to have a physical form to act out the automatic karmic script, and earth is the school where that can take place. It is confirmed over and over again in all writings about reincarnation and karma that on a soul consciousness level, we can't and don't get away with anything.

Every bit of the law must be fulfilled. The Bible says, in Luke XVI:17, "And it is easier for heaven and earth to pass, than one tittle of the law to fail." Matthew V:18 says the same thing this way: "For verily I say unto you, till heaven and earth pass, one jot or one tittle shall in no wise pass from the law, till all be fulfilled." It is only in the light of reincarnation that these biblical verses make sense, for I take them to mean that each thought and deed of every person must eventually be purified. We see, or hear about, acts of man's inhumanity to man every day. Some people seem to get away with wrongdoing and even benefit in the process. But in the final graduation exercises, every single act, every single *thought,* must be balanced on the scales of justice, or the soul remains on the wheel of karma.

Clarification of the term "karma" came forth from Cayce's readings as well. In Sanskrit, the word karma means action. In the light of reincarnation it is action and reaction, or "the law" that must be brought into play. Every action must have a consequent reaction. If an action is malefic, the return reaction will be malefic. If an action is positive and beneficial, the reaction will also be positive and beneficial. To simplify things enormously, the old Judaic principle of an eye for an eye and a tooth for a tooth can, to some degree, help explain how karma works. The idea is that every thought and deed carries an obligation and works on the principle of a boomerang. What a person sends out into the ethers eventually comes back in the exact same way and in the exact same degree. Or, what goes around comes around. That person is the only one who can rewrite his own story.

It is my feeling that major traumas on the surface of life may create an inner awakening that is life-changing. Sometimes this comes, unfortunately, in the form of illness or loss. When the person is able to recognize that the outer events or scenarios are ultimately for the purpose of inducing an inner look and question—*What is the lesson to be learned?*—he may begin to ask the Universe for even more opportunities to pass karmic tests. But there is no pressure to pass the tests until we are truly ready, for we have centuries to get everything right. To my way of thinking, life is like a school. We are able to select plenty of interesting subjects to study, but there are some requirements set by the school that, even though difficult, are necessary for graduation. One can take a few subjects at a time over a period of years, or cram everything into a few challenging semesters.

Before a change of attitude can take place, however, a person has to become aware, or awake. Life, or one's higher self, or the universe has a funny way of bringing about that awakening in exactly the way that each person needs it. Sometimes this is set in motion by something we could call divine discontent, which often precedes a more conscious search for the meaning and purpose of existence.

Perhaps what we mean by the term *awakening* is that we suddenly get the message that it is time to become better writers of our own scripts, and to be very careful about what we're putting into the heavenly computer, so to speak. If we really accepted and understood that many of the problems we create for ourselves may be due to being somewhat lazy or nonconfrontational or asleep, we'd shake ourselves, have a figurative cup of coffee, and think about what it is that we really want to bring into our lives. Sometimes it takes a shock to bring that awakening.

Painful Awakening

Elizabeth Heich describes her own awakening in her book, *Initiation*. As a young girl, her greatest dream was to be married to her sweetheart. She said, "I became engaged to him. We loved one another deeply and passionately, and I could hardly wait for the moment when I was to become his wife with body and soul, with every part of my being." Sometime after the wedding, Elizabeth had a terrible realization. "In becoming the wife of my beloved after this long period of waiting, I experienced extreme happiness as I expected I would. I had attained my goal—between us there were no longer any 'forbidden' signs. I loved him passionately, with my entire being, and he loved me in just the same way. I experienced the highest fulfillment of love in body and soul.

"And then everything collapsed around me…"

Elizabeth Heich realized that as long as she had the goal of a happy marriage to work toward, she was fulfilled. She felt she had a fixed point in her future toward which she was moving. But once she had accomplished her goal, very successfully, her future suddenly became empty. She said, "I fell into a vacuum, for I did not know what I still had to wait for." The rest of her life seemed only for the purpose of filling out the remaining time. She said, "THE REMAINING TIME, remaining time? Till when? And the answer was: UNTIL DEATH!"

Elizabeth realized that one day she would have to say good-bye to her husband, or he would have to say good-bye to her. She was devastated to think that her greatest happiness and beautiful love would come to an end. She continued, "I did not want to tell my husband anything about the desperate state of mind I was in. He was completely happy and would not have been able to understand me. If he had no such ideas and was STILL DREAMING THE DREAM OF MORTAL PEOPLE, why should I awaken him and make him unhappy?…For my part, however, I was not at all satisfied by overlooking reality…and even less satisfied by the fairy tales of religion about 'the other side' and the 'other world.' These are figments of the imagination intended to be a sedative to people. Whoever can believe in them is happy, but a thinking person insists on having proof.

"Within myself I constantly bore a heavy spiritual burden without being able to shake it off. Sooner or later, however, a constant burden on the soul is bound to affect the body.…"

Impaired eyesight was the means by which Elizabeth awakened herself, as it was with Edgar Cayce. She had made great progress in drawing and painting. Her teachers expected a lot from her in the future. Although her livelihood was not impaired with the loss of eyesight, she could no longer derive any pleasure from painting, because black spots and a heavy black lines would appear before her on the canvas. She could play the piano, however, and learned to practice with her eyes closed to be prepared for the time when she could no longer see. Closing her eyes also gave some relief from the aggravating black lines. She covered all this inner despair with an outward manifestation of cheerfulness and hope. Perhaps this was true of my older blind friend as well. Perhaps her beautiful crocheted work was her way of having purpose in her life. Or, perhaps she had become awakened and her joy was the true cosmic joy of spiritual knowledge.

Elizabeth Heich found a teacher in the form of an Indian man who taught her yoga and used ayurvedic medicine to restore her eyesight. "One autumn day I stood at the window of our apartment with my small son and watched the leaves of a chestnut tree floating slowly to earth. As I had so often done before, I meditated upon death again! Suddenly I heard the voice in me speaking: 'Death?—Why do you persist in seeing but the ONE side of truth? What do the trees and nature reveal in spring? Life!—again and again! Life and death alternate in an everlasting circle. Death is but the other side of life...'

"In this moment, I saw quite clearly, that as life recedes from the tree and its leaves in autumn, the leaves become lifeless, empty husks, fall off and die. But only empty husks!" The symbolism of the repeated cycles of Spring and Fall, with new buds on the trees and dead leaves falling again made her realize that life remains eternal, for only the leaves died. The essence of life which lived in the tree itself would once again burst forth in the Spring.

She described the next step in her awareness, "And I saw even further: The fountain of eternal existence—human beings call it 'GOD'—breathes life into man, just as the Bible says that God breathed life into Adam's nostrils. Then God inhales again, withdrawing his breath, so that the empty husk falls: The body of man dies. Yet life does not cease at this moment; it clothes itself with a new body, in an eternal cycle and moves on, as everything in this world lives and moves in rhythm, from the orbit of the planets to the breath and pulse of every living creature."

My Own Image

I was about five years old when I experienced something that must have been the beginning of my own awakening. At that tender age, I came face to face with a puzzle. I would look in a mirror and see an image that I didn't recognize. I pondered and agonized over this as I did everything else. "Who is that?" I would say to myself. "I'm in here, so who is that?" I could see a little girl.

I could watch the way she moved and behaved, but she wasn't the real ME. I could FEEL me inside, but I couldn't relate to my body and form at all. I would try to get very close to the mirror in order to see ME through my eyes. There was no one to ask, either. My family thought some of the unusual things I said and did were "cute." I wasn't being cute, and I didn't want to expose this deadly serious concern to any patronizing, even though loving, comment. I really needed an answer.

Elizabeth Heich had a similar experience as a child. She described looking in the mirror as a small girl and knowing that *she* resided inside her body. She told of wanting to see the person inside her body. She would put her eye as close as she could to that mirror trying to see inside. She said, "...when I first heard about death, I had stood before the mirror, examining the picture of the invisible, my own reflection. Even at that early age I simply could not understand that I would some day have to die, that I would someday cease to exist." This seemed impossible to Elizabeth as she continued looking at her face, her *mask*, and the two black holes from which the thinking person inside was looking at the world.

With any kind of awareness a new form of curiosity and inner questioning takes place and answers begin to appear. Unfortunately, it seems that the more tenacious or stubborn we are in clinging to the old ways of thinking and sleeping, the more difficult the event that produces the awakening. The old saying, "When the student is ready, the teacher appears," is very true. But sometimes school can be very hard.

Health Problems
As a Means of Awakening

When I attended a summer conference on astrology at Cambridge University, I met an amazing man named John Addey. His research and subsequent book on "Harmonics" is well known in the astrological community. John developed a whole new way of looking at an astrological chart that reveals deeper characteristics of a person's nature. As an example, Adolf Hitler's chart does not show the true depth of the evil of his character unless it is examined with this method.

John was not only brilliant, he was as courteous and gracious as English gentlemen are thought to be. Even though he walked with two canes, he would serve his guests extra coffee or dessert at the lunch breaks. He never mentioned his disability or discussed any pain that he might be feeling. As I sat through the lectures, I felt as though I was back in Socrates's school. We discussed, among other things, the philosophy of numbers. Since mathematics was one of my majors in school, this was particularly fascinating to me.

One day I told John about my reaction to his theories, and mentioned Socrates. His modesty was genuine. He said, "Oh my dear, no. If I had not had this fusion of my spine, I would have wasted my life playing golf and going to the race track. As it was I had to lie in bed and think!" John acknowledged the extreme measures he had to take, on a soul consciousness level, to wake himself up.

It is possible to awaken, I think, without so much pain and hardship. Life brings amazing and infinitely exciting opportunities of choice so that we can exercise our God-given gift of free will. There comes a time for everyone, however, when we consciously decide to transmute free will onto another level—that of divine will. That major life decision may be stimulated and brought about by divine discontent, illness, or hardships. We seem to know best, all by ourselves, how to create those circumstances of awakening. Sometimes the universe gives a little helping hand in our initiation process, providing traumatic external events if we're too slow in rousing ourselves. The trick is to see with an inner eye and become the observer of our own lives. It may speed things up if we learn how to ask for the right conditions needed for more growth, whether those conditions are easy or difficult. If we sincerely ask for opportunity for growth, the outer conditions may not be as traumatic as they might have been otherwise. The outer circumstances may not change, but a different perspective enables us to see things in a clearer light, creating greater healing and stronger soul connection and consciousness.

4

Hell As a State
of Consciousness

✦

WHEN WE REINCARNATE into a new life on the earth plane, we bring back the subconscious memory of all former experiences.

Just as upon awakening from sleep to start a new day we are aware that the events of yesterday condition plans and activities of the new day, so it is from life to life. But with just so many hours in the day, not every thought or activity of yesterday can be expressed in full. Each person must make choices about how to schedule his or her time. Optimally, each person intelligently evaluates the most essential tasks to be accomplished within that day and does his best to complete those tasks.

Sometimes, however, if a day was difficult we may awaken the next day with the same leftover plateful of problems. Suppose we haven't had enough time to sleep, or our nightmares have kept us tossing and turning during the night. We get up, take a shower, and put on a new suit of clothes; but we go through the day in a fog, not taking care of our daily tasks in an efficient manner. With clouds of anxiety and pressures from the previous day, it's difficult to have the good feeling of accomplishment that comes with completing one's tasks and solving one's problems within a specified time period. Matters are made worse if the problems don't disappear and sleep continues to be disturbed. Sometimes we continue the buildup of anxieties and pressures until they are overwhelming. A vacation might help us develop a new perspective on a life situation, so that daily activities seem fruitful again, but if the old patterns continue for years without a letup, it is possible that some part of the body will give way, and we become ill. Or death comes to take us away from it all.

If lifetime to lifetime is like yesterday to today, the state of consciousness at the time of death has much to do with the circumstances of rebirth into a new earthly existence. The level of awareness that can be developed in between lives plays a factor as well, for a thread of consciousness runs continuously throughout all existence.

We have discussed the fact that the spiritual realm is another kind of schoolroom, like summer school, where life events can be reviewed and decisions made about the kinds of experiences to be undertaken in the next go-round. If enough time elapses between lives for a soul to reevaluate his former times on earth, intelligent choices can be made about what to undertake on the next go-round on earth. But if a soul comes back too soon without having had enough time to recover from all of the effects of the previous lifetimes, the same traumas, fears, anxieties, insecurities, and health patterns may return as well.

If mankind has free will, and it extends onto a soul consciousness level, why would anyone come into a life of hell that was connected with Nazi Germany? What could possibly have happened previously to magnetize such conditions of atrocity? What was the soul lesson to be learned? And what if souls, back so soon from Nazi Germany, had made unthinking, hasty decisions about returning too quickly? It seems likely, from information emerging in regression sessions, that many people simply jumped into families where there were no real past life ties, as if searching for safety, or else returned to be with people who were only somewhat familiar. Without enough time between incarnations for healing to take place, incoming souls can also have a kind of hangover. A sense of disorientation in early childhood is one of the clues that might lead to a sense of having had a rapid return to earth. If one feels like a stranger to everyone in childhood, it is possible that a rapid return was like suddenly getting off at the wrong bus stop. Nothing seems familiar or comforting. A common thread among individuals who revealed past lives in Nazi Germany was some real difficulty and sadness in feeling misunderstood or even ignored by one's parents and siblings in the present time.

Denys Kelsey, regression therapist, discovered in his hypnotic regression sessions that many of these "war children" were "in search of makeshift shelter from the terrors of the bombing and extermination camps which had clung to them like malignant thought-forms after death." It is my feeling that those malignant thought-forms can represent the greatest consciousness state of hell on earth. It is particularly beneficial to go through a regression session in this instance. It can be like taking a much-needed vacation in order to develop a new perspective on life.

In *Beyond the Ashes,* Rabbi Yonassan Gershom writes, "...According to many teachings on reincarnation, there is usually a considerable waiting period between lifetimes. Ancient sources like Plato, Virgil, and the 'Bhagavad Gita' refer to intervals of a thousand years or more." Rudolf Steiner asserts that there are at least eight hundred years between each incarnation. According to Dr. Joel Whitton's subjects in *Life Between Life*, the interval ranged from ten months to more than eight hundred years, with the average being around forty years. But according to Dr. Whitton, the length of time between incarnations has been getting steadily shorter in this century. He, too, found cases of souls who died in World War II and returned in the "baby-boom" generation.

State of Consciousness in Between Lives

One of the many valid reasons for undergoing a regression session is to accomplish the kind of healing that may not have taken place in the review time between lives. There are many accounts of what happens when one dies, and a large percentage of them share striking similarities. People describe seeing a beautiful white light that is like a magnet pulling them toward something infinitely wonderful. Sometimes the soul is met by someone the individual knew and loved on earth, and who had preceded the person into death, or by a special angel or guide who surrounds them with love and gentleness. If illness has been the cause of death, it may be necessary for the soul to enter a kind of hospital where traumas to the astral or spirit body can be healed. That resting place can also act as a way station where the departed soul can become acclimated to the new sphere of existence, surrounded and protected by those beings of light who exude serenity, peace, and love.

Eventually, the newly departed spirit is led across the barriers into a schoolroom, of sorts, where he can begin to evaluate his life on earth.

Rabbi Gershom confirms my experiences in regression sessions by saying, "...There the soul is helped to evaluate its life on earth and is cleansed or purged (the original meaning of purgatory) of its sins. This purging also removes the emotional pain associated with its experiences, so that the life can be incorporated into the soul's higher consciousness....[Then the soul is] ready to descend to earth again for another round of spiritual lessons.

"All of this is assuming that death comes naturally, at the appointed time. Elderly people or those with long-term illnesses have time to prepare for their deaths and usually go peacefully when the moment finally comes. But in cases of sudden or violent death this process can be upset, and the soul leaves the body without proper preparation. It can even happen that the soul is not aware of being dead and remains an earthbound 'ghost' until it finally realizes that it is no longer incarnate....In other cases, the soul may feel that its life was not yet complete and will return to earth as soon as possible. Without the purification and healing period between incarnations, the soul often retains intense, frightening emotions carried over from its previous life."

One of the most important opportunities offered by a regression session is the ability to review events on earth, thereby speeding up soul evolution while still on this plane in an earthly body. Another major benefit in knowledge of past lives is it allows us to diminish or completely dissipate any fear of death. With awareness comes freedom.

Hasty Return to Earth

In my experience with regression sessions—not only those connected to Nazi Germany—there are many times when a soul returns almost immediately after a traumatic death. It is as if the soul doesn't understand where it is and finds the first and most convenient place to be reborn. Many things become apparent and make sense in present life conditions when a past life in war times is revealed, especially in relationship to health patterns. A weakness in the physical body is almost a certainty if suffering or starvation has occurred in a recent past lifetime.

Al, a young man who came to me for a regression session, saw quite clearly how he had set up his present life by hastily coming back to be born to the last person he saw before he died. He brought back the same feelings of loneliness and isolation as he had before his death, and he also brought in health patterns that related to the manner of his death. Al's early childhood, within the confines of his family, was not a happy one because his father hardly knew he existed. Al saw himself as an English sailor during World War II. Al's tour of duty was on a submarine. He described his sleeping quarters on the sub as having three bunks in a tier, one on top of the other. He knew that his bunk was in the middle. Suddenly, in the middle of the night, the sub was hit by a torpedo. Everyone on board was thrown into the swirling sea with tremendous pressure. Al felt himself sinking rapidly to the bottom of the sea and saw himself drowned immediately. (Al has health problems connected to lungs and breathing in his present life.) The shipmate on the top bunk, we will call him Ben, was able to grab onto something that kept him afloat. As dawn brought light to the skies, Ben found himself virtually alone in the sea. The few other men who survived were drowned during the next few days, but Ben hung on beyond what could be considered the normal limits of human endurance. When he was finally rescued, he was severely dehydrated and very ill. He spent long months in a hospital in England and was finally able to be released.

Within a short time, Ben married and moved to America. But Ben never got over his experience with the sea. He was physically impaired and psychologically damaged. When a son was born to him, Ben was too damaged to respond to his little boy. The child who was born to the couple had little or no relationship to his father. The little boy, now an adult, was the man sitting in my office doing a regression session. The little boy born to Ben was Al, Ben's shipmate. Al's attraction to Ben was simply their shared experience on the ship and the sea. They hadn't even been particularly close during their time on board the submarine. This had been borne out in Al's review of his present life. He couldn't seem to get his father's attention and felt very unloved and unwanted by him. But he had heard the stories of his father's brave battle with the sea, and survival, all through his childhood.

From all reports it is sometimes hard for a soul to realize that it has died and is in a spirit form rather than in a physical body. Some of these souls hang around the people they love, and are very sad and frustrated because no one seems to recognize that they are there. The people who have lost these loved ones through death can be sorrowful for two reasons. First, because it is difficult to lose the companionship of the one we love. Second, and less obviously, it is because the anxiety of the departed spirit is like a black cloud hovering over the person left behind, creating a double dose of grief.

Edgar Cayce says that cremation is important so that the physical body is no longer a magnet for souls who leave their earth plane existence. Attachment to the physical form and to earth plane associations can explain some psychic phenomena such as "haunted houses" where doors slam, gusts of wind blow up suddenly, or a chill appears in the air. Some of this is harmless, but sometimes, as in the case of poltergeists and possessions, the earthbound spirits are angry, malicious, and determined to do damage—even in a disincarnate form. There are too many reports from sane people who have experienced the results of this kind of mischief to ignore that it exists. There are many mediums who can "see" and make contact with these spirits. Some of these mediumistic and spiritually-advanced people take on a higher responsibility and evoke rituals or prayers to actually help these lost souls. It is possible to give them a helping hand in evolving off the earth plane to a higher spiritual level, where help on that side is available. Religious services or rites that were especially evolved throughout the centuries for this specific purpose not only promote our earthly acknowledgment and respect for our forebears who are deceased, but are important to help loved ones on the other side go on to live on a plane of higher consciousness, avoiding the entrapment on the astral plane.

In the United States, we celebrate Halloween, or All Saints Eve. Our children go out dressed in costumes with scary faces and bags in their hands to collect a ransom of candy from the neighborhood. They are convinced not to do mischief or damage in exchange for sweets or pennies. It's all done in good fun. But in Spanish-speaking countries, on the same day of October 31, everything closes down—all the shops, everything—so that people can prepare for the next two days. People go to church on October 31 to honor and pray for the departed souls of friends and families. On November 1, All Saints Day, there is a fiesta, where everyone gathers for food, dancing, and tremendous celebration. Then on November 2, everyone takes flowers to the graves of their loved ones. In Mexico, in particular, November 2, el Dia de las Muertos (the day of the deceased), is like Memorial Day. There are fireworks and celebrations. People buy lots of cakes and candy and masses of flowers to put on the graves in honor of their departed loved ones. The florists in Mexico and Spain sell more flowers on those three days than throughout the rest of the year. This kind of joyous celebration and energy helps release loved ones on the other side to go on toward the light. It is sadness and sorrow that holds souls closer to the earth plane in a static level of development. In the Jewish tradition, there are also special days that are set aside to honor the dead.

Many people on earth are walking around in a state of inner torment. Some people who are diagnosed as schizophrenics may be, in my opinion, souls living in two worlds, unable to separate past life experiences from those in the present. Or they may be polarized on the astral plane where disembodied, negative spirits prey on their sensitivity in order to continue enjoying earth plane experiences. Certainly drug addicts and alcoholics fall into the category of those souls who open themselves to other world influences. First the sensitive soul, who has difficulty coping with the "real" world, seeks drugs or alcohol to escape mental torment. By indulging in hallucinogenics of any kind, he opens himself up even more to the uglies of the astral plane. The first high of drugs may, indeed, propel the individual beyond his inner nightmares, blotting them out momentarily, but eventually the beautiful colors disappear and the scenery is not very nice. So he has to drown them out again. And so goes the cycle. Many times these nightmarish addictions relate to past life memories. The attempt to drown out the voices of the past through drugs or alcohol eventually exacerbates the conditions. The mask of a personality may hide a living hell of fear, phobias, hysteria, and mental illness.

How can these people rid themselves of negative influences in a "polluted" environment? There are healers around the country, indeed around the world, who are able to help those entities let go of their attachment to a sensitive human being and go on to higher levels of being.

It is hoped that the time is not far off when medical science will take into account the possibility of the existence of reincarnation and when drug rehabilitation centers will consider possession by spirits part of the difficulty in overcoming an addiction. I know of one therapist who first "exorcises" her alcoholic patients before beginning her therapeutic work. Psychologists and psychiatrists are beginning to acknowledge the benefit of therapy conducted with past lives in mind. When physicians can verify that health knots, tied on the thread of consciousness, continue just like memory, we will no longer put mere bandages on surface health conditions and manifestations of illness, or weak physical patterns, that continue over and over again.

Past life health hazards are particularly strong when souls incarnate too quickly. What kind of existence could one imagine if a person connected to Nazi war crimes should come back to earth too quickly? What kind of nightmarish hell would he or she have to suffer if he or she had murdered and degraded human life on a massive scale?

Not only are the obvious negative mental states, such as mental illness, brought back as a living hell, but more subtle ones return as well. I observe in many, many astrological charts an aspect that I describe as a suicidal complex. I hasten to explain that it might not lead one to actually commit suicide, but that it describes a mental state where an individual wishes he could simply go back to a higher spiritual realm instead of having to go through earth experiences. He finds himself stuck in a kind of mental restlessness and torment. Is it possible that this kind of person has come back too soon or is so sensitive that he is prone to extra special kinds of visual experiences that other people cannot share or even understand? Usually the people with this aspect in their charts feel like loners, or feel different and misunderstood in childhood. They march to the beat of a different drummer.

Actually most of the people I see who have this kind of aspect in their astrological charts can be more advanced spiritually, and somehow more awake than the norm on earth. It is as if they were polarized upside down, with their feet in the spiritual realms and their heads on the ground. It can be very difficult for these people to relate to the structure and the rules of the earth plane. They may not remember how to integrate that higher, more esoteric quality into the present life, however, and wish they could be back where everyone is blissful in a sea of consciousness. It can be easy for them to regain their memory of advanced existence and knowledge through regression therapy. This helps to polarize the person on the earth plane. Sometimes these people are geniuses and seem to tap into a universal intelligence. It is often the case that they have difficulty with traditional types of education, and sometimes they have unusual health patterns that relate to nerves, allergies, or lack of physical balance. Eventually, most of these people find themselves by associating with like-minded people and by participating in activities that are more avant-garde and freedom-oriented. Some of these highly intellectually developed people make valuable contributions to advanced spiritual and scientific theory and technology.

Nerve Damage from the Past

One young woman, whom we will call Evelyn, fit into the category of having a highly developed intellect and difficult health patterns. Evelyn described some of the problems of her childhood in her regression session. She was the youngest child born into a fairly large family already going through major problems. Evelyn's mother was exhibiting tendencies of mental imbalance, and her father was not very understanding of her mother's inability to handle life. Without previous experience of mental illness on a first-hand basis, Evelyn's father had great difficulty in coping with the situation. He hid his weariness in alcohol after a hard day at work. Evelyn was diagnosed as having multiple sclerosis as she reached her teen years, but fortunately she was able to find a medical solution that kept her on an even keel, physically. Evelyn saw several past lives in her regression session. Some of them confirmed the advanced spiritual qualities that I observed in her personality and in her astrological chart, but none of them could fully explain the physical difficulties in the present time.

I suggested that there might have been a time when Evelyn's life was suddenly cut short. Her astrological chart indicated to me that her obviously brilliant mind had been developed to a high degree in a past existence, but that somehow her achievements may have been unfulfilling, and I described a quality of "scare" that might have been related to a former time of death. With questions from me about a lifetime when she might have been in the middle of a project at the time of her death, Evelyn suddenly began to cry. She seemed to be releasing a great deal of suppressed emotion, so that it was difficult for her to speak. I asked her to share what she was seeing, and in a whisper, she described herself as a Jewish man, around the age of 40, in Italy or Germany during World War II. She realized she had been a research scientist working on an important project that seemed to be connected to health. It was as if he/she was about to make a breakthrough with a serum that would solve a major epidemic or physical problem. She saw that, in spite of her prestige and former accomplishments, she was seized by the SS and taken to a concentration camp. Evelyn, as the scientist, was killed immediately. The relationship to her life in the present time was obvious. The shock of her death must have caused severe fright and may have done damage to her nervous system. The gas that was used for her death may also have been a cause for the nerve damage, on the etheric level, that manifested in this life as multiple sclerosis.

Although Evelyn may not be able to completely cure her physical difficulties, the awareness of how they might have originated can help elevate her consciousness to the point that her own energy can be upgraded and recirculated into her system. Evelyn has a strong scientific bent in this life and may even be able to resume her former work if she chooses.

"To Die Is the Better Deal"

When Sally came to me for a regression session, she had been dealing with an illness that is usually fatal. For Sally had breast cancer. When she was first given the diagnosis, she was not really surprised, for it was her own higher intuition that sent her for a biopsy. She had been going to doctors for two years with an inverted nipple. The doctors had told her it was nothing to worry about, but some inner voice told her differently. After her instincts were confirmed by medical tests, Sally decided she would find alternative methods of healing rather than have her breast removed and go through the agony of chemotherapy and other harsh treatments. She found people she felt she could trust to point her in the right direction, followed a strict diet, and worked with a Russian healer who she believed had, indeed, cured her cancer. But the residual pain was excruciating, and that pain was taking its toll on her energy system. At the time she had her regression session she was still working in accord with the method she had chosen, and was sure the cancer was in remission. I'm terribly sad to say that cancer was suddenly discovered in other parts of her body, and Sally has since died. I can only hope that her regression session helped her, somehow, during the release from her physical body.

Sally had spent a great deal of time in her life consciously developing her awareness. She knew about her psychological patterns; she was familiar with advanced metaphysical concepts; and her life was motivated by the desire for continued spiritual growth. Sally cared about humanity. She was not a mean, nasty person. She never wanted to use force or devious methods for anything in her life. She had raised a family and was on wonderfully loving terms with her children. In short, Sally was a good person. Why should she have suffered so much in her life, especially in areas of health?

Sally suspected she had lived in Germany at the time of World War II and had somehow suffered at the hands of the Nazis.

Early on in her regression session, Sally stated that her philosophy includes a belief that some amount of pain is part of, and perhaps necessary for, life and growth. Events of Sally's childhood had reinforced that belief, and nothing could have convinced her otherwise. Her early years had been anything but carefree and happy, for they had been full of physical and psychological distress. A lot of things in her life had been unfair, but Sally had survived and was always striving toward more enlightenment. So why should she have cancer? Was more suffering necessary for her spiritual growth? Was her faith not yet strong enough? And what connection could all that suffering have to do with a past life in Nazi Germany? Sally also had no fear of death, so why the struggle to live? No answers appeared to really satisfy her questions; but once again, illness had surfaced in her life.

This was not the first time Sally's inner guidance saved her life. When she was a child, she found a little plastic ring in a box of Cracker Jack. *Something told her to swallow that ring.* When she let her mother know what had happened, a doctor was called and x-rays were taken, just as a precaution. Instead of finding a plastic ring, the x-rays located a tumor that was growing around Sally's esophagus. If it had remained undetected for much longer, Sally would have choked to death, or been unable to breathe. Some inner voice had saved Sally's life by telling her to swallow that ring. Other near-death situations reaffirmed what Sally had known from childhood: that from the age of two, she had not only been unafraid of death, but had actively wished that she could die. Throughout her regression session, it was obvious that her conscious desire to leave the earth plane had come in conflict with a strong inner will to survive. Her early life was not a happy one. There were memories of rejection from her brother, and beatings from her father if he was frustrated about something in his own life. Sally, as a middle child, felt that her mother was pleased with her older sister, a strikingly beautiful child with exceptional intelligence, and hoped for a perfect boy with her second pregnancy. So it was clear to Sally that she was a big disappointment to her mother.

In her regression session she observed that she was able to be quite objective about her existence and the behavior of the people around her until she was two. She simply thought these people were strange, but she wasn't hurt by their attitude. She didn't take things personally until her brother was born. Looking back, she realized she reached a big turning point in her life when she heard her father say that the child was so ugly he would have thrown him back if he hadn't been a boy. That's when vulnerability and hurt set in. Sally decided that her father wished he had thrown her back, wherever "back" might be. From then on, Sally was a hurt child and just wished she could die.

She did try to win favor from her family, once, by taking care of a situation involving her one-year-old brother's toys. She overheard her family discussing that the toys, left in the yard, were slowly disappearing. The little brother was too young to be asked about his toys, and there was some speculation that a neighbor's child was simply taking them to his own home. Sally decided she would confront the other child's family and went to his house. When the child's father opened the door Sally simply said, "I've come for my brother's toys!" The man called to his wife, "This little girl thinks we've taken her brother's toys. We better call the police and have her put in jail."

Sally ran home as fast as she could to tell her mother of the threat. The word "jail" terrified Sally. Her heart was pounding, and she felt as though that must be the worst thing that could ever happen. When she reached her home and breathlessly, tearfully revealed the threat, she got no sympathy or thanks for her efforts, and no reassurance about her fears. Instead, Sally was severely reprimanded and punished. Even as an adult, Sally could recall the terror she felt about that threat of jail. She also revealed knowing for certain that there was no hope of winning her family to her side.

It was very clear during Sally's session that she had a profound sense of awareness. All of her soul searching had enabled her to develop a philosophy of hope and an esoteric knowledge of truth. She had already recognized a strong pattern in her life. It seemed she had to go through difficult times over and over that turned out all right in the long run. So even with the current pain she suffered, she was not worried about the outcome of the cancer. She was sure she was cured.

Her latest health crisis was a bit different from the previous ones in her life, however. The duration was longer and the suffering more intense. It came even closer to an ultimate life or death decision than any of the others. It seemed that each health episode in Sally's life escalated in its potential to end her existence on earth. Sally knew that as each health crisis arose she had to make a more determined decision to remain on earth, whether that decision was a conscious or unconscious one. The major question Sally asked herself was why she kept on having those "tests" about remaining alive, if that was what they were.

Sally recalled a time when she was having a particularly hard time as an adult, bringing up her three children alone. She said, "A friend had breast cancer and said, 'Sally, life is so short, really take advantage of every moment.' I remember thinking very clearly, 'Not short enough for me. I wish I had breast cancer!'"

When the first past life came into view, Sally saw herself as a man around the age of fifty. She knew she had a lot of power over a group of people, as if she/he were a governor. She thought the country might be France, well before the time of more advanced civilization. It seemed that some sort of conflict sent a group of men out to defend the territory. Although Sally was not a military person, she/he was in a position to help the cause. The group of people were in some sort of danger and Sally, as a very powerful man, could have taken some action, perhaps sending reinforcements or supplies. Evidently, however, she was not very interested in the welfare of these people; she ignored their pleas for help, and many hundreds of men died.

The scene in her mind affected Sally on a deeply emotional level, and she began to cry. The fact that she had made no effort to help when help was so easily within her means was extremely hard for this loving woman to accept. She simply didn't care about them! Her cosmic, unconscious guilt was one of omission rather than commission, for she had allowed a group of people to die through neglect.

One of the men Sally neglected to help was connected to her on a more personal basis. Her sister in that lifetime was in love with a man in the endangered group and, in her session, Sally realized that by not giving aid to this man—therefore allowing him to die—she had hurt her sister very deeply.

It seemed possible that there might have been a reason for her unconcerned attitude in the French lifetime. Sally thought this particular group of people may have ostracized her at a previous time in history, perhaps very early in the history of man. The resulting neglect on her part was a completely unconscious revenge. Because she had remembered that former past life where she had been mistreated, there was an unconscious and automatic boomerang effect on an instinctual level. She had decided to get revenge without even knowing it.

Sally recognized her whole present life family as having lived and been victims of her neglect in the former time. Her sister, whose lover was allowed to die, seemed to be the same sister in the present. In this lifetime, her family didn't seem to care about Sally's existence or well-being at all.

Sally then went to another lifetime. It seemed to be during World War II. She identified the country as Austria, and she saw herself as a young Jewish girl about fourteen to sixteen years old and born into a middle-class family. Her father seemed to be a carpenter or laborer of some kind, and her mother was a homemaker. Sally saw herself as one of three children.

Her family didn't seem to be overtly religious in many ways, but they held ceremonies at home. Sally thought that was more as a private and personal tradition than because of persecution. But because Sally was just a child, she may not have known about the persecution. It was August 1938 when a troop train went through their town. The train seemed to signify that danger was near, because things changed after that. Shortly after the train was seen, Sally's family left their own home to move in with another family. Sally's father must have been involved in some kind of political movement that was potentially dangerous, and Sally's mother insisted that they go into hiding.

Both families moved into a one-room basement with a dirt floor. The room was clean and nice, however. For Sally and her two younger brothers it seemed more like an adventure than anything that might be fearful. They were able to go up into the house at night but were very cautious not to use lights. The house appeared to be deserted from the outside, as the cellar was in complete darkness with no windows to the outside. The children were quiet as mice during the daytime and had their play time at night.

After quite a long period of time, perhaps months of living in that cellar, a door was suddenly opened one day, and light flooded into the room. It was a terrible shock. Everyone was startled into immobility. They hadn't known the door existed; evidently it was an entry into a root cellar. Having lived in darkness for so long, the light was extremely painful to their eyes. It rendered them even more vulnerable because they couldn't see who was entering their formerly safe haven. Sally saw herself as being absolutely terrified and frozen with fear.

But no one screamed or ran, for everyone else was completely paralyzed with panic, as well.

SS troops entered the basement, and with guns drawn, abruptly began to separate people from each other. They took some of the members of the two families outside, and immediately shot others as they sat in the basement hideaway. There seemed no reason why some of the people were taken away and some were killed.

Sally's parents were taken away, but she was left sitting on a bench in the cellar. Sally's best girlfriend was left alive along with Sally, but her friend's family was killed before their eyes. As some of the SS soldiers came toward Sally's friend and started to drag her away, Sally became hysterical. She screamed at the soldiers, "Don't take my friend." The soldiers turned on her and began beating her and kicking her. Evidently Sally was to be taken away somewhere with her family and her friend, but when she protested and screamed hysterically, the soldiers turned on her. One major blow landed on her chest. She was evidently beaten and kicked to death.

In looking back, Sally realized she felt more fear when the soldiers took her friend than when they dragged her family away. She seemed to sense in a flash what horror lay ahead for her friend. She knew on an unconscious level she couldn't help her.

In the regression session, Sally saw that her guilt lay in the fact that she couldn't save her friend. She felt, irrationally and in retrospect, that if she had not screamed out, the soldiers might have taken her instead. She made a decision, instantly and evidently forever afterward, on that unconscious past life level, that the better deal was to die. The vicious kick to her chest left an indelible wound to her esoteric body, as well. The growth around her esophagus as a child in this life and the location of cancer in that same area of her body appear to be manifestations of a deep wound in that part of her body that has never healed. The basic impediment to allowing a healing to take place seemed to be the residual guilt over her friend's fate and her part in trying to save her. Sally said, in answer to my question, "I think I have chosen to die lots of times, then changed my mind and reversed my decision. I think that's what is going on with this cancer. I was in the fourth stage of cancer, and it had spread to my bones. But according to the most recent tests, I haven't had one single cancer cell since 1994." But Sally may have delayed her decision to live just a bit too long to save her life this time.

One of the obvious manifestations in this life, apart from the continuing punishment to the affected area of her body, was that Sally had not screamed out in protest—to her parents, her brother, to the universe. She said, "By trying to save my friend, I made it worse...except that, in the long run, by being killed it was the easier way." That courageous girl was willing to scream for the mistreatment of another human being in the German lifetime at the risk to her own existence.

It became apparent to Sally that her decision "to die is the better deal," stemming from that traumatic situation in the cellar, was still part of her conscious choice in this life. That moment of decision born of pain and panic had affected her whole life! Sally was still flirting with that notion on a conscious level, yet she worked very hard to prevent the cancer from taking hold in her body. It made the healing process infinitely more difficult, even though she wanted, on another level of consciousness, to be completely well.

Not knowing under what circumstances that original decision had been made had created serious conflicts in her life. Sally's practitioner was well aware of the healing that must take place on all levels—mental, and spiritual as well as physical—but Sally had not been able to help that healing transformation as much as she wanted to because she had been dealing with the wrong issues as the root of the situation, or the causes for her self "tests."

A further complication entered the picture as Sally began to speculate about what might have happened to her friend after she was taken away. For Sally to acknowledge the pictures and thoughts of the brutality of the SS troops in the regression session was as painful as if it were happening in the present.

She believed that her friend was taken away on a train. She felt that her friend probably starved to death in a concentration camp. With her "esoteric" eyes, she began to see her friend as if she were in the camp with her. The innocent young girl was emaciated, bald, and had cuts on her head. Sally could imagine how those cuts had come about. She knew her friend had to endure terrible torture for a very long time in that camp. She could see how they had beaten her to the point that she was hardly a person, yet she had the strongest soul and the strongest will to live. She could feel the pain and the agony of her friend's hunger. Sally's tears for her friend were heart-wrenching.

Sally re-met Janice just before Sally was diagnosed as having cancer. Their quality of friendship had not changed at all. Even though they had been away from each other since 1938, in another life, the bonds were just as strong. Neither woman knew anything of the circumstances of the basis of their friendship but it was Janice, supposedly a new friend, who had helped Sally the most when she first learned of her cancer and who was with her during the most trying times in the beginning of her illness. Sally said, "She even looks the same in this life! She's Italian now, but she looks like she used to look."

Sally finally took a long look at the soldiers who killed her. She knew she didn't have to die in that lifetime, but in a flash, she had done something that would guarantee her death. It was her spontaneous, conscious choice that "to die was the better deal." She backed up her choice, unconsciously, with her protest. When she took a closer look at the karmic situation, she realized that the SS soldiers were among the people she had neglected in her former life in France.

Was Sally so remorseful she allowed the soldiers to kill her in return? Was she so aware of what suffering lay ahead of her that she "took the easy way out" by her protestation, and did she actually make the right choice by doing so? Would this situation have to go on for hundreds of future lifetimes before Sally and the soldiers got even with each other? What kind of karma have these soldiers incurred for themselves because of their brutal way of killing Sally? Is there any way that forgiveness can take place?

Sally could stop the wheel of karma in this particular situation because she had worked very hard to evolve from the wheel of karma and the immutable law, "an eye for an eye and a tooth for a tooth." Sally may not have to seek out these people in future lives to feed them or take them into her home for her mind became her healer.

Sally volunteered that she understood that we are all one and that revenge can only boomerang again. This choice was real for Sally because she had worked very hard to get to that awareness. I'm honored to have known Sally and remember her courage and wisdom with great affection. I am still sending Sally light and love to help her on her way and hope that all who read *A Soul's Journey* will join me in that endeavor.

The answers that Sally found may be too simplistic for most of mankind. But when true objectivity is attained, and one can stand aside to watch the law in action, the process of initiation into the higher realms can begin to take place. Blame doesn't solve anything. "Whys" are not often easy or answerable. Levels of consciousness can begin to evolve with compassion, however. Try to imagine what these soldiers will suffer within their own inner computer of "an eye for an eye," and imagine how long it may take them to understand why they should suffer over and over on their own wheel of karma.

Finding the Light

There is blessed forgetfulness on a conscious level from life to life, but on a soul consciousness level, nothing is ever forgotten or erased; events can be transmuted, however, and in fact must be transmuted onto the level of spiritual mind. The ultimate realization is to know that all is mirage, a falling away from God and self. Healing occurs when one, by sheer mental effort, lifts oneself up from the baser desires and activities, and consciously brings in the light of the soul.

The first step is to desire the light. That desire is usually inflamed by such pain that the physical self cannot stand the loneliness, mental torture, and anguish that comes with whatever circumstance is mirrored to show the soul that dark side of existence. It is inflamed by hell as a state of consciousness.

I have conducted regression sessions with people who have gone through the ravages of war—on both sides. They have suffered, died, and are reincarnated. I have seen them release some of the memories that lie buried behind the conscious mind and have witnessed the beginnings of many healings take place. In the dawning of the New Age, man is beginning to understand the ultimate penalty of man's inhumanity to man.

5

Persecution Begins

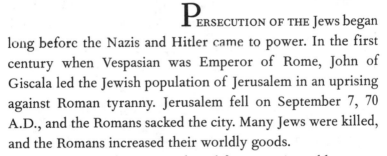

PERSECUTION OF THE Jews began long before the Nazis and Hitler came to power. In the first century when Vespasian was Emperor of Rome, John of Giscala led the Jewish population of Jerusalem in an uprising against Roman tyranny. Jerusalem fell on September 7, 70 A.D., and the Romans sacked the city. Many Jews were killed, and the Romans increased their worldly goods.

By 132 A.D., the Jews gathered forces again and began an insurrection against Rome—this time under the leadership of Simon Bar Kokhba (or Bar Chochebe). This leader had great success against the legions of Hadrian until 135 A.D., when he was killed by the Romans, and the Jewish rebellion was crushed. Once more the Roman legionnaires sacked Jerusalem. The Emperor Hadrian gave orders that the site of the city be plowed over and that a new city called Aelia Capitolina should be constructed. The only wall that was left standing later became famous as the Wailing Wall. The Jews were to be excluded from the new city, but Christians were permitted to enter if they had not sided with the Jews in the rebellion. Everything left behind could be confiscated by the Romans.

In both of these uprisings, the issue was undue taxation, and money was the bottom line issue. The sacking of Jerusalem certainly brought in more money than taxation would have.

We can skip to another time to find more organized persecution. The year was 1478 when Isabella of Castille, later of Aragon, instituted the first persecution of Jews throughout Granada. Jews were given three months to accept Christianity or leave the country. Another phase of the Inquisition was inaugurated three years later, in 1481, this time under the joint direction of state and church. Isabella directed this purge toward the Spanish Marranos. That Inquisition was broadened by 1483 to include all "heretics." The Spanish Dominican Monk Tomas de Torquemada took command of the Inquisition in all Spanish possessions at the request of Ferdinand and Isabella, and only four years later, Pope Innocent VIII named him Grand Inquisitor. This gave Torquemada permission to introduce measures of cruelty that made his name infamous. The year was 1487. By 1492, when Ferdinand and Isabella financed the expedition of Christopher Columbus to the New World, Isabella had to pledge her jewels to borrow the money, five million miravede's, for this voyage from Luis de Santangel, a wealthy Aragonese merchant, lawyer, and chief financial advisor to Ferdinand. (Christopher Columbus was so grateful for his support that he directed his first missive about the discovery of the new land to de Santangel.) In fact, this financial aid saved de Santangel's family from further persecution during the Inquisition, as he was a Conversos. Ferdinand and Isabella, in turn, expelled as many as 200,000 Jews.

In 1496, Portugal's Manoel I ordered the expulsion of all Jews from his country, and many Jews were massacred. Manoel actually took action against the Jews to please Ferdinand and Isabella, as he was to marry their daughter. Many atrocities have been committed in the so-called civilized world against groups other than Jews, but it is important to note that each time there was a major persecution of Jews, the country responsible was facing economic difficulty, if not bankruptcy. I would imagine that when the Jews were expelled from Granada and Portugal, they were not allowed to take many possessions along. Certainly any property they owned, and the goods they had to leave behind, would be confiscated or reclaimed by Spain.

The same was true of Nazi Germany. In 1938, Germany was showing a deficit of 432 million marks. (The country had been bankrupt since 1931 by ordinary capitalist standards.) The greatest pogrom in German history began on November 9, 1938. The massacre followed the assassination of Paris embassy official Ernst Edouard vom Rath the day before by a German-born Polish Jew named Herschel Grynzpan, who was only seventeen years old. This young man had heard of the mistreatment of thousands of Polish Jews, including members of his own family, after their deportation from Germany.

During the night, now known as Kristallnacht, Jewish shop windows in Austria were smashed. (Kristal means "glass" in German, Nacht means "night.") Shops, homes, and synagogues were looted, demolished, and burned. Between twenty and thirty thousand Jews were carried off to concentration camps. It is no secret that concentration camps had storehouses of clothes, furs, jewels, and even gold from the teeth of captured Jews. The hair was sold to make products, as well. The Germans were wealthy with Jewish treasures.

Why have the Jews been persecuted throughout history? We may have to trace that persecution back to the days before

Atlantis. It was said that the Jews were, indeed, a privileged and special group of people who, because of their great spiritual wealth, were given the gift of manifestation. When these gifted people needed anything—food, shelter, clothing—they knew how to bring it into the earth plane from the outer spheres.

There are two people alive today (whom I know of) who are capable of manifesting a substance called Verbuti from the ethers. One of them is Sai Baba, who lives in India. He is placed on a platform in the center of a crowd of people who come to see him perform this miracle. He is able to bring in ashes from the ethers, or from some sphere beyond the earth plane. This is no trick, either. His hands are closed, and with some meditational moments, he is able to open his palms and show that they are full of holy ashes.

I was privileged to meet the other person in the privacy of my own consultation room. I had an appointment to see an Indian man for a regression session. He had been recommended by a doctor friend of his, a woman, who had been to see me previously. This talented physician was the head of a major department in a prestigious hospital in New York. Her father had been a famous astrologer in India and had helped her with medical diagnoses by looking at the charts of some of her patients. I looked forward to working with anyone this special lady might recommend. She suggested that she stay with us to interpret, in case her friend couldn't understand my questions, but I only work with a person alone, as I feel that will facilitate the best results. As soon as I saw him, I felt a tremendous rapport between us, and I knew we would have no problem in communicating.

This gentleman, dressed in a spanking-white suit, reviewed several past lives. Then he said to me, with his eyes still closed, "Now I am bored!" I laughed and laughed because no one had ever said that to me before. He laughed with me. He then asked if he could show me something and help me in return. As he was talking to me, he put his hands on the arm of the couch. I was sitting, quite close, in a chair right next to that couch. As we were talking he suddenly opened his hands that were palm up on the arm of the couch, and there were ashes filling his hands, spilling over onto a cloth he had placed there. No smudges appeared on the cuffs of his white suit, either.

It was a stunningly emotional moment. Fortunately, I had heard about Sai Baba's ability to manifest ashes, and had also been told about an amazing man named Swami Chakradhari by a friend who had seen him in California. She had holy ashes from both Sai Baba and Swami Chakradhari. Swami had also manifested a rose for her, and had manifested a stone for her friend; later, she commented that she wished she had a stone, as the rose died soon afterward. I remarked that I would give almost anything to see this kind of manifestation. I knew that nothing like this was done without high spiritual energy and knowledge. The man sitting beside me had used his passport name to book the session, so I had no idea that this was indeed the same person my friend had told me about. I knew that Swami Chakradhari was a powerful healer as well, and I'm not sure I could have been as determined to regress him to past lives if I had known who he was.

Swami put some of the ashes on my forehead, gave me a blessing, and put the remaining ashes in a small bag so that I could keep them with me for protection and blessing. I subsequently had a gathering of friends in my home so that they, too, might see this amazing manifestation—something they might never have a chance to see again in their present lives. This time Swami wore a yellow robe with three quarter-length sleeves. This time he placed his hands over a piece of paper on a table top, and as he shook his hands over that paper, the ashes fell from his palms. He assured us that this manifestation was only "phenomena"—useful in getting someone's attention— but that it was in no way the real essence of spiritual truth, nor was it to be worshipped or praised. He said, "It is something that one could learn if he or she wanted to take the time to do so." I arranged for Swami to come to a major conference for another exhibition of the ability to manifest Verbuti. This was a gathering of people who would understand and not be skeptical of what was happening, and who would know the significance of the miracle. After Swami Chakradhari had manifested holy ashes for the group, one young lady asked a question. Swami suggested that she come up to where he was sitting. He knew that she needed some special attention, and as she kneeled beside him, he put his finger on her third eye, or brow chakra (see p. 255). As he pulled his hand away, a lovely stone appeared in his palm. As he gave that special gift to the girl, he murmured a few words to her. It was clear to the group, by the look on her face, that something unique and special had happened to her. The group was already profoundly moved by what he showed us, for it really was an example of manipulation of energy without scientific machines or hard work.

This was the closest example I could have to help me understand how Jews in prehistoric times may have been able to manifest much heavier objects than holy ashes. In the book, *Dweller on Two Planets,* written by Frederick S. Oliver, an amanuensis for the spirit Phylos, it is said that those Jews called Suernis who chose to continue their spiritual development, growing beyond the mere phenomenon of manifestation, were later incarnated as Essenes.

The Jewish mystic Isaac Luria, who lived in Spain at the time of the Inquisition and who believed in reincarnation, thought that once born a Jew, one would always be reborn a Jew. It is my belief that when I talk about the original group of people who could manifest materiality, now known as Jews, that would include many people on earth today who are no longer born into that heritage. For I have discovered in conducting regression sessions, that many people who remembered being persecuted during the Holocaust are not necessarily Jewish today.

Beginnings of Present Day Terror

Although it is generally assumed that Kristallnacht was the beginning of the most flagrant atrocities committed against the Jews, terror in Nazi Germany actually started earlier than that. In 1933 groups of terrorists, mostly young Nazis, began menacing, wounding, and killing Jews in the streets.

In a regression session, Alyce described herself as one of those ruffians. She saw herself disguised as a man and dressed in a uniform. She and her boyfriend, Henri, would spend the time after dusk running through the city, which she believed was Berlin, in an exhilarated state, beating and shooting any Jews they could find. She knew that most Jews were fearful of going out after dark because of this menace, but she and Henri were usually able to find people in alleyways who were avoiding the dangerous streets. The killings and beatings by this Nazi couple were a stimulus for wild sexual activities that would occur after their urges toward brutalism to others were satisfied. In her present life, Alyce was the victim of tragic sexual abuse.

In regression sessions, cases of evil activity, brutalism, and murder in past lives often seem to have gone hand-in-hand with sexual misconduct or violent sexuality in that same past life. The penalty each person has exacted for him- or herself in the present is extremely psychologically and physically damaging. The individuals who have recognized violence and sexual misuse in a past life almost invariably have sexual problems in the present. For the men those problems may range from impotency to premature ejaculation to other physical disorders that interfere with healthy and satisfying sexual activity. For women it can mean rape, sexual molestation in childhood, or even a tendency to prostitution in the present life. Certainly, Nazi brutality also included sexual atrocities. Rape was perhaps the mildest form of those sexual assaults; in some cases, sexual brutality was fatal.

Rape by Nazi Officers

When Jane reviewed the events of the present time, she described a fairly trouble-free existence. In fact, the conditions she revealed to me were so nice that I commented, "What a lovely way to go through life!" Jane agreed, for she had told me that she has loving parents, was able to go to good schools, and eventually married someone she loves very much. Jane's career as a singer and actress seems to be on an upward trend, and with her obvious talent, she has a potential for great success.

The only negative pattern Jane recognized was that she could overreact and be terribly upset with mishaps or difficulties. Small problems would feel like the end of the world. She recalled damaging her brother's car when she was in her twenties and dissolving in tears when her mother and father came to her aid without any criticism. She was horrified at the thought of causing any problems to anyone, especially her loving family. She also remembered that as a two-year-old her mother left her alone in the bathroom for just a moment. Jane was panicked even though she knew her mother was only in the basement, probably putting a load of clothes in the washer. Moments of anxiety could occur unexpectedly.

Jane had had a short battle with bulimia, but had passed through that phase in her life and no longer had any eating disorders. But Jane could sink into an unreasonable slump if a job or career situation ended, for instance. Logically, she always knew that something would happen to bring in new opportunities, but emotionally, it would be devastating. Fortunately, those times were like small blips on the screen of an otherwise exciting and happy life.

When I asked her to go to a past life she saw herself as a sixteen-year-old girl, running in a field, feeling pleasure and freedom. She seemed to be in France, in the 1940s. She had long, light brown hair, and she knew that she was in love with a boy who lived nearby. She described her house as a narrow, three-story stone house located in the middle of a community, perhaps a suburb of a small city. She thought that her father had a bakery in town.

"My mother and father seem to be very worried about the war. There are people in the town who are friendly to the Nazis, like the Vichy. Since we're Jewish it is very dangerous, as neighbors could lash out at us at any moment. People stop coming to our bakery, for instance, and treat us in a nasty way. We're trying to get away from the town before the Nazis get any closer, but we don't know where to go. When I come back from being in the fields, I see my mother packing a few things in suitcases. I feel overwhelmed because it seems that everything is happening very rapidly. I'm very upset because there is no time to tell my boyfriend that we're going to leave.

"I think someone comes to the house to stop us before we can get away." Jane was crying softly as she spoke. She continued, "Some German officers knock on the door, and there seems to be a town official, like a mayor, who comes with them. When my mother opens the door, they tell us we have to go with them and we have to leave everything behind. These people are cold and nasty, and I am very scared. We're put in some sort of a vehicle, like a Jeep, but with slats around the back. There is another family there too, with three children. There are about nine of us crowded into the back of this Jeep.

"We seem to travel a long way. We probably go to Germany, and we're put in a compound. Oh, it's a concentration camp." Jane started crying again at this point. The scene was very real to her. "There are a lot of people already there, and everyone is just terrified. My sister and I are huddled together because we're separated from our parents; they have been just pulled away from us. We're put in a room with lots of beds, like a barracks. I think we're working, doing menial work like cleaning a kitchen." In answer to my question, she responded, "I think I see my sister from time, but not often.

"I'm taken somewhere else. I'm taken to some officer's quarters. When I walk into this room, I know what's coming next." There was a long pause, and then Jane said, "I think I'm raped to death. I think it's only that one time, but there are a lot of people—maybe nine—who gang-rape me, and they leave my body a wreck. I probably leave my body because I can't take it. I think I only live to be about eighteen years old." Jane volunteered one more thing. She said, "I think the boyfriend in that life is my husband now. We feel very lucky to have each other. I think a lot of my overreaction in the present has to do with that time. I have a feisty side to me that comes up when I think people are going to hurt me. I came into this life fairly naive, as I had been before, but one night after the theater, I was going out to get something to eat. A man walked close to me and hit me with his shoulder. I had been moving away from him to let him by, but when he bumped into me on purpose, I turned on him and started to hit him with my bag. I yelled something and he backed away in a hurry!"

I commented, "That girl decided no one was ever going to hurt her again."

In the light of reincarnation, how could evil, as personified by Hitler and his henchmen, have developed to such a degree? How did an energy split occur that could be defined as good and evil? Was Hitler possessed by a satanic force? How could Nostradamus have known about World War II centuries before it happened, even naming "Hister" as the leading force, only getting one letter wrong?

The Beginning of Evil

Many people I have regressed into past lives have seen themselves as having lived in Atlantis, sometimes called the lost colony. Atlantis was a highly evolved and technologically developed civilization. In fact, the level of technology attributed to Atlantis may still be far ahead of what we have rediscovered today. There were three main branches of life in Atlantis: the priesthood, the intellectual, and the political-scientific. The latter two branches became intertwined as great advances in technological development reached an apex.

Many people who saw themselves as Atlanteans also saw

themselves as part of the scientific community that worked on crystals, the prime source of energy in that country. A serious political conflict arose when some of the scientists felt crystal development had reached its safest limit. They tried to convince other scientists to cease building up more crystal energy, but the levels of energy were constantly being boosted until the whole civilization was destroyed.

In every religion there is a story of the great flood. Vast damage was brought about by the abuse of crystal power in Atlantis, and at that time a whole continent went under the waves of the sea. Parts of Atlantis, sometimes thought of as a mere myth, have begun to rise from the sea near Bimini, off the coast of Florida, confirming Edgar Cayce's fifty-year-old prediction that Atlantis would rise again in that location. The continent of Atlantis stretched from the coast of Florida across the Atlantic to Spain and the coasts of Africa. Spain and some of the surrounding islands that are thought to be former Atlantean land may have been part of a route that led people to Egypt. That notion of a continent's stretching over what is now the Atlantic Ocean can explain a great deal about the simultaneous development of certain cultural habits on both sides of the Atlantic.

Ibiza is known as one of the high energy spots of the world. It seems possible that the island is located at the particular area of the Atlantean continent where positive energy and activities flourished, such as former sites of temples. According to the Cayce readings, many people who escaped the Atlantean waves brought records and advanced knowledge from Atlantis to Egypt for safekeeping and to incorporate into the Egyptian culture. Some of the people in regression sessions with me remembered surviving the devastation in Atlantis and described going to an island where they could live in safety. One woman, in particular, described going to an area of Atlantis before the great flood and knowing that she had been protected, as that location remained above the water and became a safe island. The safe islands may also have included the Spanish Canary Islands, off the West Coast of Africa, for the natives of those islands also believe they were a part of Atlantis many centuries ago. Most of the Atlanteans went further than the safe islands, however, and gravitated all the way to Egypt. The Atlanteans were also more spiritually advanced than the Egyptians, and hoped to awaken the people to help speed up their evolution.

The levels of healing in Atlantis were quite advanced and, among other techniques, included such methods as color projected into the body at certain angles, then magnified by crystals. These activities took place in the Atlantean temples, where healing on all levels was accomplished. In one regression session, Linda recounted these techniques for healing in such vivid detail that she astonished herself, for she described specific colors, angles, parts of the body and levels of crystal power that could be utilized for various maladies. She even described the architectural design for the healing rooms. Before the session began she had no idea that she had lived in Atlantis or that such precise knowledge was stored in her subconscious.

The physicians of the later days of Atlantean civilization began to practice plastic surgery to correct damage from genetic experimentation that had been conducted in the past. In an attempt to create a slave race, some physicians and scientists had experimented with inbreeding between people and animals. The later Atlantean civilization was left with a group of mutants who had highly unusual appendages. The physicians of the later Atlantean period were attempting to correct and wipe away traces of an evil practice of enslavement from the earlier times.

In the days of Nazi Germany, Dr. Josef Mengele took it upon himself to perform medical experiments with sets of twins in the concentration camp of Auschwitz, all in the name of genetic research. He performed a variety of unspeakable medical horrors and gruesome surgical practices on his twins, mostly without benefit of anesthesia.

Has anything changed over the thousands of centuries? Have patterns repeated themselves? Did the split between good and evil became so pronounced in the days of Atlantis? Are we still trying to get it right after all this time? Are the Nazi criminals the old Atlantean evil scientists and physicians returned again?

The great flood didn't seem to wipe away the evil side of man's nature after all. It seems that good and evil still coexist. And during certain periods of history, the conditions seem ripe for evil to flourish again.

When Hitler invaded Poland in September 1939, special units of SS troups were assigned to round up and kill the Jews in each village that fell to the German army. At this stage, most of the victims were simply taken into the forest and shot. Sometimes, in a perverse kind of cruelty, they were marched to the Jewish cemetery and executed there. This policy of hunting down the Jews continued in each country conquered by the Nazis, sometimes with the help of some of the local populace. Many times the Jews were forced to dig their own graves.

There are heroic tales that have emerged of people's hiding Jews at the risk of their own lives. As just one example, in 1943 a group of Danish sea captains had news of a major Jewish roundup that was to occur on the night of Rosh Hashanah, one of Judaism's high holy days. With the combined effort of the local populace, they smuggled people—Jews and others who would have been captured and killed—out of Denmark into

Sweden the night before the roundup was to occur. Their courageous action saved the lives of more than 7,000 people.

Finding a Safe House

George had an incredible past life memory of events that could easily have led to his death and burial in a forest. George saw his past life during World War II in a town that he thought might be in the Netherlands. I did not press George for details of the exact location of that lifetime. Unless such facts emerge automatically and with surety, I suggest that an individual trust his or her instincts about the location. Frequently, the picture becomes clearer as the session progresses, and the person knows exactly where he was, if those details are truly relevant. Most often more details emerge after the session has ended and the person is away from the initial intensity of the regression session and in a more familiar environment.

George quickly went to a past life after reviewing some of the difficulties he had as a child. He was born to a family who didn't seem to understand him. He felt quite alone in his life, even though he knew his mother and father loved him. His father criticized him for being unreachable and silent, and his mother resented his independent streak. Obviously George kept a lot of things to himself. Surprisingly, it was easy for him to open up to me in his regression session.

When he went to a past life, the first thing George saw was a scene that was horrifying. He saw himself as a young man around the age of twenty-one or twenty-two, unmarried, and living at home. But George had been away for a day or two visiting someone in a neighboring city. When he left home, everything was as it should have been. The news of the war was no worse and no better than before, so George had decided to risk a short trip. When he returned, he entered the town through the woods. From the vantage point of a hillside, he saw German soldiers entering his town and forcing people into lines at gunpoint.

It seemed that someone was accused of being a spy, and of passing on information to the enemy. Therefore everyone in the town was to be questioned and punished if the culprit did not confess. In most instances, the Nazis needed no excuse to roundup a whole town without any accusations at all. Since almost everyone risked his or her life in attempts to get information to the outside world, in truth, the whole town was guilty (in Nazi eyes) of something. Even though George knew who the authorities were looking for, he was intelligent enough to know that any information the police obtained would not satisfy them. People would be punished anyway, just as an example for the future. The last thing George would do under any circumstance was to betray someone.

George felt it was time to make a run for it and alert others in hiding before it was too late. So before he could be spotted by the German officers, he turned back into the woods and hid among the trees until nightfall, when he could make his way out of the immediate area a bit more safely. George described, in minute detail, the paths he took through the woods and by a canal. He described the heightened adrenaline in his system and his rapidly beating heart as he took incredible risks. He avoided going near the towns that were crawling with Gestapo. He knew of a location where a short-wave radio was hidden and his objective was to reach that point before he could be discovered. Personal safety was his last concern.

George described finding a farm house that he thought was

a "safe" house. He described the terror of working up the courage to knock on the door. Even though he was sure he had found the right place, according to the descriptions he had been given, it was not easy to trust anyone. The penalty for being caught in an escape attempt was far worse than one could imagine, not only for himself, but for those he had left behind.

It was with indescribable relief that he learned he had found the right house. The courageous family who lived there could hide him and link his SOS to the right people, beyond the Germans' reach. Although he was finally safe, George didn't want to think about what would happen to his family when it was discovered he was missing.

He was given precise instructions by the farmer about hiding in the barn. A section of flooring had been removed, and by night the family had dug a subsection that could hide one or more people at a time. The area was so closely watched they had had to take the dirt, removed little by little, to the canal or river banks and dispose of it there. Many people had been hidden in this barn and so far, no one had been caught. Food could be smuggled down by a rope to the people hiding there between the hours of patrol by the Germans. The real problem lay in disposing of feces. The only possible means of hiding this telltale evidence was to bring it up by rope in a bucket to be distributed and buried in the woods. There were no longer any pigs or pigpens at the farm that might have concealed the aroma. The Gestapo searched everything, everywhere, for clues to hidden "traitors." So the farmer and his family were incredibly brave to help George and the others they had hidden.

As soon as his communique reached the short-wave radio (that I sensed was located in Denmark), he knew he had to leave. George sneaked out of the barn at night and left the area as fast as possible; but he had no safe place to go after this. In spite of extreme caution, George was discovered in the woods by a Nazi patrol and was tortured as he was interrogated. He kept silent about everything. Before George died, he learned that whole groups of people from his town had been taken into the woods, killed, and left in mass graves. The Germans were never able to discover what they wanted to know in this particular incident, nor could they break the indomitable spirit of the people of the town.

There have also been instances in regression sessions when people remembered being involved in hiding people who were trying to find escape routes away from the Nazi searches. There were many people put into concentration camps who were not Jews, especially in Poland at the beginning of the war.

Risk of Hiding People

Valerie called me for a reading of her astrological chart as well as a past life regression. She also wanted to have a chart done for her young son, who is retarded. In the regression session, after reviewing her present life difficulties, I asked her to go to a life that would give her explanation for the present time. I told her she had a "karmic racial guilt," and I explained that I never know exactly what I mean by that terminology, but that it usually indicates guilt from another lifetime that bleeds over into the present. Usually one unconsciously deprives oneself in the present as a way of compensating for guilt of omission or commission especially if one had been in a position of responsibility for a family, group, or nation. If one has done something destructive in the past, or has not taken action, causing others to suffer, it is almost impossible to create a life of extreme ease and pleasure in present times.

In order to get Valerie to a past life, I used a system of word association to stimulate something in her mind. She had seen clouds when I asked her to go to a past life, but those clouds didn't seem to represent very much to her. After saying words such as candle, pillow, picture, etc., and asking her to respond with anything that came to mind I said, "trees." Valerie responded, "forest in Germany." I asked her where those clouds might be, and she said, "Nazi Germany." She then described herself as being female and about twenty years old.

"Everything is dark, and black, and dreary. There is fear in the air, and there are German soldiers everywhere. I'm in a small city, almost like a town, and the soldiers are walking down cobblestone streets. I'm German, not Jewish, but I'm terribly frightened of these soldiers. They could hurt us or put us in jail. I have a mother and father and several brothers and sisters. We are on the outskirts of the city and have a small-to-medium-sized farm. The whole family is involved in the farming and the making of cheese. The soldiers could take everything—our farm—and they could hurt us. They could take us to prison.

"I think we're helping to hide people. There's something underneath the ground, like a little room." I asked Valerie if her family was hiding Jews. She responded, "We're hiding people. I don't know who they are, so I don't know if they are Jews or not." I asked her how the people get to them. "There is something about a tunnel. It connects to the house. They can come from the tunnel in the forest which connects to the cellar, or come through the house and go downstairs. They can also escape through that tunnel if there are soldiers in the house. It's a short tunnel and they come when it is dark.

"The cellar holds about twelve people. We take food down

to the cellar, and we have to empty chamber pots that they use. The whole family takes care of these people, but we're really terrified we'll be caught. We live in fear all the time. Sometimes the Germans come to the house and search, but they really want our cheese, so they use a search as an excuse. They pretend to look for something but they really want the cheese." I asked if the soldiers buy the cheese. Valerie said, "No, of course not! But we always have lots of cheese out so they won't search very thoroughly. We have two cellars, and we can show them the main cellar. There is a rug over the hidden cellar door, and the table is on top of that rug.

"One day someone is moving around down below and coughing. The soldiers arrive and bring a dog. We try to signal the people, but this time there is a dog who sniffs something. There are only four or five soldiers, and half of my siblings are away from the house doing errands, but I'm there with my mother and father and some of my brothers and sisters. The soldiers kick the table over, and remove the rug, and take the people down below out of that hiding place. There are five or six people, mostly men, some young adults, and one older woman. The people are resigned to dying, and one person is dying anyway. He is the one who is coughing. Of course we are taken away with them.

"We go to a railroad track and are herded into cars. It's very dark; there's hardly any oxygen; and it's very cold. We're huddled together in a boxcar, and we're trying to lie down. The trip seems to take two days, but it feels like a very long time. We're loaded onto trucks and are taken to a camp with barbed wire around it. We're in a big camp and there are lots of people around. It's not so bad, now that we're out of those boxcars, but I'm very sad. I know this is going to be the end. I'm just resigned to this being the end of the road. It's really cold, and we just have what we had on our backs when they took us. And it's early winter.

"The people in the camp look at us curiously, and I see some of them smoking a cigarette. I don't know how they get a cigarette in here. There are guards with dogs. The commandant comes out and is so arrogant, it's easy to hate him. We go to a barracks...we don't work, we just wait. We're told that this is a better camp than most, and we do get some food—something like runny gruel. I think I just fade away and die. I'm very hungry, and lethargic, and I think I just die. It might be death from starvation. My mother is with me. She is almost dying too, but I think I die first, and she dies soon afterward."

I asked how they were punished for having helped other people. Valerie responded, "I think they question us to see if there are other people who we know of, like a network, but we've just been hiding people on our own. We try to act like stupid farm people so that they'll leave us alone. I see people from the same area. This might be in Poland, not Germany."

Valerie recognized several people from that lifetime. One was the commandant whom she hated. She believed that she had worked with him in her present life. She described her co-worker as having a Nazi-type mentality—"about as cold-hearted as they come," she said. Another person she recognized was her brother in the past life who seemed to be her younger brother in the present time. Valerie had described one incident in her childhood when she had been frantically concerned about protecting her younger brother. In the past life, the brother seemed to be especially fragile and died before any of the other members of the family. "I remember giving that brother extra food, but it didn't keep him alive. We can see each other through the fence, and we can talk to each other. Those clouds that I saw at first seem to be those bleak clouds that come with snow.

"I just wish I had given some medicine or liquor to the man who was coughing in the cellar. It might have helped to stifle the cough. I realize it was the dogs who sniffed him out, but I blamed myself for not doing something to prevent the whole situation from happening. The people down below may have been involved with the resistance, so although I feel badly about their death and I feel badly about my own, I think the worst guilt is about my family. I was only about 80 percent in favor of hiding people in the first place, but it was my mother and father who were really committed to helping. I think we were all resigned to risk death for it, but it was better than not helping at all. Oh, I think my present husband was the man who was coughing!"

Valerie then went to a life where she was burned at the stake. She realized that her husband then, and the man in the cellar, had come back to her again. She said, "He was my husband in a former life when I was accused of being a witch. I just thumbed my nose at the doctors and the establishment of the times. I knew a lot more than they did, and they knew I was a threat. I must have been a little arrogant because I knew how to heal and they didn't. In that lifetime, by my death, I left my husband with a bunch of kids and a big responsibility to care for our children. He had to pay for my trial and was left penniless. If I had been more circumspect I would have lived and I could have helped more people. I'm still acting the same way now."

Valerie's father was a doctor in this life, and she works in the medical field. She has concluded that she can accomplish more by being more moderate about her views on alternative medicine. She is, in fact, in a perfect position to introduce new techniques into the scientific field if she is careful not to step on toes of the people in authority. She realizes that she is in a dangerous situation by being aware of advanced medical techniques before her co-workers are ready to accept that knowledge. She could lose her job. That would be disastrous in her present circumstance.

Valerie has had a particularly difficult life in the present. Her father was mentally ill, even though he practiced medicine. He eventually killed her mother and then committed suicide. After she had experienced one tragedy after another, her son was born prematurely and has had both physical and mental deterioration since his birth. Valerie experiences difficulty in keeping a full-time qualified nanny, even though she pays a very high salary. Her son is becoming increasingly difficult to handle, as he can sometimes be like a wild child. The medical care for him, on top of the daily care, is extremely expensive. Once again, her husband is a wonderful father who helps with the care of his son and is very bonded with the little boy.

Valerie has an older child and has just had another baby. Yet she has an urge to have even another child, in spite of the stress of her daily life. That stress will not just go away, and there are few opportunities to get a figurative breath of fresh air. She has always protected everyone around her in this life, and can sometimes feel inadequate to do the job well. She is physically very tired, and her life can seem hopeless. She said, "I feel like I'm going to die." She knows she needs help on a spiritual level to help her cope with her routine. She also knows that if she should die in this life, she would once again leave her husband with the same responsibility of bills to pay and children to care for, and she must make the choice to live! Otherwise, lifetime after lifetime, she could carry the same guilt that is already overloading her. I asked how she might give herself some relief, occasionally, to restore and regenerate her system. She said, "I don't know, but it's nice to have permission to let myself have some ease or even pleasure in life. If I have a mission, then I must take care of myself too."

Personal caretaking seems to be the hardest thing for some people to allow themselves. In reviewing her stoic acceptance of her family's mission in Nazi Germany and their eventual death, Valerie accepts that she can, once again, make a contribution to helping humanity. But this time she has to find a way that will not be so costly to herself and everyone around her. She is planning to give birth to herself, in her imagination: "Joy—a new life, now—instead of actually getting pregnant again."

Methods of Extermination

Although there were many brave people who hid others in basements, attics, and barns, the Germans were extremely diligent in finding Jews to kill. The method they used in the beginning was simply to shoot men, women, and children. Eventually, though, the ammunition was needed elsewhere in the war effort, and this method proved to be too slow to take care of the overwhelming number of people to be executed.

By 1942, they had begun building the infamous 'showers' that were really gas chambers. But thousands of Jews had been killed before that in the most insidious ways—starvation, disease, overwork, suicide, and exposure to the elements. Jews were raped, hanged, drowned, dragged behind vehicles, burned, buried alive, and killed in medical experiments. One cannot help but be horrified by the Nazi death squads who never seemed to lack for new ways to kill their victims. The tragedy was that rumors reaching the ears of the people were too terrible to be believed.

Elie Wiesel is chairman of the United States Holocaust Memorial Council and Andrew Mellow Professor of

Humanities at Boston University. Among the thirty books he has written is the small volume entitled *Night*. It is a moving and terrifying account of his experiences in Nazi death camps. As a survivor, he was a witness to the deaths of his whole family. But most heart-wrenching was the death of his innocence and his faith in God. He described what it was like to be in Hungary at the time of the German invasion of Russia, and afterwards.

In 1941, he was a young Jewish boy living in the town of Sighet, Hungary, in Transylvania near the Polish border. He was a deeply religious child who studied the Talmud during the day and went to the synagogue at night to pray. He wanted to study the Cabbala, the mystical interpretation of the Jewish scriptures, but there was no master to teach him in Sighet.

One day he was approached by Moshe the Beadle, a familiar figure in the town. Moshe was very poor and worked at the synagogue doing odd chores. People liked him because he went about his business unobtrusively.

One evening Moshe came upon the young boy weeping, as he was praying in the synagogue, and asked him why he was crying. The young boy told him how unhappy he was because he couldn't find a master to teach him the Cabbala in Sighet. He earnestly desired to learn more. Moshe began having discussions with the young boy, talking for long hours of the revelations and secrets of the Cabbala. And so the boy had found his teacher, after all, in the unlikeliest person. Wiesel writes:

"Then one day [the Germans]...expelled all the foreign Jews from Sighet. And Moshe the Beadle was a foreigner.

"Crammed into cattle cars by Hungarian police, they wept bitterly. We stood on the platform and wept too. The train disappeared on the horizon; it left nothing behind but its thick, dirty smoke.

"I heard a Jew behind me heave a sigh.

"What can we expect?" he said. "It's war…"

"The deportees were soon forgotten. A few days after they had gone, people were saying that they had arrived in Galicia, were working there, and were even satisfied with their lot."

He then went on to describe Moshe's return to town.

"Several days passed. Several weeks. Several months. Life had returned to normal. A wind of calmness and reassurance blew through our homes. The traders were doing good business; the students lived buried in their books; and the children played in the streets.

"One day, as I was just going into the synagogue, I saw, sitting on a bench near the door, Moshe the Beadle.

"He told his story and that of his companions. The train full of deportees had crossed the Hungarian frontier and on Polish territory had been taken in charge by the Gestapo. There it had stopped. The Jews had to get out and climb into lorries. The lorries drove toward a forest. The Jews were made to get out. They were made to dig huge graves. And when they had finished their work, the Gestapo began theirs. Without passion, without haste, they slaughtered their prisoners. Each one had to go up to the hole and present his neck. Babies were thrown into the air and the machine gunners used them as targets. This was in the forest of Galicia, near Kolomaye. How had Moshe the Beadle escaped? Miraculously. He was wounded in the leg and taken for dead…

"Through the long days and nights, he went from one Jewish house to another, telling the story of Malka, the young girl who had taken three days to die, and of Tobias, the tailor, who had begged to be killed before his sons…

"Moshe had changed. There was no longer any joy in his eyes. He no longer sang. He no longer talked to me of

God or of the Cabbala, but only of what he had seen. People refused not only to believe his stories, but even to listen to them.

"'He's just trying to make us pity him. What an imagination he has!' they said. Or even: 'Poor fellow. He's gone mad.'

"And as for Moshe, he wept.

"'Jews, listen to me. It's all I ask of you. I don't want money or pity. Only listen to me,' he would cry between prayers at dusk and the evening prayers.

"I didn't believe him myself. I would often sit with him in the evening after the service, listening to his stories and trying my hardest to understand his grief. I felt only pity for him.

"'They take me for a madman,' he would whisper, and tears, like drops of wax, flowed from his eyes.

"Once, I asked him this question.

"'Why are you so anxious that people should believe what you say? In your place, I shouldn't care whether they believed me or not...'

"'You don't understand,' he said in despair. 'You can't understand. I have been saved miraculously. I managed to get back here. Where did I get the strength from? I wanted to come back to Sighet to tell you the story of my death. So that you could prepare yourselves while there was still time. To live? I don't attach any importance to my life anymore. I'm alone. No, I wanted to come back, and to warn you. And see how it is, no one will listen to me...'

"That was toward the end of 1942. Afterward life returned to normal. The London radio, which we listened to every evening, gave us heartening news; the daily bombardment of Germany; Stalingrad; preparation for the second front. And we, the Jews of Sighet, were waiting for better days, which would not be long in coming now...

"Then the year 1943 passed by:

"Spring, 1944. Good news from the Russian front. No doubt could remain now of Germany's defeat. It was only a question of time—of months or weeks perhaps.

"The trees were in blossom. This was a year like any other, with its springtime, its betrothals, its weddings, and births.

"People said: 'The Russian army's making gigantic strides forward...Hitler won't be able to do us any harm, even if he wants to.'

"Yes, we even doubted that he wanted to exterminate us.

"Was he going to wipe out a whole people? Could he exterminate a population scattered throughout so many countries? So many millions! What methods could he use? And in the middle of the twentieth century!

"Besides people were interested in everything—in strategy, in diplomacy, in politics, in Zionism—but not in their own fate.

"Even Moshe the Beadle was silent. He was weary of speaking. He wandered in the synagogue or in the streets, with his eyes down, his back bent, avoiding people's eyes.

"At that time, it was still possible to obtain emigration permits for Palestine. I had asked my father to sell out, liquidate his business, and leave.

"'I'm too old, my son,' he replied. 'I'm too old to start a new life. I'm too old to start from scratch again in a country so far away...'

"The Budapest radio announced that the Fascist party had come into power...Still this was not enough to worry us. Of course we had heard about the Fascists, but they were still just an abstraction to us. This was only a change in administration.

"The following day there was more disturbing news: with government permission, German troops had entered Hungarian territory.

"Here and there anxiety was aroused. One of our friends, Berkovitz, who had just returned from the capital, told us: 'The Jews in Budapest are living in an atmosphere of fear and terror. There are anti-Semitic incidents every day, in the streets, in the trains. The Fascists are attacking Jewish shops and synagogues. The situation is getting very serious.'

"The news spread like wildfire through Sighet. Soon it was on everyone's lips. But not for long. Optimism soon revived.

"The Germans won't get as far as this. They'll stay in Budapest. There are strategic and political reasons.

"Before three days had passed, German army cars had appeared in our streets."

Elie Wiesel and his family were deported to Auschwitz and then to Buchenwald, where his mother and a younger sister died. His father died only seventy-two days before the final evacuation, after surviving starvation, beatings, illness, and incredible hardships for almost a year. By a miracle, Elie Wiesel lived to tell the terrible story of the camps. But it was ten years after his liberation in 1945 before he could break his vow of silence and try to describe what had happened to him and more than six million other Jews.

Peter's Regression Session

In some of the regression sessions that have related to that time, details have emerged from the consciousness of the person that are similar to those written about by Elie Wiesel and others. Yet enough of that information is dissimilar to disavow that the individual doing the session had merely read the books and was repeating what he or she had absorbed. It usually comes as a complete surprise, even shock, for people to see that they may have lived during World War II, had been Jewish and had died at the hands of the Nazis. The accompanying emotion, however, makes it very real.

Peter arrived for his appointment with me dressed in the latest casual New York fashion. It was clear that he was successful and confident. His business was in advertising—producing commercials for television. Since people of all walks of life come to me for regression sessions, and I rarely meet the person beforehand, I am frequently unaware of what they might do in their business life. I don't ask those kinds of questions. I prefer to wait for whatever emerges during the session and focus on what is relevant to that experience. I am also past wondering why a person comes to me for such a session. Experience has taught that what comes forth from these sessions is rarely what the subject expects. It is almost as if the subconscious plays a trick on them just to get them there, giving some simple reason for going through the session.

The most revealing information Peter reviewed from his childhood was that he was actually shy and fearful. But he learned to mask insecurities with a charming and no-nonsense businesslike personality. He had learned how to control things in his life to his advantage. His childhood was not difficult or out of the ordinary in any way. The only thing that plagued him in adulthood was the occurrence of periodic migraine headaches. Sometimes the headaches were so severe that he would have to postpone a business meeting, but he had found medication that enabled him to get through if the occasion was critical enough.

The headaches interfered most often with his personal life. He might be on a date when the pain would commence, and he would simply have to put the woman in a taxi and give excuses for the premature ending of an evening. It was inconvenient and embarrassing at times. Peter presumed, intelligently enough, that the inherent pressures of his business were enough to cause such headaches to occur, but he would have been happier if they didn't interfere with what was otherwise a profitable and comfortable existence.

When Peter went to a past life, he saw himself as a teen-aged boy living during World War II. He had a loving, close family and had recently become infatuated with a very pretty girl in his small town. He was generally unaware of the war, except that there was tension among the inhabitants of the town, and people were less jovial than usual. Peter's mind was on a conquest of another kind. He wanted to do something heroic that would get the girl's attention and prove him a worthy suitor. Suddenly one day, German trucks rolled into the town and selected, indiscriminately it seemed, a work force to chop down some trees for firewood in the nearby forest. Peter stepped to the foreground, ignoring his mother's restraining hand on his arm, and was chosen to go in the truck. He was strong and handsome, and stood out in the crowd. He was one of the first to be chosen. There was a party of about fifty men and boys crammed into the truck.

When they arrived at their destination, instead of cutting down trees, they were given shovels and ordered to dig several huge trenches. When they finished digging the deep holes according to specifications, they were ordered to step to the edge of one of them. There they were shot, one at a time, by the officers in charge. The bodies fell into the freshly dug trench on top of each other. Peter and a few others were kept aside until the last and made to cover the bodies with dirt. There was no escape, and Peter was shot. The bullet entered his left temple.

When Peter opened his eyes after his session, many things were clear to him. In a flash, he understood his early insecurities, his rigid control over his life, and, especially, the headaches. He had revealed a life to himself that was quite the opposite of what he might have imagined. With his business acumen and drive for success leaving nothing to chance, he assumed that he had lived a life in a position of authority at a previous time.

Peter had shed some important tears during his session. As we parted, very few words were necessary to sum up the impact of what this revelation would mean to him in the future. When he tried to place some of the people he knew in that lifetime, he saw many friends and acquaintances from those former times who were obviously reincarnated as a large, loosely formed group of associations. Peter called me at a later date to report that his headaches had disappeared, and he felt he had a new lease on life. And to his great pleasure his romantic life had improved dramatically.

Will we have to have more wars, already six since World War II, so that the killer will then be killed in return? This could go on forever, for we are each other's keepers. Is it possible to find another way to heal the wounds and reconcile the karmic debt?

6

Rapid Rebirth
from Nazi Germany

✦

WE ARE CONSTANTLY changing roles from lifetime to lifetime. From a cosmic perspective, we come back over and over again as families, groups, and associates. We switch from being brothers, sisters, mothers, fathers, children, lovers, and friends and back again. The people we love or gravitate toward today are, no doubt, the people whose companionship we enjoyed in the past. The people who present problems in relationships or in associations are the same ones who gave us headaches in the past. In this book, I have only chosen to write about lives spent in Nazi Germany, but throughout the years I have been conducting regression sessions, people have uncovered lifetimes lived in all areas, and as members of all races. (See *Astrology and Your Past Lives.*) We seem to attract the same people over and over again, no matter what the external conditions, locations, and race might have been.

The interplay of characters from lifetime to lifetime is quite amazing. Ruth Montgomery says in her book, *The World Before*, "Human beings, like Cervantes' birds of a feather who flock together, tend to reincarnate in cycles with those they have known in previous earthly sojourns. By some curious law of karmic attraction we return again and again with these perennial companions to work out mutual problems left unresolved, or enjoy each other's company...But since each of us earthlings, once caught up in the wheel of karma, must experience physical life in all major creeds and geographical areas, we do not always return to the same race or locale." Nor do we necessarily return as the same sex. These memories of life spent on another stage can explain many things—attractions, relationships, sexual leanings, physical health, phobias, talent, intellect, and problems. *We don't change very easily.* So it may take effort to bridge the gap and heal rifts in the present. When a current-day relationship is so problematic that the best solution seems to be to just walk away from it (or to keep finding fault with the other person), a thought-provoking question to ask oneself is, "Do I really want to have to come back and deal with this person again in the future?" If the answer is "No," then there are some self-test questions you might begin to think about. "Where could I have possibly known this person before? What was our relationship? What could I have done in the past to create the friction and, in view of past life connections, how could I have changed things between us at that time? How can I make it right between us now? Can love and forgiveness salvage the relationship in the present?"

The dramas of the interweaving of roles, when people recognize each other in regression sessions, could provide Hollywood with enough scripts to last well into the twenty-first century. There have been so many stories of subjects in regression sessions recognizing people from the present in past lives that it is the norm rather than extraordinary. The desire to be connected again to those people who are familiar to us, even if the relationship has been painful in the past, pulls like a magnet. Difficult relationships take on a new meaning when a past life identification is made, and the relationships can be healed without much effort at all.

But the most profound examples I know of to give credence to the concept of the continuation of life and the necessity for understanding about death and rebirth are when individuals recall a past life in Nazi Germany. Many people have seen themselves as children, teenagers, and adults—both Jewish and non-Jewish—having been tortured and killed by the Nazis. Some people saw themselves as dying before being taken to a concentration camp and others recalled extremely horrifying tortures and death. Other people, relatively few, have seen themselves as Nazis and the perpetrators of crimes. The associations the victims of torture had with the perpetrators of the crimes give new meaning to the concept of healing relationships. How could it be possible to forgive these atrocities, and how can one reconcile the horror of what happened in World War II?

Everyday television shows have guests who come before the public to air their grievances against husbands, wives, children, lovers, and neighbors. Perhaps in the light of reincarnation these relationships could be resolved without such public exposure; but first, it is important to understand why these people should have been drawn together in the first place, and why these conflicts continue. In instances of marital abuse, as an example, why do people stay together? Sometimes they are risking their lives. They may be trying to get even with each other, or they may want to induce change in the other person. But in the meantime, they can be causing tremendous unhappiness for the people around them, who are forced to watch destructive behavior. The answer often lies in digging deeper than what appears to be the overt issue.

A true understanding of the joy of living may also entail gaining a greater insight into death. If people have died in concentration camps in Nazi Germany, for instance, and are back on earth again to tell the tale, there is very strong evidence for the survival of the soul.

Understanding Death

If we were so wise and evolved as to be able to understand death from a more vast plane or perspective, much of our present day suffering over the loss of loved ones could be mitigated. Much of our sadness is that we are left behind or that we will not have the comfort of physical companionship anymore.

Many of our death rituals, such as having a wake when someone dies, may have their roots in ancient times when we did understand the grandeur and celebration of a person's graduation to greater levels of consciousness. We've kept the ritual of a party, or wake, or celebration after a funeral, without remembering why such a ritual was established in the first place.

In the United States today there is a vast movement to legalize assisted suicide when a person has no hope of recovery. This is being considered as an option when incredible pain and loss of bodily function puts a terminally ill person in risk of losing not only his dignity but his quality of life. It is particularly sad when prolonged illness puts both an individual and his family in financial jeopardy.

But suicide, even assisted suicide, carries its own karmic penalty. Bringing an end to one's existence may be far from the real answer about how to leave the earth plane graciously and with ease.

Alice Bailey acted as a medium for the Master K.H. and wrote many deeply esoteric books on subjects that explain life from a cosmic perspective. The evolved Master, through that mediumship, articulates an increasingly accepted perspective on modern day medicine and death in an excerpt from *Esoteric Healing:* "The success of modern medicine is today so great that millions of people are kept alive—if not cured—who, in earlier days and with less scientific aptitude, would normally have died. In this developed skill and knowledge, and in this aptitude in the care of the physical mechanism, is today to be found a major world problem—the problem of overpopulation of the planet, leading to the herd life of humanity and the consequent economic problem—to mention only one of the incidental difficulties of this success. This 'unnatural' preservation of life is the cause of much suffering and is a fruitful source of war....It will be solved when the fear of death disappears and when humanity learns the significance of time and the meaning of cycles. It will be simplified when true astrological findings become possible, when man knows the hour of his departure from this outer plane and masters the technique of *"withdrawal"* and the methods of abstracting himself *consciously* from the prison of the body."

The Master K.H then goes on to say: "I think in terms of cycles and you think in terms of a few brief years." We tend to see life as an eternity, yet it is a mere blip on the screen of the great computer in the skies.

Two brothers, Kevin and Oliver, who were friends of mine in Ibiza, had spent many of their early years on an extended archaeological expedition, filming ancient sites and rituals in Samoa, Krakatoa; they also filmed portions of the ring of fire around the Pacific Ocean. They lived in Bali for a while and were well acquainted with an elderly artist there. He allowed them to film him and some of his art work; the story of his death was later passed on to my friends.

The artist was well into his hundreds, had lived a fruitful life, and decided it was time to leave the earth plane. He had lived on a more elevated and cosmic level of consciousness than is the usual case, and was probably quite in tune with his life cycles and his inner timing. His desire to leave the earth plane was not tinged with sadness or bitterness, but was simply a matter of awareness that a new experience was just ahead. The films of this ancient man and his art work depicted a joyous soul smiling and laughing with what appeared to be cosmic joy.

One day, he called his large extended family around him and shared a particularly lavish banquet with them. At the end of the meal, he simply announced that it was time to take leave of his earthly body. He said good-bye to everyone, went into a state of meditation for a few moments and was gone. The celebration by his family was genuine, and continued for a long time after he had left his body and was no longer present among them in the usual sense.

That kind of departure, or death, is so far removed from the tragic deaths we know about from Nazi Germany or from shootings on our own streets today it seems it is not the same experience at all. How do we prevent tragic deaths? How is it possible to change the consciousness of mankind to an acceptance of the true meaning of death?

I hesitate to write about the death of my beloved dog, Samantha, in a book about the needless deaths of so many people. But I learned a valuable lesson at that time.

Samantha was an amazing wire fox terrier. She was a healer, with vibrating limbs to prove it. If she were sitting on the lap of a friend of mine, she would put her paw on the part of their body that was weak or out of balance. More than once people volunteered what I knew to be true of Samantha by saying, "You know, she really is a healer!"

Samantha had a great honor in her short life, for Samantha sat on the lap of a very spiritually advanced soul, a beautiful and evolved person with hundreds of thousands of followers around the world. This evolved soul has come to earth to help people attain higher levels of consciousness. The energy one feels around this person is so boundless that great leaps of development of consciousness can be facilitated from merely being in the presence of this high being. If one is ready and can take the levels of energy into his or her own system, he or she is changed from that moment on.

So Samantha had a great healing. She shared this rare and extraordinary experience with one of her puppies, Peach Blossom. I had bred Samantha at a very fortunate time, astrologically, so that the puppies would have extraordinary charts, and I knew her puppies would bring great joy to their new owners. (Each puppy, inadvertently, went to live with a healer!) But Peach Blossom had made a deal with me right away. She insisted that she remain with Samantha and me. I accepted this as a hedge against the inevitability of Samantha's death, which I hoped wouldn't come until she was sixteen years or so.

Samantha and Peach Blossom went everywhere with me. They were both helpers when I conducted regression sessions, and were as quiet as could be for hours on end when I was working with someone. Samantha made it her purpose to concentrate on the subject in a session. She would either sit under the chair of the person undergoing a regression, or she would sit on the person's lap if it would help. She always knew exactly what the person needed from her. She was never wrong. My clients adored her.

One snowy March day, my car skidded on black ice and, although I was only going about fifteen miles an hour, I careened into a tree practically growing in the road. It was not until I had driven to the garage, checked out the damage, and called a tow truck that I saw my beloved Samantha on the floor of the back seat. She had evidently broken her neck and died quite quickly and painlessly. Peach Blossom had been on the front seat of the car, so I knew she was unhurt, but I had called back to Samantha as I pulled away from the tree, "Are you all right, my darling?" She, of course, had not answered.

The shock of knowing that Samantha would not be with me was just devastating. I couldn't believe it had happened—such a freak accident. I wanted to turn the clock back.

When I arrived at home after making tearful arrangements for her cremation, I called a friend who lives in a spiritual community quite a distance away from me. She volunteered to put a prayer stick in the ritualistic fire as a healing for Samantha and me. As she did so, I felt an immediate calm. My tears stopped, and I felt an inner peace. I asked my friend to write on that prayer stick that I wanted Samantha to come back to me immediately. I would look for a new little wire fox terrier puppy, and I would know immediately if it was Samantha again. Animals reincarnate, too. I could feel Samantha, now light as a feather in her spirit body, happy as could be, sitting on my shoulder, giving me her kisses. She hadn't really left me, and she was having a wonderful time, flying through the air, trying all kinds of new tricks. I was happy, as I knew she'd be back quite soon.

When I was first able to travel to the spiritual center where my friend lived after Samantha's death, I did shed a few new tears. The energy was extremely high, and the music touched me. I did miss the physical presence of Samantha. Many of the wonderful people who were at the Sunday service gave me their

kind condolences, as they adored Samantha too. We all specu-
lated about Samantha's own evolutionary progress. But comments from this amazing teacher were very clear. Knowing how
much I love Samantha, this profoundly wise person said,
"Jeannie, I understand you gave one of your dogs to God!" I
gulped inwardly, knowing that I hadn't quite done that, since I
wanted her back with me, and I said, "Well, not exactly." The
teacher continued, "But Jeannie, maybe God wants your dog!"
"Oh dear," I said. "I'd better go into the temple and give her to
God." Knowing what a struggle it was for me to say those
words, the teacher continued, "But look, you gave one dog to
God, and you have two new friends with you today."

I hadn't mentioned anything, but I had brought two new
friends with me that morning who had just moved east from
California and had expressed a desire to meet this remarkable
teacher. Later, and with great love and amusement, my friend
who lit the prayer stick said to me, "I can't believe you. You had
to be told three times!"

I learned an extremely valuable lesson from the simple
words spoken to me that morning. If God wanted Samantha,
how did I dare want to keep her for myself? I went into the
beautiful temple and gave my darling dog over to God.

Samantha did not come back as a new puppy. In retrospect,
I can only hope that my love helped her in her own evolution.
It is not only people but animals that evolve, and plants, too.

What would happen if everyone who knows about the
Holocaust could go into a physical temple, or one of the mind,
and let go of the souls of everyone who died at the hands of
the Nazis, giving them over to God's care? Claiming relationship and giving these living sparks of light to God is different
from just saying a prayer for them or feeling sadness over their
suffering. Perhaps without knowing the specifics of their

death, or even their names, we may have had intimate connections with these people. Perhaps the energy of this type of loving dedication, of giving them over to the oneness of divinity, may help all of us in our struggle to climb higher toward the light.

For we are all one—brothers, sisters, mothers, fathers, children, lovers, and friends—many times over.

Holding Hands and Walking toward the Light

A friend of mine, whom we will call Elliott, telephoned to tell me he was being married. Elliott's best friend, Michael, was married to Linda. After years of close contact with Michael's family, Elliott knew Linda and their three children very well. Michael and Linda had planned a European Christmas trip with their children. It was decided that Michael would leave a few days earlier with the children, and Linda would follow shortly.

The children and their father arrived safely, and Linda prepared to join them. Only hours before she was to leave for the airport, she received a call from her sister. "Don't leave for the airport before I get there," she said without explaining further. Within minutes she arrived to give Linda the tragic news. In Europe, Michael's car, containing all three children, as well as Elliott's niece, had collided with a bus, killing all the passengers of the car instantly. In one fell swoop, Linda lost her whole family—her husband and her three children—and Elliott lost his niece. Linda turned to Elliott quite naturally, and the trauma of the experience brought them closer together.

During the next few years, Linda's grief was so strong that she was barely able to function. Elliott married her soon after the accident and proved to be a wonderful friend as well as new husband. He gave her as much support as he could, waiting for the rawness of her grief to settle without expecting her to bond instantly in their marriage. Elliott did not hesitate to follow his heart and his head, for he loved Linda as deeply as he had cared for Michael.

Linda called me one day to ask for a regression session. She had used tranquilizers to get through the first period of shock, then went into extensive psychotherapy to deal with her grief. She hoped a regression session could give some clue as to why this should have happened.

She reviewed this life easily, as she had been born into a very loving and supportive family. She saw, very quickly, a past life in Germany during World War II. The scene before her eyes was that of a little girl about seven or eight years old, playing on a patch of grass with a little boy about her own age. They were quite absorbed in their game and were unaware of airplanes passing overhead. Suddenly a bomb was dropped at the very spot where she and her friend were playing, and they were killed instantly.

She said, "It was the strangest sensation to see that scene. And I instantly recognized the little boy I was playing with. It was Elliott!" The regression session didn't answer the major question in her mind, but it did explain why Elliott was back at her side when she needed him most. Their bonding was formed forever at the moment of their death. They may have held hands, spiritually speaking, as they walked toward the light in spirit form.

The issue of group karma continued to unfold in the relationship of Elliott and Linda. As time when on, Elliott, Linda, and I developed friendships with several other people, who had not been in our lives for very long. Elliott is a doctor and Julie was one of his patients. Julie decided to do a regression session with me and reviewed a life where she had known all of us before. She described a time as an Essene, before the birth of Christ, where we were all part of the esoteric, mystic Jewish group. She saw a karmic relationship between Linda and Michael, who were married in that life as well. Michael also died prematurely in that existence. But Elliott and Michael were brothers then. Although the Essenes were primarily a monastic group, there were some families and children in the group.

According to the Judaic law, Elliott was obligated to marry his brother's widow. Instead, in his former life, he married Julie, whom he had fallen in love with prior to Michael's death in that life. By that act, he neglected his duty, choosing his heart over his head. This time, his heart and head were in synchronicity. Elliot's and Linda's rapid rebirth after the war brought them together again.

Carryover of Responsibility from Past Life

Celeste was born in East Germany just after the end of the war. For most of her childhood she, her mother, and her sister lived with Celeste's maternal grandmother in a lovely blue house with a wonderful garden. In our regression session, Celeste's face took on a glow as she described the house, for it represented a happy time in her life. She said, "I can see that house and the beautiful garden. The house is blue and very charming." Celeste's grandmother was a wise, warm, and very spiritual woman. Celeste's mother, on the other hand, was angry, punishing, sometimes violent, and ill-tempered. Celeste's grandfather had been a soldier in the German army and was in a Russian prison after being captured. Celeste's father was in the military of the new East German regime and was away a great deal of the time. Celeste missed him, for he was very affectionate and lots of fun.

Celeste recalled that even as a very young child she hated being German. She wasn't sure what that meant, but she didn't like it when she was labeled German. Celeste had heard her mother talk about her own war experiences and knew that she had been a part of the Nazi youth groups, and was later in the army. For many years of Celeste's early life she was constantly told that life would be better if the Germans had won the war. Celeste's mother believed that under the Nazi regime things had been so organized, and said so frequently. She now felt that everything was in chaos. It was apparent that she was quite bitter about the war. For one thing, they lived in a divided Germany, and the family could not go to the west if they wanted to. Conditions were very difficult for the family in East Germany. Ideologically, Celeste's mother was still very much under the influence of Nazi thinking.

Matters seemed to come to a head in Celeste's life when she was about five years old. Her mother and father decided to get a divorce. Her grandmother had been making plans to go to West Germany, illegally if there was no other way, and she decided that now was the time to go. She would take Celeste's older sister with her, and Celeste and her mother would follow as soon as they could. When the authorities discovered that the grandmother was gone, the beautiful house was confiscated. Celeste and her mother had to move to a small, dismal apartment.

However, it was not long before their papers were approved and they were legally able to go to the West.

I asked Celeste if that change had been traumatic for her. Moving is high on the list of stress factors for adults, and it is usually a traumatic time for a child. Celeste assured me that she was excited about the change, because she would be near her beloved grandmother again, and her curiosity helped her anticipate new conditions.

The change was not what Celeste expected, however, because she lived some distance from her grandmother, and she now had to bear the brunt of her mother's ill temper without any buffer. Since her mother had to find a job and go to work, Celeste was put into a government-run facility for children. That didn't seem to be a bad experience for Celeste, because she was with other children and had a chance to play. I asked if she was lonely. Celeste replied, "I was always lonely."

When it was time to start school and she went to live with her mother again, things were different. She confessed, shyly, that she was often beaten with a cat o' nine tails that her mother kept handy. But most of the time, she managed to get through the ordeal without feeling too much pain. I wondered if she had learned to leave her body at such times, and Celeste thought that was a possibility. She also knew she had another particular way of dealing with the pain and sadness. Her refuge was in God. After the beatings, Celeste would go into the bathroom and pray to God in order to restore herself. She could always find peace during that time. As soon as she entered school, however, two new ordeals came into her life. The children made fun of her when she had to speak in class because of her East German accent. She also wore clothes that were beautifully hand-knitted but were different from what the other girls wore. She recalled going home one day and telling her mother she was not wearing a particular dress ever again! This time the beating with the cat o' nine tails was followed by her mother's kicking her, and stepping on her. Celeste thought her mother was killing her, and she just wanted to die. When she went into the bathroom this time, she knew that if she hadn't died under this savage attack, she was probably going to live. Celeste, at six years of age, had the wisdom to know that there was a purpose to her life. If she had survived this last abuse, God obviously wanted her to do something.

When Celeste reviewed her birth, she saw herself as just a few days old, feeling very, very cold. It was winter, and there was no heat. She could see herself lying on the bed next to her mother wrapped in a sheet or blanket, but not close enough to her mother to be warmed by her body heat. Her mother didn't seem to notice how cold she was, but Celeste felt that her mother didn't want her anyway. Celeste said to me, "At that moment, I wish I could go back. I wish that very, very much. I decide I'll have to just deal with things moment by moment. At least my father and my grandmother give me warmth by picking me up and holding me. When I lose both of them, it is very difficult. I become very stoic but, somehow, I never blame my mother.

"I am born fairly rapidly because my mother is in pain and I think I try to make it easier for her. I actually become very stoic even at the moment of birth. Certainly later in life I try to make it easier for her." I pointed out that she made a very early decision to take on a lot of responsibility for the happiness and welfare of others. Celeste volunteered that her mother's first thought when she saw her new baby was, "Oh no, not you again!"

Before Celeste went back to a past life, she volunteered something else. She remembered the first time she had heard about what the Nazis had done to the Jews. She was in school when the subject was brought up in class. She was horrified and couldn't help bursting into tears. Celeste realized her mother must have been part of all of that. She had heard about her involvement with Hitler's youth groups and the army. She said, "I came home and asked my mother, 'Where were you when all this was going on?'" Her mother had replied, "At that time the world was right and was very well organized." Celeste was extremely upset to hear her mother say that.

It was easy for Celeste to see a past life. She said, "I see myself as about eight years old, and I'm Jewish. My family lives in Germany—I believe it is Berlin. I have a younger brother as well. We have a beautiful apartment, but everyone is very worried. It seems that my mother and family, and even friends, are extremely nervous about something, some danger, but they don't seem to be doing anything about it. I know that, right then, I take on a kind of responsibility for their safety. It's my father's work that is the problem. My father seems to be stuck. He tries to do so many things, and once he has accomplished these tasks, we can take steps to leave Berlin and the danger. I feel like I should help him.

"I believe he is an optometrist and he has to finish the work for his clients before my family can pack up and move to another country. They are going to do this very quietly, but he feels a responsibility to the people who depend on him. I'm very nervous about the delay. I see myself riding my bicycle after school and taking my brother with me sometimes. The whole town has been changing. It is just horrible. I feel like I am much stronger than my mother, and although it becomes dangerous for me to ride my bicycle, I seem to go out every day after school. Oh, I think I am helping my father deliver the glasses to his patients.

"One day I'm stopped by a car. Two men start asking me questions—just taunting me. They are not in uniform, but they frighten me. I keep on riding, but they follow me and stop beside me, forcing me to the curb. They ask me if I'm the daughter of my father. I say, 'No,' but they keep following me and asking the same question. They want to know where he is and what he is doing. I'm so nervous I fall off my bicycle. With that, they force me into the car and take me to a big building, like a police station. I'm shaking inside. They ask me all these questions about my grandfather as well. I think my grandfather got away. They want to know where he is. For some unexplained reason, they leave me alone for a few minutes, and I run out.

"I'm panicked and I'm running as fast as I can. I stay close to the buildings, like ducking in doorways, hiding while I catch my breath and looking to see where they might be. There are very few people on the streets, but I know they are behind me, tracking me with dogs. I run through a doorway that has another entrance on the next street. As I come out on the other side of the building, just by chance, that street is full of soldiers marching by. There are some tanks as well. I run, and I trip, and I fall right under a tank. I die instantly.

"I believe my mother and father and little brother are picked up immediately and are killed. I think my mother in this life must have been there somewhere. I think she must have worked in that office where I was questioned. During the war she worked for the government." Celeste commented, "I was born again almost immediately...still feeling responsible for everything and everyone. I didn't give myself time enough to heal.

"I think I had something to do with my mother's death in a life before the last one. That's why I've had to take some punishment from her and why I didn't just leave home and go to live with my grandmother, for instance. We've made peace, however, and I also saw my father again after so many years. Both he and my grandmother have died, but I feel my grandmother's presence, helping me with my work. The past life memories help so much in filling in all the pieces of the puzzle."

My Father—My Son

Jeffrey was quiet and serious when he came to see me for his regression session, but he was eager and very open to the work we were scheduled to do. He wanted, more than anything, to understand the heaviness of his life and to be able to transmute the underlying sadness of his childhood into more joyous living. He was convinced that a regression session might do just that.

Jeffrey was born an only child into a Jewish family who had lost a very precious relative in a concentration camp during World War II. His childhood was colored by sadness because he was never allowed to forget those people who had died so tragically. Rampant good fun had never been a part of his youth, and because of his sensitive nature Jeffrey was not inclined to rebel against the strictures of his upbringing.

The great sadness in Jeffrey's family was that his paternal grandmother had probably died in a gas chamber. His father would never know, for sure, what had actually happened to her, and he couldn't forget what she might have suffered. The nagging guilt that pervaded every waking thought was that he should have done more to get her out of Nazi Germany. He couldn't forgive himself for not expending every effort to convince her to come to America while there was still time to leave. It was clearly impossible for Jeffrey's father to celebrate life when his mother had lost hers, prematurely and so needlessly.

On one hand, Jeffrey felt tremendous love and compassion for his father, but on the other, it wasn't fair for Jeffrey to spend his whole life mourning someone he'd never met. He felt cheated out of a normal existence because of the black gloom that permeated everyday life. He felt that his father barely knew he existed, so Jeffrey had no way to be reassured of any depth of love from his father. He sometimes felt that he would get more attention from his father if he, too, died.

Much of the obvious pain was reviewed and somewhat released when Jeffrey went back through the most critically traumatic times of his life. As an example, he saw himself as a two-year-old, sitting on a staircase, peering through the stair railings, watching a family gathering. He was being completely ignored. He realized that no matter how cute, charming, or smart he might be, he couldn't reach his father emotionally, even though he desperately needed him. He simply couldn't replace his grandmother.

Jeffrey gave up around that time. He developed a "what's the use?" attitude and stopped hoping and dreaming about the future. He became very stoic and serious about life. A part of him, primarily around the heart area, seemed to shut down. Jeffrey is prone to heart problems to this day.

Early on in our session, Jeffrey reviewed the birth process. Trusting his instincts, he was clearly aware of saying to himself, "Uh, oh. This life is not going to be easy." Even with that awareness, he knew that he had chosen to be born into this family to be with his father in particular. His goal was to bring him as much love and joy as he could—as only a child in a family can do—but it was obvious from the very beginning that it wouldn't be an easy task to make his father happy and lighthearted.

Jeffrey began his journey to a past life and saw himself as a woman. That came as a bit of a surprise. He seemed to be middle-aged, with a grown child. Jeffrey described her appearance, the clothes she wore, and her personality. It was vividly real to him. Although she lived alone, she was a contentedly happy person. It appeared that her husband had died some time ago and her only child, a son, lived far away. The son was happily married and quite successful in his business. The mother would travel quite a distance to visit, but always looked forward to getting home again. She had a nice house with a small garden and was very independent. She lived where she had lived most of her adult life, and her neighbors were good friends. She had her health and enough money to live moderately, so she had no reason to want to change her life.

Jeffrey suddenly realized that he/she was Jewish in that life as well, and lived in a town outside of Berlin. Hitler's storm clouds were gathering day by day, and rumors were a bit frightening, but like so many people, she thought any fearful accounts were grossly exaggerated and mostly passed on by scaremongers. At this point, Jeffrey began to relate the events of the past life as if he were seeing them on a movie screen. The details became very clear. She continued to receive mail from her son, and the son was obviously receiving her weekly missives.

Then Jeffrey realized that the son lived in America. They had always been close, and he was dutiful in his filial obligations, always on tap for help with anything in her life, even from that distance. He always wanted to make sure that she was happy and that everything went well for her. The mother knew that she had a home with her son if she ever needed it. The son and his wife always looked forward to her visits and, although it was hard to part at the end of the vacation, life in Germany was what she wanted. He never pressured her to alter anything.

But now his letters were filled with concern. His pleas and plans for her to leave Germany were urgent. "Mother, don't take any chances. Come to America right away. You can always go home again if nothing comes of this dreadful situation." She was touched, but she continued to reassure him that rumors were just that and no more. She was too independent to let a few Nazis scare her. She intended to live her comfortable life just as she had been living it, and was not going to be bullied into packing up and moving without just cause.

The mother's letters were full of reassurance to her son. "The Nazi's are actually treating us very well." She regularly reported the small changes that occurred, sometimes unexpectedly. The soldiers' presence on the streets and in the shops became an accepted reality. Some of the soldiers even stayed with Jewish families. They were courteous and polite, even though they were a bit remote in their manner. New daily edicts and regulations were so gradual that one could hardly complain. As long as everyone cooperated, matters took their course, and life was not very different. The soldiers' behavior was not at all like other people might think, one German soldier even brought chocolates to his hostess. At times, a few irrational curfews and rules were imposed, but the community was told that these mandates were for their own protection. A committee was appointed among the Jewish residents, and if there was a complaint or problem, one would simply report it to the deputy in charge and it would be taken into advisement. It was, after all, war time. Food was becoming scarce, and water was used very carefully. Her garden became all the more important to supplement diminished rations.

One night, a meeting was called. This gathering struck fear into the hearts of some people who had already been preparing for the worst—burying silver and valuables in their gardens, generally succumbing to some panic—but Jeffrey, as the woman, was quite aware of her calm acceptance of each step of the way. It was not pleasant having Nazi soldiers around, but she was one person who could be counted on to lend strength and rational counsel in times of trouble. In emergencies, people had always looked to her for kindness and consolation.

A letter was sent to her son about that meeting. A change was taking place, and she might be moving out of her house temporarily. She begged her son not to worry. The soldiers were quite concerned for their welfare, and because the inhabitants were spread out in their individual houses, some hazards were inevitable, in case of attack from the enemy. Those problems could be avoided if they were to live in apartments in the city for a short time. They would have access to more food and water and could be cared for and protected more easily. A safe place was being established for the residents of this community right in the heart of Berlin.

The soldiers suggested that people pack a few things for just a few weeks' sojourn and be ready to leave almost immediately. Actually it was an order, and the soldiers began to seem less compassionate, but she didn't want to alarm her son unnecessarily. With a heavy heart, she packed a few clothes and precious things to sustain her and prepared to leave her home. Now the soldiers seemed more abrupt. Occasionally if someone asked a question or protested, he/she was rewarded with a gun butt to the head. People began to readily comply with any orders that were given.

A huge truck was provided for the transport, and it was filled to capacity. It was so crowded it was impossible to sit down during the journey. People were packed in so tightly it was hard to breathe. During the trip which, fortunately, only lasted a short time, children were crying, and people were obviously quite frightened. There was no water, and no provisions for toilets. When they arrived at their destination, she hoped the worst would be over. Then she saw a group of dirty, dingy buildings and people from other neighborhoods being unloaded from trucks. Dreadful, nagging fears began to surface. She had carefully held her own worries at bay, but now there was no way to feel optimistic. A dawning realization of her own naivete made matters worse. She could have gotten away. The realization was debilitating. The whole group of people were beginning to panic. Rather than acting like friends and a formerly united community, they began to fight for space and clutch their children and belongings even more tightly to their chests.

In that pervasive atmosphere of danger, guards now forced everyone at gunpoint into the dilapidated buildings. They were herded into dirty apartments that were small, dingy, and unheated. There were too many people in each space, perhaps ten families in a one-room apartment, and there was nothing anyone could do. If anyone protested he or she was shot on the spot. Everyone tried to separate him- or herself from the others in the miserably crowded room.

Now the heartbreaking cries of hungry babies added to the misery. Everyone was hungry, cold, and thirsty. The smells became overpowering, as there were few toilets, and most of them didn't work. Personal hygiene gave way to necessity, and the stench became unbearable. There was no way to wash clothes or clean oneself. The sense of degradation and fear rendered the whole group more ashamed, frightened, and malleable. Each person seemed to exist in an invisible cocoon. No one dared ask questions. No one dared to stand up to the soldiers and their guns. It was each man for himself, or so it seemed.

This phase of agony was fairly short-lived. Before many days, the groups were again loaded into trucks. Rumors were rampant, but no one knew exactly what was ahead. At the end of this trip they were at least allowed to take showers and were issued clean clothes.

Actually, the clothes were never worn because the showers filled the rooms with gas instead of water. Thousands of people died, including the woman who was Jeffrey.

The impact of this awareness made conversation between Jeffrey and me quite unnecessary at that moment. I was sure more details were flooding into Jeffrey's mind. When Jeffrey opened his eyes, we simply looked at each other. After a short time, Jeffrey was able to verbalize his thoughts. "I was born very soon after that. And to my father, who was really my son in that life! I wanted desperately to be with him and to show him that I'm alive, okay, and with him again. How could my father ever accept that I am his mother returned! It's a little bit hard for me to realize it, myself." After a pause, Jeffrey said simply, "This makes sense of my whole life. I'm here to give my father as much love and comfort as possible, not the other way around."

In later conversations with Jeffrey, he told me that he had never read accounts of the Holocaust, nor had he wanted to know details of what had happened to the victims. He had heard so much about his grandmother that he had no desire to know more. The family had discussed and mourned her constantly, and had made tremendous effort to find out exactly what had happened to her. With so much uncertainty and speculation about the exact manner of her death, Jeffrey confirmed that what he saw in his regression session was from his own consciousness, not from any account he might have read.

Certainly Jeffrey's description of the way some of the Nazis disarmed the Jews in the beginning of the war has been borne out by the accounts written by Elie Wiesel and others. Elie Wiesel also described one Nazi officer as bringing a box of chocolates his Jewish hostess when he stayed in her house for a while. The officer was described as being somewhat remote, but exceptionally polite. How could anyone so polite be a killer?

The shock that comes when one realizes he has been duped is sometimes greater than anything else. The self-chastisement is one of the hooks that must be resolved and removed before a healing can take place. It is just as important to be compassionate and consoling to oneself as it is to show that kind of understanding to someone else. Sometimes it is easier to forgive others than to forgive oneself.

In the light of reincarnation, each day is a new beginning, a clean slate to write upon. Jeffrey's real task was not to forgive his father for being so remote but to, figuratively, put his arms around that kind, generous, loving mother who simply didn't know about evil. In this way, Jeffrey can allow more light and cosmic joy into his life.

That seems especially important for Jeffrey in view of the past life memory. The shock of the loss of lifestyle, dignity, and purpose during that time, as well as the loss of his life and the rapidity of his return, had prevented any subconscious healing to take place on a spiritual plane. Jeffrey would have had a difficult time in just starting all over again in this present life, even without the debilitating gloom of his childhood. An inner decision not to trust life, people, and unexpected events, especially since naivete in the past caused sadness for all, would certainly prevent a joyous and optimistic view toward the future. The ability to view the past objectively can be a most valuable tool in healing the present. In no other way could Jeffrey have truly understood his relationship with his father, and what it was that really prevented him from simply shrugging his figurative shoulders and adopting new attitudes about life.

7

Past Life Memory As a Nazi

✦

SEEING ONESELF in a past life in Nazi Germany can come as a bit of a shock, but imagine having to face the fact that it was as a person inflicting pain and torture, not as a person having to endure it. It is awesome to contemplate the kind of payback that would automatically, karmically, be incurred in a return to conscious life after having committed repeated acts of brutality as a Nazi.

The universe is not revengeful, but the law of karma brings back, in exact measure, whatever we have sent out in the past. If one could conjure up a visual image of the principle of karma, it might be as if a sad parent stood helplessly by, watching a defiant child doing something detrimental and self-destructive that could only backfire in the long run. Imagine God's tears as he watched some of his children savagely torturing other of his children, knowing what that soul would have to suffer in the future. The boomerang effect of karmic penalty for Nazi action and mentality could only lead to horrendous circumstances in the present life.

But suffering is relative. Who could determine whether it is more difficult to suffer from a terminal illness or total physical incapacitation? Is it worse to lose a child by accidental drowning or to be orphaned and left without a family at an early age? What would it be like to be tied to a chair and left in a dark room as a young child or to be consistently sexually abused by an otherwise-adored father?

All of these examples have emerged from regression sessions I've conducted, during the part of the process when the present life is reviewed. There have been instances when so much pain has been endured by a person, and brought forth during the backward travel, that I have been in awe of the resiliency and survival instincts of human nature. It seems miraculous that a person could function at all after having lived through some of the present life experiences that I've heard. As the session comes to a close, an explanation must emerge in order for a healing to take place. I often fear that nothing can possibly give explanation for such suffering in the present, but it always does. The explanation that comes forth from the person's own consciousness is meaningful enough for the individual to have complete acceptance of what may have happened in the past. Most people even comment that it explains so many things in the present. Miraculously, a healing begins to occur almost automatically.

We are told that we are never given more to bear than we can bear, but the concept of reincarnation puts a slightly different twist on the meaning. In the review time on the spiritual plane between lives, we seem able to choose just what we're willing to take on during each earthly existence.

Like paying a debt, we are given a chance to arrange our payments so that we are not completely crippled by them. But pay we must.

Three people stand out in my mind when I think of individuals who have had to pay, karmically, for their actions during World War II. These three unrelated people, one a man in his mid-forties and the other two young women in their mid-twenties, had vivid memories of being German soldiers at that time. In fact, Walter was an SS guard in a concentration camp. Each of these people has suffered almost unendurable miseries in this lifetime. The torment began in childhood and continued through adult life. When I met them, separately, each person had undergone intensive psychotherapy to attempt an understanding of their difficulties, but nothing had seemed to explain to them why certain things had happened in their lives. None of them expected to find a solution connected with a past life, much less an explanation that had its roots in Nazi Germany.

During their individual regression sessions they saw that their role, as soldiers in the German army, was to follow orders and destroy the enemy. But two of these people became aware that their zeal for killing was beyond what was demanded of them in the normal course of duty. The third person was horrified, in the German life, at what was expected of him. In Walter's case, as an SS guard in a concentration camp, his penchant for arbitrarily picking off prisoners with his pistol, was far beyond what could be tolerated by his superiors. He was eventually killed by a fellow officer at the end of the war to prevent more unrestrained destruction. Walter's story follows later in this chapter.

Sexual Violence in Childhood

Helen's penalty for the past life violence seems overtly tragic in her present existence.

On the day of her scheduled appointment, I had opened the door to the terrace for a bit of fresh air on a balmy spring day in New York. I had planned to shut the door as soon as Helen arrived, in case it might turn chilly during our session. Helen greeted me and immediately asked me to close the door. She apologized, saying she was always very cold. I shut the door and found a knitted afghan to put around her shoulders. Helen was extremely thin. She had a haunted look about her eyes and made no attempt to cover her anxiety with any small talk. She was clearly intent on the work that we were to do together.

In response to my first question, Helen told me about an incident that had occurred when she was around the age of eleven. She was visiting her beloved grandmother, her father's mother, and her adored Uncle Josh, a bachelor who still lived at home. Uncle Josh spent a lot of time with Helen and gave her special attention that was not lavished on her brothers and sisters. These periodic visits to her extended family were very important to Helen.

Helen saw herself standing by the apartment window at twilight, looking out on the cold, snowy New York scene below her, when Uncle Josh came over to stand behind her. When he put his arms around her, Helen suddenly began screaming in terror. Uncle Josh backed away from her immediately and led her away from the window. As he sat her down on the living room couch he kneeled beside her and gently caressed her hand. He was devastated and said, "Darling, what is the matter? You know I would not hurt you. Why were you screaming?"

In the panic of the moment, Helen's carefully guarded secret tumbled out. Without being able to stop herself, she told her uncle of the terror of being consistently raped by her father, Josh's brother. Uncle Josh made an effort to be calm as he heard the news and tried to extend that calm to Helen. Helen realized that she had just done the very thing she had sworn she would never do. She immediately regretted her outburst, but she had simply been unable to stop herself from telling. Helen's father had warned her, repeatedly, that if she ever revealed anything about these episodes, something terrible would happen. Her father said that he would denounce her before their church and expose the devil that was in her body. Everyone would know her for a liar and a witch.

It was, perhaps, very fortunate that Helen's grandmother could not speak English, and she evidently did not hear Helen's scream. Helen begged her uncle to protect her secret and, especially, to keep her grandmother from that knowledge. After a long while, Uncle Josh was able to reassure Helen, and he gave her some warm chocolate to drink. He said he wanted to take a short walk, but that he would be back soon. He promised, again, not to divulge anything to anyone.

Some time later, Helen heard Uncle Josh calling to her. She went to the door but he was not there. It was now growing quite dark, and Helen went in to be with her grandmother in the kitchen. Uncle Josh had been gone a very long time by now, and Helen and her grandmother wondered where he might be.

When the telephone rang, it was up to Helen to pick up the receiver, as her grandmother was not able to understand what was being said. Helen hoped it was Uncle Josh, but instead it was a stranger who informed her that her uncle had been taken to the hospital. The stranger was finally forced to tell Helen that Uncle Josh was dead. He had either slipped or had committed suicide by jumping from the roof of the building.

In addition to the devastating shock and panic she felt, Helen had to break the news to her grandmother. But the horrifying thought that ran through her head was that Daddy was right. Uncle Josh's death was proof that her father's prophecy had come true. She had told someone about the bad things in her life, and now something much worse had happened. Helen was left with the sure knowledge that she had killed her beloved Uncle Josh and she took full responsibility in her own mind. She would have to live with the guilt for the rest of her life. She could bear that pain, but nothing could ever persuade her to tell of it again.

After her uncle's death, Helen's hair began falling out. Finally, a school counselor began to worry about her and called a psychologist to interview her. During the session, Helen was given some puzzles to do, as the psychologist asked her some questions. Concentrating on the task before her, she automatically answered everything quite truthfully. It seemed that she told the psychologist about the sexual abuse without being aware of what she was saying. When she realized what she had done, she was absolutely frozen with fear and felt anger at being tricked by the man and those puzzles.

Helen's mother was called to come to the school, and Helen was terrified of what might happen when her mother arrived. It was decided that Helen must take a compulsory trip to the hospital. At the emergency room, the physical examination revealed severe internal damage. In fact, the damage was so extensive it was imperative to remove Helen's appendix along with a lot of scar tissue. Since the situation had now come under the scrutiny of the school authorities, the courts would not allow Helen to come home before the father had been removed from the premises and barred from entering the house.

Something terrible had happened again.

Helen's mother blamed Helen for ruining not only her marriage but her whole future. The family life had obviously been completely disrupted, and it was Helen's fault. Eventually their house had to be sold. In spite of the evidence, Helen's mother staunchly defended her husband. Helen was denounced, not to the church, but to the family, for Helen's mother told the other children that Helen was lying.

The repercussions extended to Helen's grandmother. She was hospitalized for a very long time and lost her eyesight. Helen called the condition "traumatic blindness," resulting from shock or trauma. During one of Helen's visits to the hospital, her grandmother begged Helen to tell her the truth. Helen said she had been lying, for she was quite certain that if she told her grandmother the truth, her beloved grandmother would die.

Finally, when Helen was about fifteen years old, one of her brothers confirmed her story. He told her that he knew what had happened. He had discovered their father raping Helen on the kitchen floor with a handkerchief stuffed in her mouth. The layout of the house included a spiral staircase leading from the kitchen to a basement playroom. At times, Helen's father would send the other children down the stairs to play, but he would keep Helen with him.

One day the boy crept up the stairs and saw what was happening. His presence remained undetected but he was afraid to defend Helen when she was accused of lying. Before his admission, Helen lived in a hell of isolation, completely alone in her knowledge of what had happened. Her mother did such a convincing job of branding her a liar that she was ostracized by the family. No one believed her, and she had no one to defend her. After her brother's admission to Helen, he stopped speaking to his mother. As soon as Helen, herself, refused to see her mother, her hair stopped falling out.

There were many suicide attempts. When Helen was about fifteen, she almost succeeded. In fact, she was pronounced dead by her doctors. Her recovery was deemed miraculous, as she had been brain dead so long it was fully expected that she would be in a vegetative state.

During her near-death experience, Helen had a visit with Uncle Josh. In that visitation, Uncle Josh convinced her to return to life to fulfill her mission. Helen had an illegitimate child at an early age, but after many years in therapy she met and married a kind, loving man. Her marriage proved to be a happy experience.

In the regression session, when Helen went back to another lifetime, she saw herself as a woman wearing a uniform. She identified that garment as a Nazi uniform, and saw herself as part of a twosome. Her vision produced the sight of running down a street with a gun in her hand along with her boyfriend, also in uniform. They both seemed to delight in their role as snipers. Helen described the street scene and the buildings quite vividly, as well as the alleyways where they would hide. The area appeared to be a ghetto.

Helen felt tremendous gusto when she was killing men, women, and children. Coupled with that thrill came violent and wild sexual urges. She and her partner alternately indulged in killing and then unrestrained, orgiastic sex. Together they killed hundreds of people.

Eventually, I asked Helen if she knew that man in her present life. Her affirmative response led me to ask if she could identify him. It came as no surprise to me that she named her father as her former lover. The violence and the attraction—at least on one side—had repeated itself in this life.

Group karma came into play as she tried to identify some of the people they had killed. She quickly saw her mother as one of her former victims. She knew she had to contact her mother again, and although she might not be able to tell her mother about her regression session, her changed attitude could not help but bring a truce between them, if not a full healing. In her mind's eye, if Helen could ask her mother's forgiveness for Nazi Germany and could forgive herself, her mother might forgive Helen for what she saw as Helen's treachery and, more importantly, acknowledge her betrayal of Helen in this life. All of this can be accomplished without saying anything to the other person. Thoughts are things, and are very potent if accompanied by sincere emotion and feeling.

Helen then went back to another life. This time she saw a life as a devoted healer in an Egyptian temple. Her particular task was working with people who had animal-like appendages.

Plastic surgery was quite common in ancient Egypt. That practice had come from Atlantis along with some survivors of the great flood. The major difference between ancient and modern-day plastic surgery was the motivation. Much of present day plastic surgery is an attempt toward the beautification and recapture of youth. Egyptian plastic surgery was an attempt to correct the corrupt Atlantean practice of breeding humans with animals to create an obvious slave class. Throughout the ages from Atlantis to ancient Egypt, the genetic experimentation had left some people with an extra appendage, such as a tail. Helen's job was to help in the removal of those extraneous parts of the body.

Helen is left with strong examples of the choice between the high road and the low. It is obvious that the guilt on a soul level has caused a tremendous amount of pain in Helen's present life. More self-punishment cannot restore the balance of right and wrong on a soul consciousness level, but self-forgiveness can.

My suggestion to Helen was that ultimate self-forgiveness had to relate not only to the acts committed in Germany, but to the awareness of the slide from the highest level of consciousness to the lowest. The climb back up to the high side of spiritual awareness and into the light is often a difficult and treacherous journey. How can one forgive oneself for such shortsighted stupidity? Better to never have climbed the heights and misstepped to a fall, than to have to painfully struggle through an eternity of lives in an effort to stand again and balance the scales. For an evolved state of consciousness demands an ever greater responsibility.

I asked Helen if she thought she had suffered enough in this life. There was no need for her to answer that question. She knows she has been more than sufficiently chastised on a soul consciousness level. She can allow herself to begin her true work in this life. Helen also has a vision of the mission she is to fulfill, as foretold by Uncle Josh. She is already beginning her training as a therapist.

Since the ultimate purpose of a regression session is to effect healing, such healing can only occur when an individual can forgive himself, on a conscious level, for what was formerly buried in the unconscious mind. In Helen's situation, the awareness of the brutal acts she committed in Nazi Germany was somewhat balanced by her awareness of the positive, healing efforts in Egypt. This may sound amazingly pat and easy. Only the individual going through the day-by-day healing process can know the depth of its reality.

Former Human Experimentation

The corruption of ancient Atlantis led to the complete destruction of that civilization. A parallel can be drawn to the practices of human experimentation in concentration camps that were condoned by the Nazis. Josef Mengele's experimentation with twins has been documented in several books, among them, *Mengele's Hoax,* and *Children of the Flames: Dr. Josef Mengele and The Untold Story of the Twins of Auschwitz*. Hitler's desire to "purify" the race by destroying anyone not of Aryan blood may trace back to unfinished business in Atlantean days.

The Essenes, living in caves in Qumran, wrote about the "Sons of Light" and the "Sons of Darkness." The writings, in the Dead Sea Scrolls, seem to confirm what Edgar Cayce said about the "Sons of God," who came in to uplift the consciousness of the Egyptians. The "Sons of Darkness" may also have been the "Sons of Belial" described in the Bible, who were still trying to create class consciousness and enslavement. The Sons of Belial are synonymous with the Biblical Satan. Throughout history, there have always been periods when one class of people tried to enslave another.

The "Sons of Light" were trying to uplift everyone's consciousness, acknowledging the existence of a soul, even in those poor beings who still bore the genetic markings of animal appendages. It may be that some souls were still trapped in partial animal bodies from the beginning of time, when some of the more curious spirits became trapped in the sensationalism of animals' activities.

. . .

Ellen went back to a past life in Druid times in England in her regression session. Little by little she began to see herself as deformed in some way. She was somewhat of an outcast in a small village, living alone and scrounging an existence from a few compassionate people. She was not mistreated and did not seem to be too unhappy in that life. Then a vision came to her of a Midsummer's Eve celebration. Her deformity was ignored in that celebration, even mildly accepted as part of the pageantry. She wasn't quite sure why this should be true, but she saw many people dancing in a meadow, and knew that her participation in the yearly ceremony was a joyous occasion for her. During the rest of the year, she lived virtually alone. In her session the vision that gradually came into focus was that she was human, but that her legs were similar to the hind legs of a lamb or ewe. She had a great deal of hair on her legs, like fur, and hooves, even though her upper body was human. Some other people dancing and celebrating in the meadow also seemed to have some sort of animal characteristics or appendages. The people in this group were intelligent, definitely human, with spiritual consciousness. They were not primitive except for their appearance, but they were ostracized from society except at the time of those Midsummer's Eve celebrations.

One might think that this young lady would be horrified at what she saw. Instead, a light of acceptance and awareness came into her eyes and she shyly said, "This explains so much about my life!"

Was Hitler back again from the days of Atlantis and Egypt, still trying to "purify the race" according to his twisted concepts? One of the little-known facts about Hitler is that he was a student of the occult. He began to use astrologers in 1939, when the SS captured an astrologer named Wilhelm Wulff and coerced him into working for the Third Reich. Publicly, Hitler decreed that the practice of astrology was banned in Germany, but Wulff cast horoscopes for individuals, nations, groups, and movements. Wulff later wrote a book entitled *Zodiac and the Swastika*. He quotes Heinrich Himmler as saying, "In the Third Reich we have forbidden astrology. We cannot permit any astrologer to follow their calling except those who are working for us. In the National Socialist state, astrology must remain a privilegium singulorum. It is not for the broad masses."

An astrologer tempted fate if he dared cast Hitler's horoscope without official approval. However, a Swiss astrologer, Karl Ernst Krafft, having used his knowledge to predict trends in the commodities market, said that Hitler's life would hang in the balance between November 7 and 10 in 1939. When a bomb went off on November 7, just a few moments after Hitler had left an anniversary celebration, Krafft wired Rudolf Hess of the SS to warn him that Hitler would still not be safe for a few more days. He was promptly arrested. Later, however, he was released to work for the German cause.

Information came to the British about Krafft's astrological service to Hitler, and the British decided to hire the best astrologer they could find to second-guess Krafft. In this way, the British might know not only what Hitler was thinking, but might also slip pro-Allied propaganda through forecasts similar to Krafft's into Hitler's hands. Churchill said, "After all, why should Hitler have a monopoly on astrologers?" and he promptly hired Louis de Wohl. (In 1931, De Wohl had accurately predicted the breakout of the war and the future invasion of Poland at a dinner party attended by Lord Halifax. De Wohl knew all five astrologers presumed to be working for Hitler, and had worked at some point with Krafft and was familiar with his methods.) In his first memo to the British War Office in

1940, he advised that the Germans would not invade England because he was sure Hitler's astrologers would counsel Hitler against it. Confirmation of the accuracy of this prediction was discovered after the war in Gestapo files by a friend of Wilhelm Wulff's who worked in the British Secret Service. He wrote a book entitled *Astrology: A Recent History, Including the Untold Story of Its Role in World War II.*

Before his rise to power, Hitler had been greatly influenced by a German metaphysician named Horbiger, who taught that there had been many cataclysmic events when civilizations had risen and had been destroyed, and monstrous mutations had occurred. Was he teaching about Atlantis? Horbiger's theory was that one of these periods of mutation had produced the Jews, whom Horbiger blamed for the "degeneration" of Nordic supremacy. When Hitler came into power, he brought Horbiger's theories of racism with him onto the official Nazi platform.

Another person who influenced Hitler's thinking was Alfred Rosenberg, whose book, *Myth of the Twentieth Century,* became a fundamental part of Nazi thinking. Rabbi Gershom writes in *Beyond the Ashes,* "If Hitler's *Mein Kampf* was the bible of Naziism, then Rosenberg's *Myth* was its catechism." He goes on to say, "Rosenberg and Hitler were both initiated into an occult lodge called the Thule society. Hitler appointed Rosenberg the official 'theologian' of the Third Reich, with the task of rewriting history and creating a neopagan religion. Rosenberg's *Myth* attempted to purge Western civilization of all Jewish influences and resurrect the ancient gods of Nordic mythology. (Jesus, to Rosenberg, was a blond-haired, blue-eyed Aryan child kidnapped into slavery.) Although people in metaphysical circles often think of paganism as a gentle, life-affirming earth religion, the type of neopaganism preached by Rosenberg and his cronies was heartless and barbaric."

Rabbi Gershom continues: "Whether or not Hitler's soul was literally from among the Sons of Belial, it is well known that he was interested in the occult, and many believe that he was a student of black magic. Hitler wanted nothing less than the complete reversal of the laws of God, as symbolized by his version of the swastika. This design, which appears in the art and rituals of tribal peoples around the world, is known as the 'whirling logs' to the Navajos and Hopis. It was used in mosaic borders by the Romans and appears in Tibetan Buddhism. It is also used in India, which is apparently what led Hitler to see it as an 'Aryan' symbol. Drawn in the ancient way, with the logs whirling clockwise, the swastika symbolizes the four directions and the harmony of the universe. But, in true Satanic fashion, Hitler purposely *reversed* the swastika, turning it into a symbol of utter chaos.

"...If Hitler was indeed a black magician, then he would have greatly feared the 'white magic' of the thirty-six 'Lamedvavniks'—the hidden Jewish saints—as well as the spiritual power of the kabbalists and Hasidic Rebbes whose lives were so totally devoted to God."

Was that an unconscious motivation for Hitler's desire to exterminate all the Jews in Europe? Was Hitler really trying to rid the world of a karmic group who invoked the light through their prayers?

Former SS Officer

Walter's story was documented in my book *Astrology and Your Past Lives,* but it bears retelling. Walter's comprehension of the ramifications of that life and why it should have happened in the first place only came full cycle over a period of time. Walter's awareness produced a tremendous healing as he understood the deep, underlying patterns of the difficult events of this life.

Suffering is relative to the individual who is experiencing the pain. The events of Walter's childhood may not seem to be so extraordinarily difficult, and therefore the retelling of the events of his childhood may not be compelling enough to touch a chord of response. The actual events only scratch the surface in describing how Walter felt. But the retelling of his dreams is enough to call forth a response of terror in anyone. It was these nightmares that led Walter to call me with the idea of attempting a regression session.

Imagine awakening morning after morning after yet another night of horrifying spectacles of tortured animals seeking shelter in one's bedroom. For the underlying theme of Walter's dreams was always the same—that of innocence being tortured. If I were writing a film script, I would show Walter being jolted awake in the early dawn with wringing wet pajamas, twisted sheets, and disheveled hair, reaching for a cigarette to help him adjust to the reality of daylight. I might imagine that after a long time of such nightmares Walter would dread night and the time for sleep. I could certainly imagine Walter seeking companionship in the evenings and looking for anything that might help the transition from day to night. I would show him heading for his favorite bar, consuming drink after drink in hopes that he could simply leap into unconsciousness without the awareness of what was to come.

I could imagine the agony of having to pull oneself together after a hellish night to face a responsible job, and the effort of adjusting to the world around without revealing those inner horrors to anyone else. I would show Walter's development of a personality: a facade of toughness and tight control over his emotions. I would certainly expect Walter to erect a huge wall between himself and the rest of the world.

This script would accurately describe how Walter has dealt with his life. He is an alcoholic. Walter is one of the lucky ones. He reached such a low point in his existence that he joined Alcoholics Anonymous, and he has been sober now for many years. He works very hard to help other alcoholics find the treatment offered by AA. Walter had been sober for some years before he came to me for a regression session. In spite of his new understanding of himself and his sobriety, the nightmares had not stopped.

First Walter asked me to interpret his astrological chart. My description of the subconscious patterns I saw in his chart confirmed what he'd experienced in his life and led him to tell me about the nightmares. I suggested a regression session to help him get to the bottom of the problems. A tremendous healing can take place when demons are brought into daylight. Walter asked for an intermediate session so that we could analyze his dreams.

From my perspective, it took a lot of courage for Walter to get ready for his session. He was well-acquainted with the dynamics of psychotherapy and other kinds of healing, and he had no assurance that the situation might not become worse after bringing things into daylight. Walter did indeed confess that he was quite nervous when he arrived for his scheduled appointment with me. I did my best to encourage him. I have seen almost miraculous results, time after time, after only a few hours of regression therapy, instead of months or years of traditional therapy. (It is after a regression session that traditional methods of therapy can be very beneficial. The regression session speeds up the results of other forms of therapy quite amazingly.)

In one of Walter's recurring dreams, he saw a beautiful Palomino horse that had been given to him. He loved the horse so much that he kept it in the room with him. It was necessary to take the horse to someone for an "adjustment" before he could ride him, and it was with great reluctance that he gave his treasure into the care of someone he didn't really trust. When he returned for the horse, he discovered that it had been beheaded and skinned, and had shrunk to the size of a small dog.

Walter would awaken from this dream in total panic. He had been trying to find the poor animal, which was hiding in agony somewhere in his room. After analyzing this dream, Walter was ready to go on to a regression session.

Walter's childhood had been made difficult because of an invalid in the family who lived in his house as he was growing up. He was forced to assume additional responsibility and was unable to be frivolous in the face of the suffering of a relative. He had an unhappy marriage that ended in divorce and was now in an unhappy, unfulfilling relationship in which sex was withheld from him. Walter reviewed his birth and became cognizant of a birth survival decision that described his life perfectly. It confirmed the patterns he had discovered while he was in therapy.

Walter went to a past life scene quite easily. After a few moments of quiet, he said, "I think I am a German officer, a member of the Gestapo. I seem to be in charge of a camp—I don't think I want to see what I did."

He went on to describe his daily activity in the camp. He then saw himself deliberately selecting his victims for the day. With tears pouring down his face, he described his abusive treatment of the prisoners. He talked about the people he murdered in cold blood, shooting them with his pistol. He next described the women he had brutally raped.

Walter said, "It is like I pick and choose certain people with a particular kind of sadistic cruelty. I am not arbitrary about whom I brutalize. I pick specific people." Walter recognized his ex-wife as one of the women he had savagely raped. He continued, "I think I am shot by one of my own officers. I am just too sadistic for them to deal with. I think I was tried and found guilty at Nuremberg, posthumously."

After these insights, Walter was visibly shaken. I asked him to look at his childhood in pre-war Germany. He saw that he had been orphaned and as a sensitive young man had been a prime target for the Hitler Youth groups. Without any family love to counterbalance the messages that were drilled into his head in his formative years, he took the injunctions of the Nazis to heart. Walter's sense of the lack of family love in his early years helped him cope with what he had seen; still he had the feeling that there was further information yet to come to light. In spite of what he had learned about himself, he felt lighter and relieved after our session.

Most often, as time goes on after a regression session, new information comes to the surface. New insights may come about as a result of additional sessions with me, or quite often, spontaneously. Additional information just seems to float up into consciousness. Walter was profoundly open to new pieces of the puzzle that began to come to mind. Not long after our session, the whole picture became quite clear.

Walter had volunteered to help with a project of mine, so we saw each other again outside of a formal appointment. We were taking a break from work one day, when we happened to talk about the possibility of a past life association between us. As we sat talking, with our eyes open and with no kind of preparation, I told him that I could only trust my instincts, but I felt we might have been together in a previous time in Japan. In contemplating our association, I suddenly *felt,* rather than saw, the delicacy of the clothes I was wearing. The robe was fashioned of a kind of gossamer silk that I've never seen in my present lifetime. I also knew that I was very tiny and delicate, not my present build in this life at all. Walter seemed to be wearing a gray silk robe, and I knew he was a man of great dignity and position. I could see exactly how we looked in those clothes.

Walter contributed some of his own insights. He thought we had been married, but that our relationship didn't last very long, in spite of a tenderness in our association. He sensed an element of danger around us that made our time together even more poignant. He knew that we lived a very elegant lifestyle, but that we were apart most of the time, and the quality of our life was not sustained. He confirmed my sense of our appearance and added even more details.

I happened to be talking to a new friend, Eleanor, the next day, who was also working on the project. Since they knew each other, I had Walter's permission to tell her about our experiences outside of the regression session. After I finished my story she said, "Don't you remember my regression session? I was an infant in a room full of Japanese elders when a Samurai burst in the door and chopped me in half!" My own reaction to that was sudden and real. I burst into tears and said, "Oh my God, you were my baby, and I couldn't save you." She continued, "But you weren't even there. Somehow you couldn't get to me."

I had become friends with Eleanor almost the moment I met her. We had similar experiences and associations long before we were acquainted. I would mention someone's name in casual conversation, and Eleanor would have a story to tell. It was always "what a small world," between us. It was not by accident that we felt an instant bond of friendship. Eleanor raised an interesting question. "How is it that I don't feel the same closeness to Walter as I do for you?" My answer was, "Because he wasn't there. He may never have seen you, in fact. There was some kind of political movement that kept him away. I think I was tied up when the Samurai killed you, and I don't think I lived very long after you."

The climax of the story came when I asked Walter if he wanted to hear our mutual fantasy. "I think I do," he said somewhat reluctantly. Afterward he added, very quietly, "I have always suspected that alcoholism doesn't develop in just one lifetime, that it must take many lives of drinking to develop an addiction. I think my disease began when I returned home and found that my whole family had been murdered by my political enemies. I was just so sad, I sat and drank my life away."

One more bit of information emerged that seemed to tie everything together for Walter. I asked him if he thought that perhaps some of the people he had so deliberately murdered during his time as an SS officer in the concentration camp could have been the same people who had been involved in the massacre in Japan. He didn't answer me, but his silence was more eloquent than words.

One of the women Walter had raped in the life in Germany was his ex-wife in the present time. Because of the violence of the act, a karmic hook was forged between them that brought them back together for an extended period. His relationship with me and with Eleanor, although sad, had no sting involved such as revenge, anger, or overt acts of cruelty. So we were privileged to meet again for a very short time, under pleasant and caring circumstances without any karma to be resolved. Eleanor and I have not been in touch for several years, yet I think of her often and with great fondness. She was my baby, but for less than a year. There was no blame attached to me, as she knew I was unable to protect her from the murder. In the present time, Eleanor showed great kindness to me in sharing her apartment while I was in New York for a few months, away from my home in Spain.

Surprise Twist to Past Life

Before beginning our telephone regression session, Eileen told me that she had had a recurring dream since childhood. The dream was especially frightening because she saw herself being chased by dogs. As soon as she was old enough to attempt an understanding of this dream, she realized that it might have taken place in Nazi Germany. After reviewing two former lifetimes that explained her present day relationships with family and friends, I asked Eileen if she could find a previous existence that would qualify for a "karmic racial guilt."

I explained to Eileen what I meant by that term. In this instance, "racial" doesn't mean color or present day genetic racial heritage, but relates to a time when she might have felt responsible for a race, group, or person because of something she had done in a past life. That guilt is usually associated with the thought of "if only I had done something more" or "if only I hadn't done something." It is either guilt of omission or guilt of commission. In either case, if someone else has suffered because of the individual's actions in the past, the boomerang effect in the present time is a sense of deprivation. Usually life has not been easy for people with this kind of subconscious programming. That sense of deprivation may relate to lack of love, less than ease of living, elusive success, or sadness and unhappiness. If the guilt that resides in the subconscious is connected to the former death or lifelong suffering of another person or group, the individual cannot seem to allow himself or herself a life free of some self-punishment.

After I gave Eileen that information, she said, "Uh-oh, here we go. This one is scary. This is the one I've been waiting for. It's not what we think…Oh, my God!" Eileen burst into tears and said, "It's the dream I've had, but I'm not the one getting chased; I'm the one holding the dog! Oh my God!" After a moment of consoling Eileen, I asked if she had been male or female, and how old she was. She replied, "I'm a man, and I'm in my twenties. I'm German; and I'm the one holding the dog!" Eileen was sobbing. Through her tears she said, "It's a German Shepherd, and I'm chasing kids. Oh God, I thought it was me, and it was the other way around." I gave Eileen as much comfort as possible and assured her that she would experience a healing effect if she could just look more closely at the circumstances.

Eileen continued, "There are other soldiers with me. We're in the country—I see a dirt road—and there is a farmhouse. I'm in uniform and I'm holding the dog. There are people running in every direction." I asked her to tell me how many soldiers and children were there. She continued, "There are three or four kids. Someone else finds the children and chases them out of a barn. I am outside with the dogs." She paused for a moment and I could hear a fresh batch of tears as she said, "I'm just a kid myself. I'm among a group of soldiers. We are supposed to find people who are hiding." I asked if they were to go from house to house searching for Jews in hiding. She replied, "There is only one house that we go to. We may have been tipped off that people were hiding here, or we may just stumble across this particular place. This farm is off by itself in the country with no houses nearby.

"We're going from a city through a small town to another destination. I see four of us in a jeep, and I'm sitting in the front passenger seat. The person in charge is a mean person. He's driving the jeep. We're all fairly young. One of the soldiers goes to the door of the house and just walks in, surprising the family inside." I asked her about the farm family. She replied, "There is a mother, and a father, and a teen-age son. Oh, these children are not their kids. The family is not Jewish, but they are hiding these Jewish children in the barn. Two of us are left standing outside, each of us holding a dog by a lead." I asked Eileen what happened after her fellow soldiers found the children. "Everyone is shouting and yelling. There is so much chaos and noise. The dogs are just barking like crazy. There are only two dogs, but they're making a great deal of noise.

"My dog starts barking. I hold onto him with all my strength but he's pulling me, trying to chase the running children. The children are so scared and running as fast as they can, but of course we catch them. The family is in the house. They don't come out." I asked what the soldiers do to the family as punishment for hiding the children. She said, "They're upset but there is nothing they can do. We need them to work the farm for the crops.

"I'm terribly upset over finding these children. The person in charge opens the door to the barn and finds the children in the hay. One of them is a little boy just about three years old. Oh no! I didn't think I'd have to do something like this. I know I'm not a Nazi. I'm just drafted, and I had to go into the army. I really don't want to do this job, but I'm a soldier, and I have to do this. The kids are captured except for one of them who gets away." I asked Eileen how the child managed to elude the dogs and soldiers. She gasped and said, "Oh, I let him get away. There is so much confusion, that as I am supposed to be chasing this boy—he appears to be about twelve years old—I hold onto my dog until he can run off into the woods, and he runs really fast."

There was a moment of silence before I asked Eileen what happened when the other soldiers discovered that one child had escaped. She thought for a moment and said, "Well, I'm back in the car, and there is an explosion." After trying to decide what kind of explosion that might be, Eileen reluctantly saw what really happened. "Oh no. I don't want to believe this. We're back in the jeep, and I'm shot in the back. Oh, I'm shot by my friend. I don't believe my fellow soldier would do this." I asked Eileen if she knew that soldier in this life. She replied, "I think that person is my brother in this life!" Eileen had already described a difficult relationship with her sibling. He stayed away from her as much as possible and refused to share family responsibilities when crisis times forced Eileen to take charge. She said, "That would explain a lot of things." I asked Eileen how this brother would feel about shooting her in the back, on a soul consciousness level. She replied, "Terrible. No wonder he doesn't want to have anything to do with me."

She suddenly took a deep breath and said, "I think the boy who got away is my fiancee!" I said, "He must love you so much." She said, "I think he does." In concluding my session with Eileen I commented how fortunate it is, after difficult childhood experiences, to have attracted someone who will be very loyal and loving.

I spoke to Eileen the following morning to make sure she was feeling comfortable about our session. After telling me she was fine, she said, "It surely has given me a lot to think about. After we hung up, I spoke to my fiance last night. I didn't tell him I was doing a regression session, but as he was saying good-bye he told me that he loved me. That is not something he would ordinarily say over the phone." The spontaneous expression of his love for her may have been stimulated by her memory of the sacrifice for him in Germany.

8

Mengele and His Twins: The Two Lives of Eve

Aᴎᴅ ᴛʜᴇɴ ᴛʜᴇʀᴇ was Dr. Josef Mengele.
Of all the atrocities that were committed by the Nazis, Dr. Mengele's medical experiments at Auschwitz rank as among the most heinous. These experiments he conducted in the name of science had no scientific basis at all. It is difficult to imagine a more insidious lust than Mengele's passion for his work. Mengele's subjects for experimentation were children—more specifically, twins.

An amazing event occurred in my life when I met two young women unacquainted with each other, who had been twins at the time of World War II. These women, who each had past life memories of Nazi Germany, revealed to themselves in their regression sessions their memory of Auschwitz where Josef Mengele conducted his experiments on twins. In fact, there are *four* people who discovered a connection from that lifetime. They have come together again in the present life in a complex and very dramatic web of interactive relationships. One of these four people was a young American man at the time of World War II and was never in Nazi Germany. He is still alive today. He is in a unique position to confirm the information gleaned from the individual regression sessions of the twins because of his present day connection to them. The fourth person was not a victim, but was part of the daily camp activities at Auschwitz and was lovingly remembered by one of the twins.

But before I tell their story, there are many sets of twins who actually survived Mengele's torturous experimentation and have come together again today in a support group that stretches from the United States to Europe to Israel. They have actually revisited Auschwitz in an attempt to purge some of their memories, but they will never forget what they suffered at the hands of this sadistic man. They lost not only their families but their childhood. Their stories have been told in a profoundly moving book, *Children of the Flames: Dr. Josef Mengele and The Untold Story of the Twins of Auschwitz,* by Lucette Matalon Lagnado and Sheila Cohn Dekel. The two young women I met, and regressed to that time, had never read the book about the twins who survived, and yet their past life descriptions match exactly what the survivors have said. I have used quotes from that book to confirm some of the statements made during the individual regression sessions cited in this chapter.

One of Mengele's twin victims, Vera Blau, who survived the camps and her terror of his fearful cruelty, swears that Mengele loved the children. In *Children of the Flames,** Vera said, "They took blood from us every day. But when Mengele made the blood tests, he was much more gentle than the nurses. He liked

---

*Unless otherwise noted, quoted material in this chapter is taken from *Children of the Flames,* published in 1991 by William Morrow and Company, Inc. and republished in 1992 by Penguin Books. Reprinted with permission.

little children and was strict about keeping them well. He would get very angry if a twin was sick." Mengele seemed to dote on one child, in particular. Vera continued, "Mengele loved this child. He had a twin brother, but Mengele played only with him. I believe Josef Mengele loved children—even though he was a murderer and a killer. Yes! I remember him as a gentle man." Eva Kupas, another survivor said, "Once, I wanted to go see my twin brother. So Dr. Mengele took me by the hand and walked with me over to where he was staying. Mengele held my hand the whole way." Yet a former nurse at Auschwitz recalled watching Mengele "sew" twins together in an effort to make them Siamese. Most of his operations were performed without benefit of anesthesia.

Moshe Offer remembers, "One day, my twin brother, Tibi, was taken away for some special experiments. Dr. Mengele had always been more interested in Tibi. I am not sure why, perhaps because he was the older twin. Mengele made several operations on Tibi. One surgery on his spine left my brother paralyzed. He could not walk anymore. Then they took out his sexual organs. After the fourth operation I did not see Tibi anymore. I cannot tell you how I felt. It is impossible to put into words how I felt. They had taken away my father, my mother, my two older brothers—and now, my twin." Moshe never learned what happened to his twin.

In the descriptions of the young peoples' reactions to Mengele, we can see the classic example of a victimized child, who always seeks the attention and runs to the parent who is abusing him. Even after Mengele performed the most horrible experiments, he would give the child a reward of a piece of candy, hold his or her hand, and then tell stories that brought those children to his side, with pride, to be called "Mengele's twins." As these twins were liberated and grew older, they became more consciously aware of the terrible burden of hating him for what he did to them, while owing him their lives. None of these victims of Mengele's torture ever got over their fear of him. They grew into adulthood with their haunting memories and nightmares and mourned for their lost childhood.

In all accounts of the arrival of a train full of captive Jews disembarking at Auschwitz—whether those accounts have been written by survivors of the camps or brought to the surface in regression sessions—the description of the reception committee is the same. They include the sight of a handsome man who stood out among the soldiers because of his grandeur and demeanor. Evidently, Mengele looked forward to the arrival of the trains full of panicked, starving Jews.

Impeccably dressed in a crisp, well tailored uniform and wearing shiny black boots, he always had a pair of spanking white gloves in one hand, never worn, but held quite elegantly and casually. As people poured out of the openings of the boxcars— half starved, half dead, fully terrified—this smiling, genteel man greeted them as if they were coming to his home for a lawn party.

Mengele had a passion for his work, and because he was conducting genetic experiments, he was always excited to see the new batches of twins he could collect from the arriving groups. He also instructed the guards to be on the lookout for any misfits such as dwarfs or hunchbacks. As families tried to stay together and mothers frantically clutched their children to their sides, he quickly looked them over before flicking his finger to signal to the guards which way they should go. One way led to the gas chamber and the other to the barracks. If someone was ill and feeble, it was guaranteed he or she would pass immediately to the gas chambers. If a person was still somewhat robust and healthy, he or she might go to the work areas.

But for all of his natural graciousness and charm, Dr. Josef Mengele was dubbed the "Angel of Death." In his early days as a doctor in the army, he had been in charge of the triage section, picking the wounded who needed medical attention most rapidly and leaving the less critical patients for later treatment. It was as if he were back on the battlefield, but this time making genetic judgment about the prisoners. He seemed to have no remorse for those condemned to die, for he had absolutely no regard for human life. But he could woo, captivate, trick, and seduce almost everyone he met. If it were necessary, he could force mothers to let go of their children's hands, and head them off to the gas chambers, leaving the children behind before they knew what was happening. He would then charm the children and distract them until they were led to the children's quarters. It was a bit later that the full impact hit these children, when they would cry and cry, and beg for their mothers.

Most mothers heard rumors that it was fortunate if they had twins, for twins were under the special protection of Dr. Mengele. They were allowed to keep their hair and their clothes. They were given a somewhat better diet, including some potatoes, occasionally. But they were still always hungry. The real treat was the candy that Dr. Mengele lovingly fed to his "children" at certain times. Some of these twins were in their twenties; some were tiny toddlers.

There is no way of knowing how many twins died after Mengele was through with them. Sometimes they died as a result of the experimentation. Sometimes their organs were removed while they were still alive, and then they were mercifully thrown into the fire. Sometimes they were simply murdered in cold blood.

But some of the twins did stay alive to tell the terrible tale. And some have been reborn to tell the tale.

Unfortunately there was little delicacy about revealing to the children what had happened to their mothers, fathers, or siblings. The fires blazed away day and night right in front of the twins' barracks. When a new group of children first arrived and would ask for their mothers, other children simply told them, "Your mother is in the fire!"

Zvi Spiegel was an older boy with a twin sister. He was given the job of looking after the boys in the segregated twins barracks. They called him the "Twins' Father." He watched every new batch of children come to the realization that they would never go home or see their parents again. He did his best to protect the young boys (the girls were left on their own, with no one to turn to); but if he had not done what he was told by Mengele, he would have been shot right away, and there would have been no one to try to ease the pain of the little ones. But Zvi Spiegel could not be everywhere. There were many very young children who were simply left on their own to cry for their mothers or for food.

"The children would stand for hours just watching the flames," he said when interviewed by Lagnado and Dekel for *Children of the Flames*. The crematoriums were located only 100 meters away from the twins' barracks. There was just a small fence in-between. The twins could see the transports—the trains pulling into Birkenau. They missed nothing that was going on at Auschwitz.

"All day, the twins observed Mengele motioning people to go to the right and to the left. They watched the masses of people going into the crematoriums."

Peter Somogyi said, "It took nearly four days to get to Auschwitz (from a town near Budapest, Hungary). Since this was the summer, it was extremely hot inside our car. We were given no food, no water. I remember a little boy crying incessantly for water. We arrived at Auschwitz on July 9, 1944. It was early evening, and when we stepped out of the cattle cars, we could see the chimneys with very, very high flames leaping out from them.

"'What is this?' my brother and I asked our mother. 'Oh, it's probably just a big factory,' she told us. Uniformed guards walked up and down the selection line asking for twins. They asked for them both in German and Hungarian. But it wasn't until the third time the guards asked that my mother admitted we were twins. The first two times she kept silent. She didn't know what it meant, whether it was good or bad. And because my brother and I didn't look alike at all, it was easy for her to pretend we were not twins.

"My brother and I were quickly plucked out of the line. It was the last time I ever saw my mother or my sister.

"We were placed in an ambulance and whisked off to the twins' barracks. There, we were greeted by Zvi Spiegel, who told us he was the 'Twins' Father,' in charge of all the boy twins.

"We didn't know what had happened to our mother, and so we asked him when we could see her. He hedged. He didn't want to tell us yet what had happened, what was probably happening that very moment—that she had gone up in the flames."

Mentors of Hitler and Mengele

Just as Hitler was influenced in his occult search by Alfred Rosenberg, whose book, *Myth of the Twentieth Century*, became a fundamental part of Nazi thinking, Mengele had his mentor as well. Professor Otmar von Verschuer was the most acclaimed racial scientist of his day. His work at the University of

Frankfurt fit in with Nazi thinking about eugenics and helped give scientific credibility to the Nuremberg Laws, one of which was to forbid sexual relationship and marriage between Jews and "people of German blood." Verschuer's Institute for Heredity, Biology, and Racial Purity in Frankfurt, Germany, was largely financed by the Nazi Party.

Mengele became fired up with the thought of creating a superior race. His passion for Social Darwinism led to a Ph.D. in anthropology after obtaining his medical degree.

With excellent credentials and having graduated summa cum laude, he was able to obtain a position as an assistant to Verschuer at the Institute. It was here that Mengele perfected his "ability" to evaluate and determine who was and who was not a Jew. If he decided that an individual possessed a drop of Jewish blood, even from former centuries, the person was inevitably marked for deportation to the death camps.

Verschuer helped Mengele obtain a position as an SS doctor at Auschwitz. He also helped him win grants to undertake two research projects at the camp, beginning in April 1943. At Auschwitz, there was no one to stand in Mengele's way vis-à-vis *in vivo* experiments, that is on live bodies; and the human laboratory there was the ultimate realization of a dream of both Mengele's and Verschuer's. Verschuer was closely involved with his protege's work, and Mengele sent laboratory samples to Verschuer from his experiments. It is ironic that Verschuer gained even greater recognition and glory after the war, winning many prizes. He denied any responsibility for death camp practices, pretending horror at what Mengele had been doing, even though they had corresponded the whole time Mengele was experimenting on twins. Mengele evidently did not begrudge the honors heaped on his hero's head, even though he, himself, was forced into hiding.

In *Children of the Flames,* the authors say, "The line between science and quackery was not a very fine one at Auschwitz. Mengele's experiments, although ostensibly performed in the name of scientific truth, followed few scientific principles. Mengele would test one twin and not the other. At times, siblings were injected simultaneously as they stood naked side by side. Despite the preferential treatment, the show of kindness, the children endured unspeakable pain and humiliation....

"The strict veil of secrecy imposed over the experiments enabled Mengele to work more effectively. Twins who were subjected to the most grotesque procedures took his secrets to their graves. And those as yet unhurt had only secondhand stories about what was being done. No one at Auschwitz—not the prisoners, not the SS guards, not even other doctors—knew precisely what Mengele was doing with his twins, either while they were alive or after they had died. Even the children who themselves were the subjects of his tests did not know what the objectives of the experiments were. Rumors were rampant, especially when children were taken out in Red Cross trucks, never to be seen again."

There was a calculated effort by Mengele to limit information, presumably to keep his "guinea pigs" from panicking. One can only guess how the twins would have reacted had they known of the existence of Mengele's unbelievable pathology laboratory, where bodies of live children were daily brought over to his assistants to have still more "tests" performed.

Mengele especially seemed to dote on the youngest twins, the toddlers who could hardly walk and talk, and who were completely dependent on him. There was a little boy, about three or four years old, who bore a striking resemblance to Mengele himself. He was a dark child, with large brown eyes, a round face, and a gentle disposition. Mengele came to the barracks often to visit this one child, scooping him up in his arms, kissing him, and showering him with toys and chocolates. When asked his name, the boy would reply, "My name is Mengele." The Auschwitz doctor himself had taught the child to say this, as a father would teach his son.

"The youngest children were not aware of the darker side of the man they affectionately called 'Uncle Mengele.' They did not know about the surgeries of unspeakable horror. It is not that Mengele confined the more gruesome and painful studies to the older children, but that they were too young to comprehend the sinister experiments. They saw only a cheerful, avuncular doctor who rewarded them with candy if they behaved. But the older twins and the adults, such as the twins' mothers and the Jewish doctors who saw Mengele at work, recognized his kindness as a deception—yet another of his perverse experiments, whose aim was to test their mental endurance. The fact that Mengele could behave so nicely even as he inflicted pain, torture, and death made him the most feared man at Auschwitz.

"Mengele would plunder a twin's body, sometimes removing organs and limbs. He injected the children with lethal germs, including typhus and tuberculosis, to see how quickly they succumbed to the diseases. Many became infected and died. He also attempted to change the sex of some twins. Female twins were sterilized; male twins were castrated. What was the point of these ghoulish experiments? No one, neither the child-victims nor the adult witnesses, ever really knew. Mengele constantly probed the children, trying to wrest from them secrets they did not possess.

"Once in a while, Mengele seemed to be drawn physically to one of the older, female Jewish inmates, in spite of the efforts of their Nazi captors to strip them of their beauty. Shortly after arriving at Auschwitz, women were herded into Hitler's version of a 'beauty parlor,' where their heads were shaved. The women were then given either a regulation striped uniform or absurd, ill-fitting rags to wear. Their shoes were usually too large or too small, often consisting of a 'pair' of one flat slipper and one high heel. The effect was to make the women look ridiculous and thoroughly unalluring to everyone—including their Aryan guards.

"Occasionally, the Nazi system failed, and a woman radiated beauty, her shapeless garments and shorn hair notwithstanding. Mengele encountered such a woman in Ibi Hillman. Tall, blond, and statuesque, fifteen-year-old Ibi had been the pride of her small village in Transylvania. When Ibi removed her uniform in the course of an 'inspection,' Mengele found himself staring at her, transfixed. The other female inmates, and even his own assistants, watched him, aware of his attraction to the young woman. Any other SS officer would have simply made her his mistress. But Mengele evidently would not concede feeling an attraction toward a Jew. In a loud voice, he dispatched Ibi to the infamous Block Ten, where the Nazis were performing sinister gynecological experiments. Few women survived Block Ten.

"A few weeks later, Ibi was spotted by some inmates wandering by herself, in a daze. They hardly recognized her. The beautiful young girl looked like a shriveled old woman. Her slender limbs were now swollen and disfigured, while her stomach was bloated from the numerous surgeries that had been performed on her. Sickly and grotesque, Ibi Hillman no longer held any possible attraction—for Dr. Mengele or any other man."

Among all these people—before Ibi Hillman, however—was one special girl.

The Lives of Eve

Eve came for a regression session after having her astrological chart interpreted by me on the telephone. The chart had actually been a gift to her from a man we will call Brett, who was an old friend of hers and a client of mine. He had told me nothing about her, except that he wanted to give her a chart as a gift, and if she wanted to do a regression session he would include this as well. Eve had interned with Brett's company for work experience while she was in college. She had now graduated from law school and was working for a law firm. He was considering asking her to work for him again, this time in a very prestigious position with his organization.

Eve decided she did want a regression session after hearing her chart, but since I reside some distance from where she lives, she wanted to wait until I was in her city to work with other clients in her area so that we could do this in person. The next time I traveled to her location she booked a time for an appointment. When she arrived I couldn't help but notice her exceptionally pretty face, good figure, a lovely smile and bright eyes. Her intelligence and personality made her come alive with sparkling vivacity and energy.

After we had said our hellos, she laughed and said, "I think I was Brett's first wife!" I dismissed this statement immediately, as I happened to know that Brett's former wife was still alive. I thought to myself, "The things that emerge from a regression session are rarely what people expect," so I didn't comment one way or another about her statement. I actually forgot that she had said that until much later.

She went through her childhood, which had not been traumatic to any extreme degree. Some things emerged that would help clear her conscience, as she was not quite the sweet little southern girl her family thought her to be. She was extremely intelligent, diligently went to church every Sunday with her parents, and was polite and nice. But she had more boyfriends than girlfriends, and she understood that some jealousy from girls was due to her popularity. She was lucky. She had a loving mother and father, horses of her own to ride, and a nice lifestyle.

Eve had entered a few beauty contests and won, hands down. When she was voted college queen, however, the friction this created made her decide that she was through with beauty contests. It wasn't worth the isolation she felt from other girls, who labeled her as stuck-up and unfriendly. No one seemed to see her as she really was. It hurt, but she shrugged it off and decided to focus on intellectual achievements. That was actually a very major decision in her life, for she had two distinct paths in front of her. Although she knew she had made a conscious choice not to model or study acting, thereby denying a certain part of herself that enjoyed the lure of the glamour world, the regression session showed how important that choice had been for her, how strong that decision was, and how it had changed her life. This lawyer was obviously not just another girl with a pretty face.

Eve had had a steady boyfriend in school, but when she met Ed she knew she had met her mate. They fell in love, had a decent engagement time, and a perfectly beautiful marriage ceremony. She said over and over again, "He is everything to me. He is a brother, lover, husband, and best friend. The big problem is that we hardly need anyone else. We don't go out seeking new friends. We're very content just to be together."

With his dark good looks, Ed was a complement to Eve in every way. He was the solid citizen, allowing her to be a free soul. Their love for each other was so secure that he was never jealous if she went to important social functions with Brett, her boss. Since she was now part of Brett's organization, those social functions were partly for work, but there was also an element of glamour involved that was a lot of fun for her. Ed didn't begrudge her those experiences. In fact, Ed's agreeable nature surprised people. She seemed to have a lot of freedom for a woman in a happy marriage. Once again, other people misunderstood. But Ed knew she needed a certain amount of independence, and it was easy for him to go along with it. Ed's job took him away from home on short trips, but neither one of them, both young and exceptionally good-looking, ever worried about infidelity.

Eve had one problem that didn't fully emerge in the regression session. She had recurring nightmares about a menacing Hitler-like figure from early childhood. She was afraid she must have done something terrible in a past life. It was as though Satan were haunting her in her dreams. But she dismissed this by saying that Ed would simply hold her when it happened and make it go away.

Eve's past life memory explained her marriage and comfortable relationship to Ed in the present. She saw that in a past life in Egypt they had been married and were part of a religious group that had some unusual conditions attached to the worship. No one grew old in that society. When a person reached a certain age, it was fully expected that he or she would simply end life by a painless method of suicide, knowing that a better existence awaited on the other side. Loved ones on earth were never burdened with care for elderly people, and they could continue their work unencumbered.

When it came time for Eve to go, she wasn't sure she wanted to honor the tradition. She balked a bit, not feeling ready to depart the earth plane, but Ed, her husband in that life also, was fully oriented toward the rules, and felt she should respect the custom and do what was expected of her. There didn't seem to be any real reason to die, from Eve's point of view, but she agreed and followed the ritual of ending her life.

After she was gone, Ed was devastated. He was alone, missed her dreadfully and, in retrospect, couldn't see why her death had been necessary at all. He changed his mind about the group doctrine and was a lost soul for the rest of his life. He not only lost Eve, but the security of his religious beliefs.

Then, in the same session, Eve went to another lifetime. This time she saw herself as a very young, single woman living in an area that resembled Greece. She lived in a small city with her mother and father. Eve saw an exciting trip ahead that seemed to be connected to her father's business. It was similar to a conference of today, and it was to be held in a large city. It would be a change of pace, at least, and promised to bring some new adventures into her life. During a large gathering, which may have been political in nature, she met a man who dazzled her. He seemed to be equally enchanted by Eve, and they made plans to see each other soon after that chance meeting. Their love blossomed rapidly, and since the conference would only last a short time, their future plans had to be made quickly. The only hitch was that this man was already married.

He swore his undying love, and to prove he meant to be with her for the rest of his life, he asked her to go to a distant city to wait for him. Eve couldn't go back home now for she was no longer a virgin and would disgrace her family if she announced she was involved with this man. Evidently he had a degree of prominence, and it was well known that he was married and already had a family. Eve was so completely smitten with him that she was willing to do anything just to be with him.

He sent a servant to accompany her to another country and located a place for her to live. She was well provided for financially and had the protection of this servant. Eve thought the city might be Rome. It seemed clear that she had plenty of time on her hands to enjoy the culture, create a home environment, and occupy herself pleasantly while awaiting the arrival of her love. But the man never returned to be with her. Eve never doubted his love or that he was trying to return to her. But she had no word from him in all the remaining years of her life. She felt in her heart that he was detained somewhere and was unable even to get a message to her. She passed the time until her death by just getting through each day, one after another.

When I asked Eve to identify the man, her servant and her family she quickly said, "Oh the man is Brett! And I think the faithful servant is Ed. He became a friend to me, because we only had each other, but he stayed by me and took care of me."

After talking a bit more about her present day relationship with Brett, and the fact that she had worked for him when she was in college, she was still unsure as to why he hadn't returned to her in the days of Greece and Italy. She knew that she had faithfully awaited his return until she died.

(In the meantime Geoffrey, a friend of Brett's, also did a regression session with me. He identified himself and Brett as officers in Alexander's army. Alexander was insatiable in his desire to conquer, loot, and gather treasures. Geoffrey realized that a group of soldiers tried to convince Alexander to cease his campaigns. Everyone was tired, and they hadn't been home to see their families in many years. And it was becoming increasingly difficult to transport all of the treasures Alexander had appropriated for himself. Alexander ordered the group of dissenting soldiers shot. Both Geoffrey and Brett died along with the rest of that group. If that were the case, it would explain why Brett was never able to return to Eve and why he couldn't even get a message to her.)

When Eve finished her session, she was amazed at the information that had come from her subconscious. She felt lighter and knew that she had explained a lot about her life through her new awareness. In particular, her relationships with Ed and Brett were completely clear. Regarding her relationship to Ed, she said, "No wonder. It feels like we've always been married, lifetime after lifetime. Even in that life in Rome, he was there to take care of me. It also explains why Ed lets me do whatever I feel is right for me at the moment!" Her relationship with Brett was a bit more complicated, as she has a deep attraction and love for Brett, in spite of her contentment and happy marriage.

Eve and I might never had gone further with the investigation into her past lives if it hadn't been for two factors. Eve's terrible Hitler/Satan dreams got worse and, shortly thereafter, it was decided that she was to accompany me on a five-day conference in another city. I suggested that we do another session while we were at that conference; but a friend who had her best interests at heart had advised her against it, fearing that it might make things worse instead of better. I suggested that we take some time and at least analyze her dream. She agreed.

One evening, after a full day in the conference, we set the stage for the dream analysis. In a dream analysis, only, I use two chairs so that the person can fully appreciate his inner conflicts as manifested in the dream, and as he moves between the two chairs, he learns how to dialogue with himself. Soon the meaning of the dream becomes clear.

Sometimes it is difficult to keep a person going in such an exercise, especially if he or she considers himself or herself to be psychologically savvy. It is like getting a piano student to practice scales for half an hour until his fingers are warmed up for the big recital. The seemingly unimportant details that come forth before the real issue breaks loose can seem boring and even ridiculous. But keeping the left brain busy with this exercise allows the right brain to come up with the real information and the "good stuff." I use this technique of a dialoging with one's subconscious in both dream analysis and regression sessions.

Both Eve and Brett had experienced great frustration in their individual regression sessions with me as I was urging them in the phase of practicing their scales. Just as each one of them was about to get up and tell me they were fed up and finished, their memory broke through in vivid color and detail. For Brett, this had been especially astounding, as suddenly his sense of smell from a past life was equally as strong as his unexpected visual sense. Eve was just getting to that moment of annoyance in her dream analysis when, with her eyes wide open and staring straight at me, something became very vivid indeed. I shall never forget the look on her face. Her eyes became wide, frightened, and tearful. She said, "I think I was in Nazi Germany. I see myself with this very handsome man, and I think he betrayed me."

As Eve was no longer moving between chairs, I began to ask her the kinds of questions I ask in a regression session, for I had already suspected that the dream analysis would probably lead to a full regression to a past life. In a regression session I ask the person to close her eyes, so the present environment will not be distracting. But in a dream analysis the eyes are wide open. Eve was obviously not seeing anything in the room we were in, nor in the present time, even though she was looking right at me. (At this point I didn't have to ask any questions, either.) I was like a person with dark glasses at a movie theater, with Eve giving me a frame by frame description of the movie on the screen.

Eve described herself as a young girl, perhaps fourteen or fifteen years old with the budding quality of great, exceptional beauty in its virginal state. She said, "I look somewhat like I look now, with dark hair, but I'm really a knockout. I have a sophistication that is far beyond my years, and I think I'm older than I really am....I think I really do know it all, and my instincts for flirtation and sexual attraction are all there, even though I haven't had a chance to practice them."

Eve described a garden where people were gathered as if it were a party. But it seemed to have a more serious overtone than just a social situation. She was standing by herself near a hedge, rather bored with the whole thing. As she looked around, she saw a devastatingly handsome man at the bar, getting himself a drink. Within seconds she was walking to the bar to get herself a soft drink as well. They made eye contact, and she had a chance to practice the flirtation that was instinctive. Eve thought that they probably didn't speak to each other just then, but the die was cast. He knew what she was doing, and as they wandered throughout the party, the eye contact continued until they found themselves at the bar again. This time, with very few words, they made arrangements to meet at another time, away from the party. They couldn't speak many words to each other, for if Eve's parents or friends had glanced at them, they would have known in a second what was going on. There seemed to be something else that occupied her parents' attention, and Eve knew it probably had to do with the beginning of the war.

I resisted asking Eve for more details because the look in her eyes told me that something truly frightening was ready to emerge. She needed no help from me. She said, "I become the mistress of this man. I know he is a high-ranking Nazi officer.

I see myself at a really elegant party where the men are all very important officers in uniform and the women are really dressed up. I'm wearing a red satin dress." I volunteered, "And ankle strap shoes." She said, "Exactly." I could see what she was wearing and what she looked like as if it were a photograph.

"I am quite drunk, and I may even take some drugs, occasionally. It feels like it is difficult to keep up the pretense of the situation and this facade. I'm really just a young girl pretending to be a grown-up and this man is an SS officer, high up in the Nazi hierarchy. He's older and very sophisticated. These other women are the girlfriends of the other officers, not the wives. There are lots of these parties, and I just drink more and more champagne to get through them.

"Oh my God—I'm Jewish! I feel like I'm betraying my whole family by what I'm doing. But then I rationalize that I'm keeping them safe by being with him. He loves me so much, he'd never let anything happen to them. A part of me is saying, 'I'm not going down with the sinking ship.' But I mainly tell myself I'm helping my family.

"I think I have a brother and a sister. I'm much closer to my brother. That sister is almost like an inconvenience to me. She might as well be a little brother I don't pay any attention to. My whole family would consider that what I'm doing is so wrong and a real betrayal of them. I feel so guilty."

Eve went on, as if it had happened yesterday. "One day I go home to see my family and when I get to the apartment, *they're not there!* Everything is gone, the apartment is empty, cleaned out. I'm devastated, shaken to the core. I race back to him to confront him, and he becomes very angry. He beats me up and says, 'You little Jewish bitch. Who do you think you are? Do you really think you mean anything more to me than a pet dog on a chain?'

"At that moment, my life is over. I don't think I die, but I might as well have died. I'm not there. I've betrayed my family, fooled myself into thinking I could save everyone, and he didn't even love me. I think he gives me twenty-four hours to leave Germany. I don't think I go to a concentration camp. I think I get out somehow. I think my brother comes with me."

I asked Eve where they went. She thought a long time and said, "I really don't know. I don't know much of anything after that. We may go to the Orient, but I'm not sure. Everything that happens afterward is completely blank. I just know that somehow my brother is with me. I may be on drugs. I don't know what happens to my father and mother or that sister—she's always been a thorn in my side, but now I feel so guilty about everything. What a fool I've been. I certainly understand why I chose not to be a model or an actress in this life. I consciously chose to develop my mind and become involved in politics!"

Eve and I spent a lot of time on the healing of that experience. Among other healing techniques, I suggested that she figuratively and mentally give comfort to that girl by putting her arms around her. That young girl was really scared, in over her head, and so ashamed. She needed to forgive herself for making a wrong choice in her young life. Eve knew that she'd have to forgive herself, as if she were a mother who never blames her child but only wants to protect. She said, "At least I know that I didn't do anything really evil. I was so afraid from my dreams that I had done something much worse."

To digress for a moment, when Brett knew that I was attending this particular conference, he suggested that Eve come with me. He felt that the conference would give her some new information, and it might be important for a special job he had in mind for her. She happened to tell him she hoped I would analyze her dream/nightmare while we were there. He thought it would be a good idea. Then Brett called me to volunteer something I couldn't have known about. As Eve was describing her life in Nazi Germany, I was even more flabbergasted because of what Brett had divulged. Brett was married, but was currently separated, and he had been married twice previously. I was unaware of that fact—I had known about only one previous wife—for in my work with Brett it was information we wouldn't have discussed.

When Brett was a young man in his twenties, he had met a stunningly gorgeous girl at the Copacabana, a popular nightclub in New York that was one of *the* places to go in the fifties. After a short engagement, he had a brief marriage to her. Tragically, she was a drug addict. Brett had sent her to a drug rehabilitation center and knew that she would be safe and protected while he was away from New York on a business trip. But while Brett was away, the girl had discovered that she was pregnant, had run away from the center, and had committed suicide. Her life was too far over the edge of horror to think of bearing a child.

Before this gorgeous creature had come to New York, she had been in a concentration camp, and although she was Jewish, she had been the girlfriend of a very high-ranking Nazi officer! She had been a victim of Mengele's horrible experiments. The sister had been thrown in a fire, and their mother had jumped in after her. Brett's wife and her brother had been released from the camp at the end of the war, and they were living together in New York when Brett met her. Brett told me a bit more about the situation, but Brett was quite sure that Eve was Bobbi, whom he had married and lost.

As Eve was going through her wide-awake regression back to Nazi Germany, I was holding my breath from shock. I remembered her statement before her first regression session with me, "I think I was Brett's first wife!" During the wide-awake session I watched her face, her eyes, the emotion, her tears, and knew this information was all new to her. Brett had not set her up to tell this story.

I was sure Eve would hear very little that was being said at the conference the next day.

Since Brett was very anxious to know if Eve had confirmed the information about his first wife, I told him what I could without betraying Eve's confidence and trust in me, and I did not tell Eve what Brett had revealed to me. In a situation where two people recall the same scene, I always ask the individuals involved to talk about it between themselves. This way I'm not imposing my thoughts and feelings but asking what they think, and how they see a situation. But I had to swallow hard when I was talking to Brett, because I still felt overwhelmed from the information Eve revealed. I said to Brett, "There are a lot of similarities, but there's enough difference to cast some doubt. You'll have to ask her for the details." Brett and Eve subsequently discussed this session together, but Brett was still reluctant to tell Eve everything he knew about Bobbi, his first wife. He knew that Eve might do more sessions with me, and he didn't want to prejudice her in any way. Brett had also told me that the gorgeous girl he married had just a drop of Jewish blood dating back to the fifth century. The Jewish blood came through Bobbi's mother's side of the family, making Eve and her siblings technically Jewish. The Nazis were meticulous in tracing racial heritage, even back to earlier centuries. I volunteered one more thing. I said, "Eve thinks she and her brother went to the Orient, not New York." Brett said quietly, "Bobbi and her brother *did* go to the Orient first, and then came to New York."

Eve and Mengele

Eve and I stayed in touch after our sessions together and our time at the conference. Neither she nor Brett told me what, if anything, had happened between them after Eve's memory of Nazi Germany. Some time later, however, Eve called to tell me that a lot of the missing details had been popping into her mind at the oddest moments, and she'd like to share them with me. This time she knew the name of the handsome SS officer.

It was Josef Mengele!

We set a time for another telephone session. At that time, Eve volunteered some of the things that had popped into her mind, but I also asked her a lot questions to help fill in as many pieces of the puzzle as possible. Our sessions together, and her close working relationship with Brett, had stirred up tremendous feelings within all of us. Eve and I had shared something so strongly emotional that my association with her was now beyond that of consultant/client. I cared a lot about what had happened to Bobbi/Eve.

One of my strongest impressions of Bobbi, after we had talked, was that she must have been so heavily addicted by the time she met Brett, and so terribly traumatized, she would hardly have known what was happening in their relationship, for she had told me earlier, "I'm just not there." Eve said, "I think you're right." In our telephone session, Eve alternated between "I" and "She."

"I'm not that old. I have the feeling that I think I'm older than I really am. I may be very young, like fourteen, fifteen playing older. I have dark hair and a lot of it. She has really pretty wavy hair, long, darker than mine, but not really black."

Mengele's fascination with hair had led him to allow the twins to wear it long.

"She's very trim. She's so thin that she has enough breasts that they stand out. She has enough to play grown-up with. She's really a knockout. I'm wearing a red dress at that party. Satin and really clingy, almost like a wraparound dress. The dress is long, like calf-length, and it has a slit in it and a deep V neckline. I do get a feeling of a bracelet, and she probably smokes. This is a little girl trying to play grown-up, and I must say she's very good at passing herself off as older. No one really knows how old she is; they see her as no age, but as a timeless woman who has some polish and sophistication. I don't think people look at her and think of age first. I see her as trying desperately to hold on to this illusion of being sophisticated and trying not to overdo it. It's her own illusion that is shattered if she overdoes it."

I asked, "Where does she get this sophistication?"

Eve responded, "She's just born with it. She comes from a long line of past lives that made her this way. As a little girl she dreamed of things like movie stars and glamour. She has a cultured background; she knows music, she knows some art, and she's very intelligent."

Eve began telling me about her family life. I asked, "What does your father do as a profession?" Eve thought and then said, "I'm not sure I even understand what he does. He's somebody in government or a political type. I get the sense that he's a little above it all. He's not someone who serves at the direction of another person. He is a little like a college professor, in that sense. It almost doesn't matter whose political ideas are prevailing at the time. His intellect gives him the ability to see both sides, and he's such a gentleman and so well thought of— everyone knows him to be so honest—that even if he holds views that are different from the people he's supposed to serve they know they can trust him. He keeps being honored because of those traits. My mother has almost black hair. She looks almost Portuguese or Italian. She wears her hair short. She's pretty and she's the perfect match to her husband. The problem is I think she lacks depth. I'm not sure how smart she really is."

I asked if they entertained a great deal. Eve said, "It's more like they're always invited other places. They don't seem to do much entertaining themselves. We live modestly."

Eve described how she first met the man who she is sure was Josef Mengele.

"I meet this man at a party where children are invited, which is not usual. It's outside. Someone has a beautiful house with landscaped lawn. I'm wearing something white, and the dress is a little casual. It seems to be a Sunday afternoon. I don't fit in. The kids are such kids, and I'm not accepted by the adults, so I'm almost sulking, standing by a hedge watching a game of croquet.

"I notice this man first. Then he notices me noticing him. He's about thirty and very handsome. He's tall and very commanding with dark hair. He has on a uniform. He's an officer and he's movie-star handsome.

Beppo Mengele was extremely handsome, with a slight enigmatic smile. Though he acted like an angel, he looked more like a young Gypsy. His appearance was later described as similar to that of French actor Charles Boyer.

"I don't even know who he is. I don't go to these parties. But I know how to flirt, and I know how to make eye contact. I make certain that he sees, and I just smile."

I ask, "Don't you feel dangerous doing this?"

"Absolutely! I've never done this before. I make myself be somewhere he'll be—I follow him around. I'm just obsessed with him. Just by a look, I know he's noticed me, and he's pleased. It's dangerous for him too. He's not married, but I don't even think to ask. I have some kid's drink in my hand, and he has a drink. I manage to go up as he's ordering his drink, and we step away for a moment. He cuts straight to the chase. I don't know exactly what he says, but he asks me to arrange to meet him some place...like dinner. He's smart. He knows he can't stand around there and talk to me, and he knows that my standing there at the bar was contrived and that I arranged to meet with him. I go home and daydream about him constantly."

I ask, "How in the world are you going to sneak out of the house to meet him?

Eve responds, "I arrange it with a friend. He gives me an address, and I meet him about two days later. It's summer time, so I tell my mother I'm spending the night with a friend. I think my mother isn't in the house when I get dressed, but I get out of there before she sees me. I even think I manage to wear something of my mother's... I don't seem terribly concerned, but I do put a coat over what I'm wearing in case someone should see me.

"I spend all of my allowance on a cab to get there...It's a small restaurant, dark and cozy, and he almost has his own little private room where they cater to him. I'm terribly nervous. As I get a bit older, I kind of laugh at how little I knew. I just smile and nod and let him talk. He doesn't do anything that night. He's a gentleman and takes me home. It works out very well because my parents aren't there. It worked out so well that night it was like fate contrived it. They weren't suspicious. I get the feeling it is never that easy again. It doesn't take long before everyone is on notice. "

I say, "You have siblings, don't you?"

"I have a brother, and the other sibling is someone I don't feel close to. I'm close to my brother, and I feel like my mother is close to this other sibling. My father is the figurehead. That's how it breaks down in the house.

"It seems like it is not very long before everything falls apart. I am totally infatuated with him and can't do anything or think of anything else."

I can't resist asking, "Who catches you?"

"It's my brother who catches me. He's older than I am, and he's jealous and feels protective, especially since our father is not there very much...he really is a professorial type. My brother has all these male hormones raging and thinks he is the peacock. I find it really annoying that I can't go and come as I want.

"It is at night, coming back, and it is only the second or third time, but he's up, and my Mom and sister are asleep. It's like he's waiting for me, because he knows something is up. I don't know how he knows, and it really aggravates me. I can't figure out how I alerted him. I never really know why he knows or is suspicious, but he is very threatening. He is going to tell Mom and Dad. I guess I decide to act like a teen-ager and say, 'I'm doing this and you can't stop me.' I just throw tantrums. It provokes my brother more than either my mother or my father.

"It's a Sunday again...a Sunday afternoon. Sundays are the only days we (the family) spend together. We probably go to church and have our family meal together, but then I'm going to go out. I guess I become very proficient at dressing like a grown-up and putting a sweater over a blouse that's a little too revealing. I whisk past them after I've changed after lunch. They don't really notice. But my brother notices. He's in my room taunting me...He's trying to blackmail me, so I tell my parents. My father is smoking a pipe, and my mother is cleaning up after dinner, and my sister, the perfect little sister, is helping her and—I shouldn't say it that way, but it's that she has no interest in growing up. She's in her little cocoon, and I find it maddening. I feel so guilty, feeling what I feel.

"It's only been a few times, but I'm not going to let my brother stop me, and with my parents...I come storming out of my room and tell them I'm going off for the afternoon with this man and I leave. No one yet knows who it is. I don't give anyone a chance to know."

I interject, "Where has he taken you?"

"Like the ballet or something cultural. It's not that public in a dark theater, and I think he has his own box. We haven't done a lot yet. I think we meet this Sunday in a park. I see a park with a lake, and ducks, and geese, or swans. I think we end up going somewhere then. It feels so queasy, but I think we go to a hotel room. The hotel is very nice; I see red velvet. It's small and cozy, not really public and elegant.

"I'm a little nervous, and I think it's almost at my instigation. I even think he's a little surprised. I think I'm the aggressor and that may be why it's a hotel room...he's unprepared. I don't think he has all that liberty where he lives. He may live in an officer's quarters, but he's not free to come and go and bring whoever he wants. He's privileged in a certain way, and where he lives is very nice, but he can't take me there.

(Josef Mengele may have a wife at this point. He married Irene Mengele in 1939, but throughout their whole married life, they were rarely together.)

"Obviously I'm a virgin—I refuse to be miserable, but it was really nothing. I'm not sure I'm all that attracted to him at this point, and I'm not sure what's propelling me. I sleep with him, and he's very handsome, but I'm not doing it for those reasons. It may be because he's glamorous.

Much as they loathed to admit it, several of his female victims...were not immune to Mengele's sexual magnetism... Mengele seemed almost a romantic figure.

"I do go home that night because he can't stay out. I feel guilty as sin after I get home. I'm really surprised that my family hasn't waited up for me. I don't get in really late, and I do get away with it at this point. My mother seems incapable of really confronting me. She doesn't know what to do with teenage rebellion, and I think my Dad has some idea about what's going on but he uses his absence to avoid it.

"It seems like a lot happens in a short amount of time. I do this thing with him and then I don't hear from him. It's not like he's falling all over himself with puppy love for me, and then I find out that I don't hear from him for a reason. It's work-related. Also my Dad gets much busier, and I think we move soon.

"Now I'm totally distraught. I've slept with this man, and I don't even hear from him. I'm totally consumed by this. We've evidently moved somewhere for the summer, as if we went north, and now we're going back. My father's work seems to force us to live somewhere else for part of the year, and it's not a place I'm attached to. The apartment is in a city, somewhere that is hustling and bustling and cosmopolitan. I'm very upset that we have to leave, because where we live is isolated and dull. I feel like a caged bird...but I have to go home with my family. Our home is well appointed and it's nice, but I don't feel alive there.

"I think I contact him before I leave, or I think he knows I have to leave, and I think he even calls me at home. He tells me not to worry, that it won't be for very long. I don't know how he knows that. He says not to worry, that I'll see him soon!

"The whole trip to the city is not something we do every summer—this is different. I don't quite realize what this trip is about. I don't think this man tells me a lot. He tells me things that are like riddles—such as I won't be away very long—he tells me enough that makes me reflect. He indicates that he knows my father and knows why we were in the city all summer long. He certainly tells me enough to make me understand that there are serious things going on.

"As the young, naive girl that I am, when he tells me we will be back together, I take that as if he's trying to console me and trying to make me happy. He wasn't saying it for my benefit, but almost like a cat and mouse game. It's as if there was too much pleasure in it for him.

"We take the train back—I see myself in a dark traveling outfit. We're home for two or three months, and it's before Christmas when something happens…you know I think I suddenly realize we're at war! I'm suddenly angry at myself that I could have just completely ignored the facts or could have been so thoughtless or naive not to think about what it means to be at war—My father is involved, somehow, and we suddenly…I think we lose our father.

"I don't think he's dead, but the news I get makes me so angry at myself, that I haven't seen this coming. I'm sure my anger is a defense mechanism against the pain of what happens to him. I think we're lied to about where he is, because he doesn't come to tell us, himself, what is going on. Someone else comes…some little military person shows up at the door and says my father's been called away to serve his country, like he's been drafted. I think we're in Italy, but we're told he's been called into German service. We all know pretty quickly that something is wrong. He would have let us know.

"My Mom aggravates me so. She can't be the person she pretends to be. She's got to be smarter than that. She won't discuss it with us and tries to make it seem as though it's nothing! Even my dumb sister knows something is going on. But my Mom won't try to find out anything. She knows just enough not to

ask questions. I still don't understand that she can't try to find
out where my father is, and that makes me so mad.

"Now I think it's the holidays, and I'm not living at home. I
have an apartment and a female roommate. I think I finally put
things together, and I understand the political situation. I'm eons
away from where I was with my family. I probably must have just
left. I just can't sit there doing nothing, and I just go. I don't think
of it as running away. I think I just leave home, and in order to
do that, I have to contact this man. I feel really badly about my
brother. I miss him. The tug with my brother is that he is too
loyal and feels too much responsibility for my mother and my sister, so he stays with them. He is fully as enlightened as I am."

I reminded Eve of something she had previously said. "You
told me that you decided, 'I'm not going down with the sinking
ship.' Are you Jewish?"

"I certainly don't think of myself that way. As a matter of
fact, no one that I know of in my family is Jewish. We go to
church, and I think we're Catholic. At this point, I don't know
I'm Jewish, but I am. I find out about being Jewish later on! I'm
made aware that there is Jewish heritage somewhere. I think my
mother knows because it seems to be on her side. My father is not
Jewish. He's wanted for a different reason.

"At some point I know that my father is dead. His death has
to do with principle. He's probably anti-Nazi.

"I don't tell my mother I'm leaving. My brother and I agree
that it's not good news when we haven't heard from our father.
We're worried about him. There's an understanding between us,
and we're in total agreement about what it means to the family...for there certainly is a problem, but we make different choices about how to handle it. Of course he has a way of making me
feel I've made the wrong one. I resolve that I have to go to find
out. I'm not going to be like a sitting duck—I'm going to have to

take charge. He says, 'I can't leave Mom,' whereas I feel I have a moral obligation.

"I have to contact this man before I leave, to get passes. He does help me get there, and in fact I may have been escorted. I think he sends someone to get me. This escort is very deferential, and I'm totally impressed. We travel by trains but it's first class. I'm so quiet and withdrawn and consumed with what I'm doing that, as I look back on it, I must have seemed almost queenly. I'm so reserved, so standoffish...he treats me like I'm a person of stature.

"When we arrive, my lover sets me up in an apartment, and I have a roommate. She's the first inkling I have that I really don't know what I'm getting into. I pretty much think of her as a prostitute. She's kept by somebody, and I realize that it's going to happen to me, too. I don't really have much of a choice.

"My lover doesn't call on me when I first get there, for the same reason I don't see him before I go. This roommate tries to tell me that it's not like you spend every night of your life with them. You have a lot of time on your own. They're too busy. They just want you there when they want you.

"The party that I saw before is soon after I get there. I get terribly drunk. I don't even want to think about being kept. I don't relate to my roommate at all, and I don't want to accept that it's my position as well. I go to the party with her, but he'll be there. I don't think I've gotten to the point at this particular party where I can enjoy myself. I get drunk to block it out and dull my senses.

"Now I begin to realize exactly who he is, and I begin to formulate a plan. That happens over a fairly short period of time, and then I begin to enjoy myself! I'm not just a victim—I've gotten myself into this situation, but I'm in a position to overhear a lot and learn a lot. I've ended up in a situation that I can possibly turn to some good and possibly turn to my advantage."

I'm compelled to ask Eve how she feels about this man, once she's with him.

"I'm not sure I was ever really attracted to him except for his looks. But by being with him, I get a sense of power. He's a very important person, and that's the enjoyment of it. I get an allowance; my rent is paid; and there are accounts everywhere so that I can buy clothes and anything I want. I don't really get cash. If he goes shopping with me, he says he likes that or not, but he doesn't come across as domineering. I flatter myself that he doesn't have to impose his taste, that I know enough without it. Unfortunately that gives me a false sense of security and makes me think I know more than I do and...that he agrees with me more than he really does. I think that there is a rapport between us that really isn't there.

"There is a sufficient number of times to be with him, but there's a lot of time off. It's a pretty normal life. I read or go to the movies with this girl, and he gets me a job. I work at a museum or something. That's where I get my little bit of spending money for movies and cab fares and odds and ends. As I look back, it's yet again an instrument to create a facade of normalcy.

"My roommate points out the celebrities at the parties. They're all pretty high up in the Nazi regime. The parties are for the officers to show off—one upsmanship—They don't want their wives there. I feel very much like what I am—the date and the lover of a person they look up to and perhaps fear a little. He does treat me affectionately in a crowd of men, but I don't get a lot of attention otherwise.

"I definitely want more! There's ambition there. I don't think I want to become his wife, but I want to be important so

I can control the situation. I start drinking a lot, but it doesn't do anything. I'm still shoving my conscience aside. But I still feel like my best answer is being here. The thing that is most frustrating is that I can't really talk to him. The only time I really see him is at parties—I don't think I even sleep with him—maybe occasionally.

"I think I do try to find out about my father and I think I get hit, publicly. He backhands me at a party. Since I can't see him or talk to him, I become bold and...it's more than his just slapping me. And that's when I think I know—Uh oh! I think I am shocked at that, but I don't think I dissolve into tears. All eyes are on me. I have to carry it off, so I turn and head to the bathroom. I don't run—I have a busted lip, and it's already swollen, but it's not severe—no broken bones but I'm shocked. I couldn't believe he would do that, but I have to remain cool as I'm dependent on him."

...At Auschwitz, he would smile and act kindly, then fly into a rage at the slightest provocation.

"I had been back to our apartment in the city, and it wasn't that my family wasn't there—all of our possessions were gone. It was cleaned out, empty. When I saw everything gone, I was in shock. I start out by asking about my father, and he won't give me any answers. Then I ask him about the apartment, and he hits me. He turns his back and walks away. It's only later that I realize he said, under his breath, 'You little Jewish bitch. Who do you think you are?'

"Things continue the way they are. We don't acknowledge that scene, but he seems even more distant now. I know I've blown it! Although I continue to play the game I have been playing, I realize how little I really have. I thought I could make him fall madly in love with me, and I could control the whole thing."

Dawn of Awareness

"One day someone shows up at the door to take me away. Mengele is in the apartment, and it appears like he tortures himself. He tells me I need to go back with my family, that they've moved, and I'm going to be taken to be with them.

"It's the daytime. Mengele knew they were coming—it's the Gestapo! He's pretending to be the good guy. He says, 'Don't be too worried when they show up. I'll take care of things but you need to go with them now. Give it a little time, it'll be okay.' I don't know about my Jewish blood at this point, but I know as soon as he says this that I'm in danger. I'm terrified. But I carry this off with great dignity. I'm on shaky ground, but I don't know why.

"I do know that because my father had disappeared something is wrong, but I still don't know any details. My roommate is there, but she is very quiet, and she hides in a corner. When the Gestapo come to the door, he greets them and pretends to me that I just have to get some papers together. I don't have to ask him about my father—I know he's dead. I'm still maintaining the play, and I go with the Gestapo."

I can hardly speak at this point, but Eve is silent, so after a while I ask her, "Where do they take you?"

"I'm at some place, small and dark, like a holding cell...I don't know where I am, and I'm numb. I get the impression that I do get back to the apartment again for a very short period of time, like a day or two. Going back was almost like a small amount of humanitarianism, and I get a small sense of security. There was a little bit of compassion. Then I'm taken away again, later, and I do meet up with my mother, and brother, and sister. My family has been brought back to the city for questioning. This is not a camp just yet, it's more like a jail.

"When I saw my family in jail cells, and I was put in there with them, a couple of things happened. I was relieved and happy to see them. I also realized what a fool I had been, and I was envious that my brother had made a choice that he could live with, and I hadn't. That is when I found out that we were definitely Jewish. I think I did know it and didn't want to acknowledge it to myself. There were certain things—when he hit me and we argued, certain things were said and done—but to acknowledge it would mean defeat. I wasn't ready to admit defeat. His words may not have been harsh, but I didn't want to hear things. If he had said something blatant, it was at a moment that was so full of emotion it would have been lost. But there was an undercurrent. He had a smile or smirk that was almost malicious. He was thinking or taking pleasure in things I didn't know about. When he lost his temper that one moment, I took the blame for it and thought it was my own damn fault for pushing it.

"There was no blame from anyone in my family. That makes me feel even more guilty. I don't think the pretense is totally dropped. We talk about how the war is going and take some hope in the fact that things won't last. We think Hitler will be defeated, and there's an end in sight. But things go from bad to worse. There's still some dignity where we are now. We're the only ones in this place. My family has been brought there directly from home, and we're questioned individually. They harass my brother, but it's mainly because he's a man, and they want to wield a little power. They want us to cooperate."

More emotion and sadness crept into Eve's voice as she described what she was seeing.

"We are taken from the place where we can deceive ourselves and we're put on a train to one of these camps. Suddenly there's no dignity. We're with a lot of people who are poor and starving and have lost all dignity. It's hard to find hope. The real shock sets in when we get to the camp.

"I don't think I ever drop my dignity; I dare not drop the facade now, or I'll identify with these poor people, and become one of them, and go into despair. My sister is so scared, my mother has to keep her arms around her just to hold her up. I can't even allow myself to feel sorry for her. We don't look like them. We stick out like sore thumbs. When we get to the camp and they try to separate us, my brother exerts some resistance. He stands up to them, and it sets in motion a very swift chain of events.

"A big change comes over me. It is worse than if I could accept just being a victim. I had to take responsibility: 'I pushed him too hard.' 'If I had only been more diplomatic...' I moved like a robot. I think I managed to keep some drugs on me—I don't know how—we were strip searched before we got on the train. I take drugs just to get through this ordeal. I don't let anyone know I have them. I want to be able to give some to my brother and sister, and I regret not being able to do that, but my brother would have disapproved. I don't panic; I'm numb. Whatever state I'm in now, I'm not incoherent, but I'm not there.

"We're separated. We all end up alone. I don't have a chance to say good-bye. I know my mother and sister die, and I think that I've seen what happens to them. I didn't want to remember, it was so horrible.

"I'm treated very differently than a lot of people are. Alternately I'm treated well and then poorly. I am told that I'm being punished for something my mother did, but I don't know what that was. They supply me with drugs. It may be because of him, but I see a nurse giving me drugs. I think I even hallucinate sometimes. She is compassionate and gives them to me. I think I know that nurse in this life! I think it could be Annette, Brett's daughter. I think there's no question it's her. She was so compassionate."

At Auschwitz, a nurse had saved my life. She was a Jewish inmate who worked at the infirmary where they placed me when I got very sick. If it hadn't been for her, I would not have survived the concentration camp.

"I don't die. The war ends. Now I know that my mother and sister were not gassed, but I think they were killed somehow. I think something happened when we got off the train, but they weren't gassed.

"I think I have opportunities to see my brother. It's almost like I'm a guinea pig. They let me see him, and it makes me happy to see my brother, and then they take him away because it makes me unhappy. I think they torture me. I think they do awful things—all kinds of perverted things. But I'm not there—I'm not a person.

"This woman, the nurse, in her compassion, gives me the drugs. I'm in a hospital sometimes—an experimental hospital, but I don't know what kind of experiments. The thing I remember about this nurse is that she has on a white uniform and white bulky shoes. Stereotypical nurse, and she gives me candy—chocolates. I'm forcing myself to eat them. I'm forcing down this sticky sweet candy because it makes me feel better. I guess that candy held the drugs. I think that nurse *is* Brett's daughter, Annette!

"I guess I was an object of his perverted pleasure. On one hand I would be treated commonly, coldly, just for experiments.

On the other hand, he'd bring me to his office, and dress me up for classical music on the radio, and give me champagne, and pretend like I was special. It was perverted."

Josef Mengele loved music and often whistled a phrase from a classical piece when he was choosing Jews to go to the gas chambers.

"They would bring my brother to me in the night. My brother and I had an incestuous relationship. It was the only way I could remain sane—for both of us—I think that's why we couldn't stay anywhere we were known when we were released from the camp. We couldn't go back to Italy because we were lovers.

Several twins believed that Mengele had pairs of twins mate. There are hushed testimonies to that effect. Although all the twins deny firsthand knowledge—and many insist it never happened— there were rumors around the barracks that such perverse experiments were indeed taking place. No twin will elaborate on what he or she knew. Even in the nightmare world of Auschwitz there were taboos, and this was the ultimate one. That Mengele breached it is not unlikely, given the awful scope of his experiments. We will probably never know for sure. Unless, of course, one twin, haunted by the memory of the forcible coupling, steps forward and testifies.

"I don't know how I'm liberated. I leave with my brother. I think we probably go to Italy. But things are not the same, so we couldn't stay with the people who are there. It's just…I'm just a zombie. I haven't died, but I think I'm dead. I'm on drugs. I rely on my brother. He takes care of me, but now he gives me drugs. He doesn't know what else to do. I get to the United States eventually, but one of the good things that happens is that we end up with some money. I think that's why we go back to Italy, to get some money. We probably go to the Orient before we go to the United States to get drugs. I don't remember any details about that time."

Eve told me there must be a bit more that was haunting her for she said, "I don't know if I've told you about another nightmare I've had. They stopped, thankfully, after the regression session with you—thank you, counselor. I was sitting on a cot, and this is the reason I'm firmly convinced that this was a flash from that life. I'm sitting in this room, long and narrow with wood floors. The room is not decorated at all, and there is a row of cots along the wall. They are steel cots with mattresses and white sheets. I'm sitting with my back against the wall, with my feet cross-legged. In my dream, I see Satan—he's small—and he's just to the left of my bed, and he's saying something to me. I'm sobbing. I'm just so emotionally uncontrollable, I can barely talk. I don't know what he says to me, but I responded to him, and it was an effort to talk. I said, 'That's the meanest thing I've ever heard.'

"The other thing is that I think my sister was my twin...in my recollection and in my feelings. But I'm so different from this sister, she almost seems like a little brother...we're just so different. That's consistent with the way it feels, but I don't know that for sure...was just horrific to acknowledge. I chose to feel responsible that I could have done something to prevent this. It feels so right that this man was Mengele!

"There are things that suggest to me that certain people are who I think they are. My maiden name in this lifetime is as close to Mengele as one could get! I think Bobbi's twin sister was named Baba. I named my dog Bubba, but the way I say it makes people think it's Baba! I've always been fascinated by girls' names that sound like boys' names. I used to wish I was a twin, and I've always said I want to have twins."

After we'd had a chance to let all that sink in, I told Eve about a theory of mine: that there is one moment in time when we make a wrong turn that could change the course of our lives.

I asked her when that might have been for her. She replied, "It was when I agreed to meet him for dinner. The flirtation was innocent enough, but I could have walked away." I continued, "But how did you feel inside when you made that choice?" She knew immediately. "It felt like something destined. I felt powerless to resist it. If I could have resisted that pull, I would have ended up exactly where I did, I just wouldn't have felt so responsible. I don't think I would have had such a torturous experience. Looking back, I think I made it worse. In many ways, I've faced the same issues in this life. The glitz and the glamour versus the family. The glitz and glamour are still a lure! It's difficult, and I'm tantalized. Assuming that Bobbi had the means, I think she would have wanted to escape to one of the Allied countries. She might have gotten involved in issues that were relevant. I think she would have joined the resistance. She is most likely to have met a man on the other side who would have fought for justice."

I asked, "Isn't that your issue now as a lawyer? Justice?"

She replied, "I haven't let myself get upset about injustice now. I can't let it in. I can cry over a commercial. I'm so drawn to being a foster mother and working with inner-city kids. But when I think about how emotionally involved I would get, I just can't do it. I would float away in a river of tears. Bobbi couldn't let those feelings out, and neither can I.

"After our session together, I'm a lot more forgiving of myself. I'm beginning to have more compassion, and it's just beginning to affect the decisions I have to make. I allow myself to make mistakes, and I don't feel like a prostitute or whore just because I like the glitz and glamour.

"You know my brother was Ed! He died shortly after I did. He is still keeping me safe. Brett offers the glitz and the glamour. That may be why it's scary for me to become too involved in the social side of our work together. But Ed is no slouch. He is going to become a very successful attorney, and he has a taste for the finer things in life. He represents a secure lifestyle for me.

"Isn't it amazing that I should have worked for Brett not once but twice in my life? We're still not together after Rome and the life in New York. You know that I committed suicide after I was married to Brett in that life—his present one—because I discovered I was pregnant. I just couldn't handle it. Whew! So far, Ed and I have no children and haven't wanted to take that next step. Maybe now, I can begin thinking about motherhood."

The Nurse at Auschwitz

I had done a regression session with Annette at Christmastime one year, and upon meeting her, I had felt not only a deep respect for her, but a strong emotional connection as well. That reaction was augmented by what emerged from her regression session. Annette had taken on a tremendous amount of responsibility for her siblings when she was very young, and that information could only endear her to me even more. Clearly, she was intelligent, caring, and sensitive, and her appearance was that of elegance and good taste. I was very impressed by her manner.

About a year later, as I was writing Eve's story, another "coincidence" happened. Annette is Brett's daughter, and therefore came to know Eve while Eve was working on a project with Brett. Annette had told Eve about a dream she had, and Eve thought it might have relevance to her, Eve's, life in Nazi Germany. Apparently, many things had floated up for Annette after our only session together. I called Annette to ask if she would share that new information with me. She began by saying, "Sometime after you and I had done a regression session together, I had a dream about a past life in Nazi Germany. In fact, this dream was so vivid and real, I awakened crying out and just sobbing. I have had dreams where I'm crying, but I'm only crying in the dream. This time my pillow was completely soaked. My husband is a very sound sleeper, but I woke him up and asked him to just hold me."

I asked Annette what she saw and she replied, "I saw an area that looked like a bullpen, with fences and dirt—almost like where you would keep animals. People are being brought into this fenced-in area by the soldiers." After some questions by me, Annette continued, "I see myself in some sort of a uniform that might be a nurse's outfit. I'm not sure if I'm a nurse, but it appears like that. I have something on my head, like a hat or scarf that ties in the back, and I'm wearing an apron." "How old are you?" I asked. "I seem to be in my early twenties." "Are you Jewish?" I asked. Annette responded, "I don't think so. But I'm forced to be here. It's not like I can come and go. I don't have a choice about being here." I asked how many people she saw and if there were men, women, and children. Annette continued, "There are perhaps hundreds of people being brought in, but they are being separated into these different pens; the men going one way, and women and children another. There is a big building with a huge door, almost like a factory door where they are supposed to go. When they come into these pens, they are so scared they are just shaking. These people are very dirty. Their clothes are just filthy, and they're so scared they are huddled together."

"What are you doing?" I ask. "I seem to be washing them—both women and children. I have a bucket of water and some cloths, and I take these dirty clothes off them and wash some of the dirt from their arms, and legs, and bodies." I asked if the huge door was where the bogus showers were located. "No, I don't think so. I think they're handing out clothes and blankets inside that building. I know these people don't have long to live, but I don't think they're killed immediately."

I continued, "Do you know what happens to these people once they go in the door of that building? Is that where they shave their heads?" "No, their heads are already shaved before they get to me, and I don't know what happens after they leave me. I think I'm just supposed to disrobe them before they go inside, but I think I get water and wash them because I think it will make them feel better. I think I go inside that building to get the water. I just feel so sorry for them, and they are so frightened—so terribly scared—they're just shaking. There is someone else helping me clean these people off. It's another nurse—but I'm the one in charge and I'm taking the risk of getting the water. I say to her, 'I just want to let them go.' She says, 'You know the soldiers would kill you if you did that. At least what you're doing is helping them and making them feel so much better.' I do seem to soothe them, and they do relax a little bit when I bathe them. But that makes me feel even worse! I'm making them feel better to face something horrible. It's like leading lambs to slaughter."

I ask what would happen to her if the Germans knew she was helping them. She said, "I'm sure what I'm doing is dangerous, and eventually I'm taken somewhere else. Oh, I think they are conducting medical experiments inside that building!" I asked Annette to go a bit further in time and tell me what she saw. She continued, "I remember twins. I see two little girls—they seem to be twins, and they have brown hair. I believe there are others. "One of these little girls is very sick and is left outside but the other one is inside. They are very scared because they are separated. I hear someone say the sick child is no good to them and to get rid of her. I see myself talking to one little girl who is going to die—it might be this sick twin—and I tell her not to be afraid. I ask her if she knows who Jesus Christ is and, of course, she doesn't know. I tell her to think about him and to keep repeating a certain phrase over and over again. I don't know what I tell her to say…I can almost recall the words…but I stress that she must keep saying these words and thinking of Christ, and he'll take care of her. I was very compelled to tell her that. I really, really felt in my heart that she would be safe. I knew she was going to die, but I felt that Jesus Christ would be with her. I'm just so heartbroken, and I can't think of anything else I can do to help her.

"I think these medical experiments are really bad, just horrible," she continued. "I see this little girl—the other twin, I believe—who is inside the building lying on a table. There is a doctor there too." I asked Annette to describe the doctor. She responded, "He is attractive. I remember thinking, 'How could you be so cruel?' He is charming, but he shows no compassion. He's very matter-of-fact. He's charming in the respect that if a friend or an equal came in, he could be very gracious. I could hardly believe it was the same person. He was performing the medical experiments." I asked Annette what kind of medical experiments. She gasped and said, "This twin—this little girl—seems to have a different arm on her body. Oh no, I think he's putting another arm on her body. She has a man's arm sewn on her instead of her own arm. I hear the doctor saying, 'This girl is not doing well. Get her out of here. She's not going to make it.' "

Annette suddenly saw something and said, "Oh, Oh. I have candy that I'm giving them. I'm not sure the Nazis know I'm giving them this candy. I'm going to get into a lot of trouble, so

I have to sneak it to them. My gut reaction tells me that I'm giving them drugs inside that candy. I'm not sure, but my instinct tells me that's so. I just feel so badly that I was involved in something as horrible as this. I don't know why I'm selected to be there, but I know I'm not there from free will—I have to do what I'm told and I can't leave. I'm watched a lot. I feel so close to the people's fear and I can identify with that so much that I know I'm close to danger myself.

"After this dream, I was so upset I told my father about it. (Annette's father is Brett!) I just couldn't shake it. He tried to reassure me by telling me that I had helped them so much. But I feel even worse because I think I gave something to one little girl and killed her. And I think it was the little girl I told to pray to Jesus."

I asked Annette if she had read anything about Mengele and his medical experiments, for Annette's description of the doctor and his invalid scientific work at Auschwitz certainly sounded like other descriptions of Josef Mengele. She said she had been too upset to want to read anything about the war years.

I related some of what I had read from *Children of the Flames* and told her that the twins who had survived Mengele's experiments described one nurse who had been very kind to them and who had made all the difference in the world to them by her acts of kindness. In spite of that, Annette still feels that she didn't do enough to help the women and children who were suffering so much.

Annette said, "I think the lady who works for me now in my business was the other nurse. There are so many similarities in the way she works with me. It's funny that the only other person I told about this dream, except my father, was Eve. I just happened to speak to her the next day—just coincidence—as she was working on a project for my father, and I told her about my dream." Annette paused for a moment. "I think I knew Eve in that camp, too. I think she was mistreated even more because she was attractive."

Finding Eve's Twin

After the last session I had with Eve I transcribed her tape to include it in the book. Several months later, I happened to be in the same city where Sarah, another exceptionally beautiful young woman, a client and friend, lived. We decided to have dinner together and began talking about her regression session. I had told her I wanted to do another session with her, but after several attempts to set a time for a second look at a past life, I had let go of the whole idea. Sarah had commented that for some reason she was a bit hesitant to go into a full, intense regression again, as I had sensed she might be. I suspected that she might dredge up some painful information.

Both Eve and Brett thought that Sarah might have been Eve's twin sister. If she did remember a past life as Eve's twin, the emotional reaction might be difficult for her to handle at the moment. Sarah was under a lot of pressure with her work and had very little spare time.

As we were having dinner, Sarah began talking about her rather short-lived association with Eve. She described some of the problems she had in communicating with Eve.

The two women had met over the phone when Brett hired them for a project they could work on together. Since they lived in different cities, most of their association on this project was at a distance. I had met the two women through Brett, individually in their respective cities, and had done both astrological charts and regression sessions for each of them. In fact, by a twist of fate, the first time they were meeting face to face was when we were all in the same city at the same time, and I had the pleasure of introducing them to each other. We three had breakfast together, and they seemed to like each other immediately. The two beautiful, intelligent, very successful young women seemed to have a lot in common. It was later on, after a bit of time had passed and they had been working together for some months, that problems developed between them.

At dinner, Sarah told me she had been especially frustrated because she didn't know how to resolve the situation that had built up between them. She hesitated to say anything to Brett, for fear of going behind Eve's back, so she started writing a letter to Eve. After almost completing the letter she stopped writing and never sent it. She said, "I realized it was a total waste of time. Working with Eve was frustrating to me, as she was not a 'team player.' Eve seemed more concerned about being in the position of authority and living up to her title than completing the actual work.

"Eve had no prior experience with the phase of the work I was trying to do, but because she had been put in a power position, I had to get her approval on matters she knew nothing about. I spent a lot of time explaining why certain things had to be done or how they had to be done. It slowed things down considerably. It seemed to me that her behavior became more irrational and unreasonable. I could never discuss a problem with her, as it appeared as though she took things personally. Things seemed to get worse and, depending on her mood, sometimes unbearable for me. There seemed to be a bond between Brett and Eve that I couldn't penetrate, and I had no one to talk to about the problems I was having with her. I felt that I was between a rock and a hard place, a no-win situation. My hands were tied, and I worked overtime trying to do my best for Brett. I am still flabbergasted by all this. When I think about the money that was wasted on unnecessary parts of the project, I know that for half the cost, so much could have been accomplished. I feel sick about it all."

Sarah continued telling me about her frustrations with Eve. A year earlier, Eve had been in the city where Sarah lived and they were having a business dinner with a lawyer friend of Sarah's. She said, "I had arranged a dinner in a restaurant that I frequent. I wanted Eve to meet an attorney who specialized in deals that related to our project. Because I go to this restaurant often, the waiter was especially nice. He made a special appetizer for me and brought us wine and dessert on the house. When the bill came, both Eve and I reached for it. Brett would have been picking up the tab for our expenses anyway, so it really didn't matter, but I wanted to make sure the waiter got a very good tip because of his attention and gifts to us. Eve insisted on using her card to pay the bill, and when I saw that Eve barely left a 15 percent tip, I put an extra ten dollars on the table from my own funds. She was furious with me and made a scene in the restaurant. She said how dare I second guess her, and how could I care more about the waiter's feelings than hers, and that I had humiliated her. I was mortified, and the attorney tried to try to calm her down. Eve turned on the attorney, an older woman, and verbally attacked her. So the attorney said goodnight to me and left immediately. I was speechless. This took place in a restaurant that I frequent and in the city where I live. I felt like I was in a twilight zone. Then the ranting about Brett and irrational things continued in the car on the way home." Sarah's comment to me was, "That girl almost gave me an ulcer."

As Sarah was describing her shock and frustration, I thought to myself that Sarah's reaction to Eve's behavior was like a re-stimulation of a past life tie. For as we talked, almost a year after the incident, Sarah's annoyance toward Eve hadn't dissipated. Sarah was enjoying some special success in the present moment, and that former incident might easily have been forgotten because of the excitement of the moment. I commented, "That's really why I wanted to do another session with you. I think you two had a past life together." Sarah said, "You mean in Nazi Germany?"

I was somewhat stunned because that *was* what I thought, and both Eve and Brett had independently offered that opinion to me. I asked her why she said that. She confirmed that she had done some work on her own after our first session and had sensed many things about a life during the Holocaust. I asked if we could put her comments on tape. Sarah agreed, and we went to my hotel room where it was quiet. Sarah began talking to me without even closing her eyes. (I usually ask people to close their eyes, just to block out the present environment.) The information seemed very fresh in her mind, and more details seemed to emerge as we talked.

"After I did the first regression session with you...you told me that I could probably easily access more information about past lives without any help from anyone else. You said to just let things float up into consciousness, so I did just that.

"What I remembered was that Eve was my twin sister and that we lived in Germany during the time of Hitler. We were young girls, and we were very different in our ideas about life, and our approach—the way we viewed things and about our duty to our family. I felt very strongly about my parents and about doing the right thing. She had an attitude—not a carefree attitude—just an attitude of a person on a suicide mission. That's the best way I can describe it. Like a person who just doesn't care about anything and has no regard for other people's feelings—she's on a pleasure binge.

"I remember that as issues were coming up in Nazi Germany, certain things were scary. People in the Jewish community were frightened, and she scoffed at it, initially." Sarah stopped talking for a moment and said, "Oh, my tears are starting again. I've cried about this every time I have thought about it." I got some tissues for Sarah and encouraged her to cry if she felt like it. I waited until she was ready to start talking again. "There were discussions in our family, and we wondered what Hitler was going to get away with. There were lots of different points of view about that. In fact, we didn't want to believe that certain things could happen. You just can't believe that people could be that evil. Some part of you says, 'Oh, it's just all propaganda, or maybe it's too late!' There were families who were moving very fast, selling businesses to get away, and these people were being laughed at.

"There was a night when a lot of men were rounded up to be taken to a concentration camp. My father was taken away, and my brother, and some neighbors. It was like a city that was just wiped out. All the men were just taken off. Then we tried to figure out ways to get them out. I think my father was taken to Dachau. I remember wanting to use legal means to find ways to get them released or to help everyone to escape. Now that I think about it, there wasn't very much help from Eve. She's too busy "f-----g" around. I'm sorry to use such strong language, but I'm getting angry just remembering that she was "s------g" around instead of doing what she should have been doing to help the family. Oh my God, it's just like what I felt she was doing with me in the business situation! No wonder I was so upset about it all.

"It gets very painful because we are taken away. As I think

about it, there was a Nazi soldier who was like a border guard. She had some kind of deal with him, supposedly, that we were going to be taken care of. As it turned out, we didn't get taken care of. Only she got taken care of, and we got taken off. She betrayed us. I guess it's kind of muddled for me because I don't really remember how we got betrayed, but it's something I figured out on my own. I can't know for sure what she did to me, but I remember that we suddenly ended up in a concentration camp and I don't know what happened to her. She was "f-----g" this guy—at least that's the conclusion we reached."

It was interesting to me that Sarah thought the soldier was a border guard. Eve had talked about being escorted from her home by a soldier, sent by Mengele, for her safe conduct. Evidently the family thought he was her lover. More than likely, he *was* a border guard.

I asked Sarah what she remembered about her death. "My death? We were marched into an oven! My mother died with me." Sarah began crying in earnest now. Then she turned to me and asked a very significant question. Her tone of voice was very demanding and angry, not directed toward me, but because of what had just occurred to her. "What was she doing with my brother?" I couldn't answer that question for her at that point. I knew that what she had said dovetailed almost exactly with Eve's detailed recollections.

Realizing that she had been a twin in that life, Sarah continued. "When my mother was pregnant with me, in this life that is, I *was* actually a twin. The other twin didn't develop, so I was the only twin who lived. Did I tell you that?" Sarah reminded me of comments I had made when I first gave her an interpretation of her astrological chart. I had told her she might have been a twin in the womb, but that the other baby died well before birth, and that she might have been unaware of the existence of a sibling.

Evidently, as soon as I had finished the interpretation, Sarah had confirmed that bit of information with her mother.

Suddenly Sarah became very agitated. "I'm just now realizing that the other twin was Eve!" She appeared quite shocked, and then hesitated a moment before stating, "Eve is younger than I am." I nodded "Yes." She said, very heatedly, "I was darned sure I wasn't going to spend another lifetime with her. My mother was pregnant with twins, but I was the only child who made it through the pregnancy. I was supposed to be a twin to Eve again!" Then Sarah laughed and said, "Okay, I think I've had just about enough!" But she continued a bit longer anyway. "Did I tell you that my grandmother is Jewish in this life? It's the same situation. My father is not Jewish."

She said, "If she had been my twin sister again and had done *something like she'd done in Nazi Germany*, I would have kicked her butt. I'm not a wimp in this life! In fact, I felt like that a year ago when we were working together. I was so angry at her, I just wanted to kick her butt! But for some reason, I couldn't respond to her as I normally would have. She really almost gave me an ulcer. It was beyond…it was all because I sensed her being manipulative and not being sincere with me. She told me when we first met that she usually doesn't get along with other women because they are so jealous of her. But believe me, I was not jealous of her. I thought to myself, 'That wouldn't happen with me. I have a lot of beautiful friends, so that won't ever be an issue.' My strong reaction to her came from her inability to communicate with me fairly, to be honest, and her manipulating me behind my back. I could sense all of it. I felt she just couldn't work with me as a partner, and that she was constantly trying to outdo me. She sabotaged everything I tried to do."

Evidently the twins' reaction to each other had not changed from one lifetime to the next. There were several things that amazed me about Sarah's recollections. Sarah confirmed what Eve had seen when she described her twin as being the 'perfect little sister,' helping her mother clean up after dinner. Sarah described it by saying, "I felt strongly about my parents and about doing the right thing." Eve recalled suddenly being angry at herself that she could have completely ignored the facts or been so thoughtless or naive not to think about what it meant to be at war. She said, "Even my dumb little sister knows something is going on." Sarah had said, "Eve scoffed at people's fears, initially."

Sarah had described Eve as if she were on a suicide mission. Eve had that impression about herself, too. Sarah said, "She betrayed us...it's something I figured out on my own." Eve had said, "My family would feel that I betrayed them."

I thought it was very significant that not only had Sarah known about a brother, but that she started to become very agitated and indignant over something about Eve and their brother. One memory was different in the former twins' accounts. Eve thought only their father had been taken away, whereas Sarah thought that both her father and brother had been taken to a concentration camp. Sarah saw that both she and her mother died by being thrown into the oven, whereas Eve had said she didn't know what happened to her mother and sister. She had then clarified that statement by saying, "I think I know, but I've blocked that out."

Brett's First Wife

Brett was kind enough to meet with me to tell me about his first marriage. It was clear that the tragedy of this relationship had left its mark, and Brett had probably never fully recovered from the emotional events of that time. As previously explained, the marriage took place when he was a very young man, living in New York City after the war. He was a theatrical manager at the time, and a client of his was playing at the Copacabana, a popular nightclub of the day. Bobbi was there quite often with her brother and his friends, who chose this nightclub as their favorite party spot. Brett said, "I saw her on a repeated number of nights and just stared at her. Bobbi was very exotic looking. One night when she was on the dance floor alone, I asked her to dance. She said, 'Didn't you want to ask me to dance four months ago? What took you so long?' Bobbi was a singer and had a job as understudy for a major role in a popular Broadway musical. An important producer was planning to star her in a future Broadway show.

"Bobbi and her brother had been in Auschwitz during the war. Her father, mother, and twin sister had been killed by the Nazis. After the war, when they were refugees, her brother had started dealing drugs in order to supply Bobbi, who had become an addict. When they came out of Auschwitz, it was not a terrible thing to deal drugs. After what they had been through, their attitude was 'Who gives a "f--k."' Her brother took Bobbi to the Orient at first and later to South America before coming to New York. Bobbi was so out of it with drugs, she really didn't know what was going on." I asked if she was able to handle being on Broadway and if it was obvious to people that she was hooked on drugs. He replied, "Nobody knew. I couldn't even tell, but of course I was totally naive at the time. She would use heroin at night to help her sleep."

When they first arrived in New York, Bobbi and her brother shared an apartment, but later on the brother found a penthouse apartment for Bobbi on top of a hotel on Central Park

South. The brother paid her rent and gave her money to buy whatever she wanted. He had plenty of cash as a drug dealer. Brett said, "They had separate residences for several reasons. She didn't like the people he associated with, but more importantly, he had an appetite for her, and they both tried to fight it." I asked if Brett had any sense of this relationship when he met her. He said, "I didn't know until I was given a letter from her after she died. She had written to me just before she committed suicide.

"We were married by a priest about a year after I met her, but we didn't actually have a marriage license because she couldn't pass the blood tests. The tests would have revealed her drug addiction. She was actually Catholic. She had only a drop of Jewish blood from the fifth century in Italy, and she had been raised as a Catholic. I went to a priest who had known the family in Italy to help her break her habit. The priest helped us find a rehabilitation center outside of New York City, and he married us without the blood tests.

"Bobbi's brother agreed to help convince her to go into a rehabilitation center if I would take a trip to Turkey. I was to take two of my friends along who had diplomatic passports to bring back some furniture for our penthouse apartment. I suspected I was bringing back more than furniture, but it was a deal so that he would help me put her into the center, and then keep her there until I got back. She only spent two days there and came out after I was gone. He let her come out because he really didn't care whether she was off drugs or not. He just wanted to mess me up. I was gone for three weeks, and she was to be in the center for a month.

"When I returned, she had killed herself two days before. I went to the apartment—the penthouse—and everything was gone—it was stripped of the furniture. The doorman took me to the manager, who gave me a note that she had left. I then went to the police station to find out what had happened.

"Her note said a lot of things she never felt she could tell me. She wrote how difficult it was for her to exist with the pattern of evil she had learned to accept in order to live. She told me that she was three months pregnant and didn't know whether the child was mine or her brother's. That was the first I knew of their incestuous relationship." I asked Brett how he was able to deal with this tragedy. He replied, "The anger and hatred took the form of revenge. My life was ruined. I eventually went to Tibet and entered a monastery for six months.

"She left me all her money, and I remember the exact amount after taxes. I tried to call her brother, but he wouldn't talk to me or deal with me. I was contacted by a lawyer and was told I was the principal beneficiary of her will. She left me about $1.2 million after taxes. It was all drug money that she had put in a bank account." Brett paused and then said, "I was so angry and full of revenge and hatred for him that I used that money to have him killed." The room reverberated with silence.

Brett continued in a very sad, soft voice, "Part of my anger and grief was, 'How much of this am I responsible for?' I have carried all this guilt throughout all other relationships. I had pushed Bobbi too hard. In those days things were not very clear to me—everything was black and white. There was no understanding on my part that people can be psychologically innocent but behaviorally evil."

Then Brett looked very intently at me and asked, "Did Eve tell you anything about dogs?" I answered, "Only that she had inadvertently given her dog, in this lifetime, her twin sister's name from the German lifetime. Was her sister's name Baba?" Brett nodded, "Yes." In response to Brett's question, I asked,

"What happened with the dogs?" He said in a very quiet, shaken voice, "She told me in her letter that they had trained the German Shepherds to have sex with her." Brett and I sat quietly for a while before he asked me if Eve had told me why they had brought her brother to her. My recollection was that Eve told me they would bring her brother to her in the night, on occasion, to calm her down. She couldn't stop screaming in the night. Brett continued to tell me what had been in Bobbi's letter to him. He said, "On Christmas night, they made her brother rape her to give a gift to Christ." Then he asked if she had told me how her mother and sister died. My response was that Eve had said, "My mother and sister died, and I think I must know how, but I blocked it out even then."

Brett continued, "They arrived in the camp on Christmas Eve 1944. The war was almost ended. The Germans had built a big bonfire in front of the Christmas tree to welcome those who arrived at the camp that night. They had decided that every Jew who arrived would have to give a gift to Christ. Because Eve and her sister were twins, they were treated in a special way. The evening got totally out of hand, and one German SS officer decided that Eve's mother should choose one of the twins to be thrown into the pit and burned alive. If the mother didn't choose, then the whole family would be burned alive. The mother finally chose Eve's sister and then jumped in with her. Bobbi always wondered why her mother loved her sister more, by choosing her for the fire and leaving Bobbi behind. The Nazis were infuriated that the mother had done that. They had wanted to see the psychological reaction of the mother and her child."

I told Brett that Eve had remembered that she was punished even more because of something her mother had done, but she didn't know what that was. I remarked that Eve had said her brother was very judgmental about drugs before they got to the camp, but that after that, he would supply her with drugs because he knew she needed them.

Both Eve and Sarah were hurt by the mother's choice of the twin to be killed. Eve felt that her mother loved her sister more by choosing to spare her the horror of the camp. Brett told me that he has been very afraid not to be compassionate and understanding since that tragedy.

It would be hoped that these three people—Brett, Eve, and Sarah—could find a way to heal the past through love and forgiveness. The sadness and tragedy of the circumstances seemed almost beyond each person's control. Eve had commented that if she had only resisted having dinner with the dashing officer, who she believed was Josef Mengele, she might have suffered the same consequences, but without such guilt for the circumstances of her family. Sarah and Eve might be able to resolve their relationship by discussing the conflict of the twins' different personalities, rather than trying to heal the situation that occurred in the present. Brett can only know that he did what he sincerely thought was right at the moment, and he is back now with Eve to send love and healing energy to her on a higher, more esoteric level. Eve and Ed have each other and are in a position to heal many past lives through their devotion to each other.

When groups of people who have been involved in such heavy karmic circumstances can bring themselves to put all the others in the light of the universal consciousness, and if there can be a sincere desire on the part of each individual involved to send energy, love, and best wishes that each of the other people will have in his or her life that which is best for his or her soul development, the law of the universe can allow the best circumstances to come in for the self as well. Ultimately, each person needs to love and heal the self.

9
Methods of Growth Toward Unity

The Akashic Records

Now that we have entered the computer age, it is easier to understand the workings of the universe. Imagine that space is like the hard drive of a PC, except that the number of gigabytes is unlimited. There are files in that hard drive—called the "Akasha"—for each and every human being who ever lived on earth. Those files are called the "Akashic Records." Every single solitary thought and deed of each person is permanently recorded in those records, just like information recorded in the files in a hard drive.

When I came to grips with the concept of the Akashic Records in my early thirties, I took a figurative gulp and decided I'd better begin to watch every thought that went through my mind each second of each day! Deepak Chopra says in his book, *The Seven Spiritual Laws of Success,* "This moment—the one you're experiencing right now—is the culmination of all the moments you have experienced in the past. This moment is as it is because the entire universe is as it is."

The entire history of human collective and individual activity exists in the Akashic Records, to be tapped whenever someone finds the key that fits the lock. There are no secrets in the universe! Mercifully, we have little access to those records until we have developed a sense of the responsibility and wisdom that must go along with possession of this knowledge. It would bring very negative results if we were able to read someone else's records to be used against him or her.

Thankfully, we are blissfully unaware of what we may have done in the past, until the day comes when we are ready to handle that information without threat to our survival and growth. A valid reason to conduct regression sessions without hypnosis is that the left brain acts like a filter and allows us to accept only what we can deal with at the moment. Otherwise the knowledge (perhaps the same knowledge of good and evil described in the Bible) might be more than we could cope with.

At some point in our evolutionary development, soul consciousness causes us to become curious about unseen matters. This can come as a result of many external events, such as trauma, or merely from a sense of divine discontent. As we develop new awareness of the continuation of life, we begin to make a connection to our interaction with everything around us. We can correlate our own lives and all manner of life, including relationships with people, animals, and plants.

Within the ethers exists a substance that penetrates all manner of matter. This can explain our magnetic connection to some people and the ability to heal relationships through the power of the mind, even if we don't use words. Thoughts are *things* and carry their own very potent energy. How many times have you thought of someone, only to have the phone ring with that person on the line calling you? This may also explain why inventors in different parts of the world suddenly come up with the same ideas. (If this weren't so, there would be no scramble for government patents.) The potent energy of thoughts can also explain universal cyclical trends and is a reasonable explanation for the "hundredth monkey" phenomenon.

Curiosity can lead to an incredible journey that may only take place in the mind. A process of deliberately observing what is going through your own mind in each second of time is the first step toward changing your life. You may not be able to *erase* the recorded thoughts and deeds from the past, but you can start, right now, to type into your own files, or Akashic Records, those thoughts and deeds that you choose to record. This is like writing your own script or movie that will play for the rest of your life—until you decide to create a new script, or movie.

For true understanding of life on earth we eventually learn that we are writers of our own scripts, and co-creators with God or the universe. The writing of these scripts can only be done while we reside in the physical body. The release of creative energy through *the activity of making conscious life choices* can be one of the most exciting and challenging things you will ever experience. Not only can you tap sources of stimulation and mental energy, but what you program into your own computer, or subconscious mind, to be stored in the Akashic Records can bring boundless rewards. The only limits are your own imagination.

Let's say you are a successful business executive and you have a product that you want to promote. You may have decided on an advertising campaign in the past that produced less than satisfying rewards. So the new advertising campaign can make or break the sales results. It won't do any good to berate yourself for not having found the most successful method of promotion the first time around, because that is past history. And the campaign you work on in the present may or may not be the absolute best way to release information, but it's a risk you have to take.

You sit at your desk and begin to think. With a review of the previous campaign you can see where you might have gone off the track in the past. You may doodle around with several ideas and ultimately come up with a dynamic new concept for your product. After you have decided on that new plan you may share your ideas with co-workers or your employees, ask other people for their input, and then turn it over to an advertising agency for refinement and design. You can place the ad in strategic places in magazines or newspapers, send out mailings, or find other ways to let the public know what you have to offer. You may then have to allow time for the results to come in so that you can evaluate the effectiveness of your efforts. You may never have left your desk or your office to set this new campaign in motion.

Suppose you decide to do this with the rest of your life. You probably need to take time to review what went wrong before and objectively view your past mistakes. It is not only unnecessary to blame yourself for having made a wrong choice in the past, but this can actually be detrimental. Moreover, it wastes time and valuable energy. But if you have hurt someone else, it is important to find a way to make amends; you may have to come back over and over again in a karmic relationship with that very person for many future lifetimes. When you view your life as your own creative product and step outside of yourself, you give yourself the opportunity to make conscious new choices. That means taking ultimate responsibility for what happens in your life, rather than blaming others for outer conditions. We all act as mirrors for each other and tend to project onto someone else what we are really trying to tell ourselves.

First, there is a need for reflection and review. A regression session can put you in touch with your own records so that you can see exactly what you have written in the past. This releases you to make positive decisions about how to restore balance in your own life and in relationship to other people.

Secondly, you need time for that reflection on a daily basis. Meditation is one of the most powerful tools you can use for deep, productive reflections, and it will be discussed more fully later in this chapter. Meditation is not passive, but active. It is a process that helps you develop the ability to clear the mind. Just as with a computer, you need to start with a blank screen in front of you. However, first you have to learn how to turn the computer on and focus on the right key to push in order to access that blank screen.

Finally, you need to allow time for the results of your new decisions to manifest in your life. If you become impatient and delete what you put in your computer, write over the text with something new, or put in doubtful words that obfuscate the message you've sent out to the universe (your advertising campaign), the results will be confusing.

A. Self-Regression

It is possible to conduct a dialogue with your higher self all by yourself. You can do it, *if* you can do it. It is a matter of asking yourself one question at a time and learning how to listen for the answer. With the practice of daily meditation, you're already primed to take this next step. It can be easy or difficult, depending on how much you can focus your mind on the exact questions you're asking and how much you can dedicate yourself to hearing the answer.

I conduct regression sessions without the use of hypnosis so that people can learn how to reveal inner information in a conscious state of awareness. I always suggest that new information will come into consciousness after a regression session is over and that it is important to trust whatever might pop into the mind later on. On many occasions, a person has called me to tell me amazing information that has come forth after the session is over. Working in this way can have long range benefit as that new data continues to surface. You are actually learning how to open your own doors to the Akashic Records by dialoguing with your own subconscious.

In so doing, the conscious part of the intellect plays a valuable part in assessing the information that is revealed. That is especially true if one is aiming at new spiritual and psychological awareness with the *intention* of creating new conditions in his or her life. This creation of positive conditions leads to the upgrading of the quality of relationships, and could eventually lead to the creation of a better world.

It is not important to be concerned about whether the information you receive is "accurate" or not. Fantasy belongs to each person as much as if the thoughts can be proven and verified. What is important about the process you undertake is how those past impressions relate to patterns in the present. If any revelation can give explanation or can clarify situations in the present, it has great value in your ability to create anew.

Before beginning self regression, an explanation of the process I use when working with people might be helpful. I use the analogy of knitting to explain the process. Imagine knitting a sweater. As you are working on the twenty-fifth row, you suddenly realize that you've dropped a stitch on the eighteenth row. Your sweater won't be a very good sweater unless you go back and pick up the stitch. It is my opinion that in traditional therapeutic practices, the work you do is similar to picking up a crochet hook and weaving that dropped stitch into the whole sweater again. It is then necessary to pull and stretch the knitting around that dropped stitch to integrate it into the weave of the sweater. Sometimes that stitch shows and the pile isn't very smooth. It may be necessary to go back once more to pick out that stitch and try again to blend it into the whole garment more evenly.

A regression session can augment a traditional therapeutic process, because in the regression session, a person unravels the *whole* row of knitting, or many rows of knitting, to pick up that dropped stitch. After that, the sweater begins to knit itself up again. (By that I mean that with one or two regression sessions you allow new information to float up to the surface, filling in information about the patterns of life without any further assistance from an external source.) In a regression session, I do not leave a person until he or she has reached that dropped stitch. After that type of inner work, any time spent with more traditional types of psychotherapy will be enriched and will make the therapeutic work even more effective. As the individual understands the basic formula he or she has set up for his or her life, the pieces of the puzzle will continue to fall into place. The important thing is that the individual now has a new perspective on almost everything around him. This is like wiping off a dusty mirror so that you can really see the reflection with great clarity and in all its glorious detail.

B. Steps for Self-Regression

First, sit erect rather than lying down. A position similar to a meditation pose not only helps you with the concentration necessary but allows energy to flow downward from a higher sphere of consciousness into the brain.

Next, close your eyes. That is helpful in blocking out the current environment and all the Pavlovian responses connected to your present conditions.

Then, direct yourself to review some of the hardships, pain or traumas you've experienced in this lifetime. After you've thought through a recent difficult time from the perspective of your higher, objective mind, direct yourself to go back to an earlier moment of pain or loss. That may be physical pain or emotional pain, physical loss or emotional loss. After you've reviewed several situations, ask yourself what the connection might be between them.

A very simplistic example may be that you've just had a minor automobile accident after having had a fight with your spouse. In an earlier moment you may have fallen down and skinned your knee just after you've been angry at something your mother or father said or did. You may be able to trace those patterns quite far back. The new perspective you gain is that you better observe and acknowledge anger or frustration and take time to cool down before racing out to your automobile or before crossing streets against the light. That kind of awareness may not be very difficult to attain. But, of course, one can go much deeper.

I've used an example in my book *Astrology and Your Past Lives* that describes a baby lying in a crib. Say that you've asked yourself for a very early moment of pain or loss, and you see a small baby. You don't see anything to indicate that the moment is significant, however, and you may be ready to dismiss that image as simply your imagination. However, if you persist and ask yourself, "What am I doing in that crib?" you may get an impression that you are crying. You may then ask yourself "What time of day or night is this?" The answer might be, "Three o'clock in the afternoon." Perhaps you are stuck for the next question. Take a look around the room to observe the furniture, the color of the walls, whether there is a rug on the floor and or curtains on the window. This process helps to place you in that moment and enables more insights to come to mind. You may realize that you are feeling alone or frightened and you may realize that you know Mother is not in the house. Then you can ask yourself, "Where is she?" You might draw a blank again, but please refrain from saying to yourself, "I don't know." You actually know everything if you persist in asking. If necessary, ask five times until you bore yourself into coming up with an answer! Eventually what you realize is that the next-door neighbor had an emergency and asked your Mother to come over for a moment to help her. You can then ask if Mother is coming back soon, and if the answer is "Yes," you can convince yourself to play with the mobile above your bed, count your fingers and toes, and wait patiently for mother's return. If the answer is "No, she's not coming back soon," you can observe the panic that sets in. That observation may explain what happens to you in later life when you don't get an immediate response from a person or situation. You might tend to panic when panic is an inappropriate response in adult life.

Be sure to review the past in the present tense. That allows you to tune into emotions that are connected to the scene before your eyes. Be sure to trust what comes into your mind, even if it doesn't make sense at the moment. Keep asking yourself about the significance of what you're getting. You may actually see pictures or just get an impression. You may find it works best to be quite logical by asking simple "Yes" or "No" questions, as if you were taking a test in school. Would the answer be found in Column A or in column B?

You can also learn to work with a pendulum to get yes and no answers. You can purchase a pendulum that has either a crystal at the end or a metal tip. Practice asking questions with answers you can verify. Observe which way the pendulum swings when the answer is "Yes" and which way the pendulum swings when the answer is "No."

Treat your own regression session as if you were making a personal film. Make choices along the way in the observation of your film. You are the screenwriter, the director, and the actor. Trust your fantasy first, but in observing objects in the room, as an example, you can make a choice about the color of the wall or the curtains at the window. That attention to detail only serves to get you to the real meat of the moment.

Birth Patterns

A very valuable moment in a regression session is the observation of the birth process itself. In a self-regression, ask yourself how it feels to be in the womb. Is it crowded, cozy, warm, or cold? Ask yourself if you know that you're going to be born. Some people are not aware of what lies ahead of them, and the beginning of the birth process comes as a great shock. You can be sure that later on in life, when that person is suddenly faced with events that may appear out of the blue, his or her reaction will be the same—a great shock.

You can finally rewrite your birth survival script by asking yourself how you would have ideally been born into this world. You may not be able to change the reactions of other people in that scenario, however. If, as an example, you observe that when you were born, the doctors and nurses were tired and they were just going about their job in a perfunctory manner without any real excitement, you may realize that life brings in changes relating to outer circumstances where other people seem unenthusiastic.

The important thing is that *you* have a choice about your reaction to their complacency. You can be enthusiastic about your new life even if the doctors and nurses are tired. The choices we make early in life are the same kind of choices we make right down the line.

One of the great values of understanding life from a different perspective comes from realizing that we cannot change other people! You cannot change the reactions of other people in the original scenario, of course. We can only change ourselves and our *reactions* to others. But that awareness can make all the difference in the way we lead our lives.

Meditation

Many people operate on a humanitarian and spiritually-elevated level without daily meditation, but meditation enables a person to consciously and deliberately go into an alpha state that builds the quality and strength of the aura. Consequently, this higher level of energy feeds the brain with supercharged fuel. Creatively active people must be able to tap a source of inspiration, whether conscious or unconscious, that enables them to express a greater degree of creative results. Actors and musicians, for example, study their craft for years to learn how to develop techniques they can fall back on if they are not "up" for a performance. For an actor, dancer, or musician must give a performance that transcends his personal feelings, even if he is sick or emotionally devastated. Many dancers, for instance, have given truly great performances when they are in great pain from injured muscles or torn ligaments. Artists have painted their greatest masterpieces when they were in true agony of the soul. Mozart composed soul-soaring music when he was terribly ill.

Sanford Meisner, a superb acting teacher, created an exercise for his students that helped develop a higher level of interaction between two actors. He used the term *independent activity* to direct his students' attention onto a transcendent level and away from acting a part. One student is to concentrate on an activity that is enormously compelling, such as carving a sonnet on the head of a pin. After a moment or so, the other student enters and focuses on getting the attention of the first actor away from his activity so that a creative friction can exist. When the two actors are completely involved in their tasks, it is as if the left hemispheres of their brains are so fully occupied that the right hemispheres are free to soar to new levels of inspiration. (This is the kind of concentration that is developed with meditation, so that loftier thoughts and energy become part of the individual system.) When the second actor enters, it has to be done in such a way that it automatically pulls the first actor's attention away from his or her activity; otherwise the first actor continues concentrating on that activity. When true interaction takes place, something special happens. Higher energy is released, sparks are generated, and electricity is in the air. It is my contention that everyone should study acting (and singing) as a way of learning about life.

Great singers, such as Joan Sutherland, can produce almost other worldly sounds that seem to emerge from the ethers by concentrating on techniques that free the vocal cords from any strain. These techniques enable a pure sound to emerge that seems to reverberate outside of the singer's aura. This quality of attention and concentration is, in itself, a form of meditation. All great singers, dancers, and actors use their bodies as vehicles and learn how to allow a quality of energy and activity to pour forth that is distinctly beyond the norm. This is meditation in action, for the meditation process must be accompanied by creative work or it is purely mystical. That in itself is not futile, but it is a more passive than active way of dealing with life. Most people living under the stress of modern-day activity cannot take the time, or may not choose to live on that purely mystical level.

If a person has chosen to walk the path of enlightenment and to tap a universality within himself, daily meditation is the single most important activity in which he can engage. It is only through this concentrated practice that a firm connection is made between the spiritual nature and the physical, mental, and emotional vehicles. There are no shortcuts. The regular, deliberate attempt to bring higher energy into all daily activities stabilizes that mystical process of creativity. Meditation then becomes the greatest platform of security in life, for daily meditation eventually brings profound changes into the external events in one's existence. Motivation to use this higher energy for the well-being of mankind is the match that lights the cosmic fire which must, then, boomerang in a positive way. Most importantly, meditation enables each person to touch the people around him on a higher level of consciousness. The supercharged energy produces a magnetic force that enables others to tap their own level of soul consciousness. And energy that is sent out must return in kind, magnified many times. Therefore, inadvertently, when the underlying motivation is for the well-being of all of mankind, a higher energy is released in one's own life. This concept of motivation is the key to unlocking many of the riches of life.

There is a cosmic stratum of energy where all doors can be opened. The deliberate and conscious choice to transmute the little will (I want what I want when I want it) onto the higher level (I want only what is right for all concerned) brings a release from the burden of making a wrong choice in life. That is like putting something or someone in the "light" or giving the thought or plan over into God's hands. This can be the greatest struggle in life, this wrestling between free will and the conscious choice to live on a level of higher will. The struggle can make itself felt over small things or over what appear to be well-motivated desires. I illustrated this point when I described losing my darling dog, Samantha, in an earlier chapter.

In the practice of meditation, the coordination of tapping higher levels of consciousness and integrating the concrete mind allows man to walk with his feet on the ground and his head in the skies. Meditation facilitates that kind of coordination and puts the power of the mind into proper perspective.

Although prayer is an important religious activity, its function is quite different from that of meditation. Prayer is basically a function of asking, whereas meditation opens avenues for listening. Visualization is similar to prayer in that it creates an avenue for the manifestation of higher spiritual concepts to materialize on the earth plane. Meditation makes the results of visualization easier, as the mind gains more control over random and even unwanted thoughts, rather than the other way around.

There are many methods of meditation and many misconceptions about its practice. Meditation is more than just a way of establishing a peaceful inner feeling. It serves a very practical purpose in the everyday process of living, of raising the vibrational and health level within the human system. More importantly, daily meditation creates the actual bridge, called the Antaskarana of subtle etheric structure that serves as a conduit for the free passage of energy from the higher etheric level down through the denser bodies. Conversely, it allows the spiritual part of man, trapped in his dense physical vehicle, to bring forth a higher level of energy to light up the heavy physical body. Each individual has his own specific atomic point in the ethers. Through meditation, each person can find his own point in the heavens and actually come into contact with his soul. The yearning for the soul connection is the basis of all longings in life. For with the awareness of that higher point, man can tap an eternal wellspring of abundant joy and health. (See *Astrology and Your Health: A Practical Guide to Physical, Mental, and Spiritual Well-being*, revised edition published by Plutoh Publications, 1317 Third Ave., Suite 100, New York, NY 10021.)

Perhaps the greatest misconception about meditation is that it is a passive activity. Certain kinds of music serve an important inspirational function, for example, creating an external ambiance that can penetrate the very pores and cells of all the systems of the body, but listening to music is a passive experience rather than an active one. Meditation must incorporate active concentration to bring about the desired results. Many individuals are concerned about an inability to control the mind and thoughts during meditation. Some may try to create a mental void. This focus on deficiency and failure disappears with the true method of meditation, which is active. Meditation is a profoundly engrossing process of concentration, but that concentration must be on *something* rather than on *nothing*. The end result is a dynamic ability to build more creative thought forms.

By the very nature of man's descent into the earth plane, the focus of his existence is brought down into density. One of the physical laws ruling existence on the earth plane is the law of gravity. And it is important for man to be grounded in order to exist on the physical level. It is difficult to function efficiently if one is flying above the earth like Peter Pan. Before entering the physical plane, each individual builds a heavy framework in the form of a bony skeleton to protect the fragile spiritual nature from the force of the elements—a process not unlike choosing an automobile that will make travel safer and easier. In our imagination we could color gravity and the physical body in dark tones. But meditation is the science of light, and its practice develops the ability to work with the substance of light energy. With meditation, the physical vehicle becomes illuminated with the light of the spirit, which shines through darkness on the physical plane. The difference in the quality of life before and after the practice of meditation is the difference between walking on a road on a very dark night without a flashlight and walking on the same road on a night brilliantly illuminated by the full moon. Meditation turns on an inner lamp and fans a brighter inner flame.

The spiritual nature of man is the true driver of his vehicle. If the driver of a car is tired, asleep, or not properly positioned in the driver's seat, the automobile may take an erratic or even dangerous course on the roads. When the spiritual part of man enters the body before birth, during birth, or shortly thereafter, it is not uncommon to feel reluctant about taking another trip on the highway of life. A person may consciously or unconsciously avoid taking full control of the operation of his own automobile. He may try to drive with half of his spiritual body hanging out of the window or slumped down so that he can't really see the road ahead. Meditation enables the spiritual body to sit upright, fasten the seat belt, and take conscious, efficient, and effective control. At an even higher level, meditation allows the spiritual self to attune to a protective automatic pilot that is clearly more sophisticated and always aware of the road conditions ahead.

The ideal meditative state is to live each moment in touch with one's own specific atomic point in the ethers. Then every activity is a form of meditation. Joseph Campbell stated that underlining sentences in books was his form of meditation. No matter what method one chooses, what is important is the daily exercise of controlling the thoughts formed by the mind so that those thoughts are born on a higher level of consciousness. The mind is the builder. When one can focus attention and concentration at will, thoughts are directed from an inner state of clarity rather than from reactions to outer circumstances. At that point, a person is on the way to greater liberation and freedom. Fear, anxieties, and worries have no room to grow roots when the calm inner light is bright. The condition of the physical body may or may not always reflect that inner state of being, but there is one window into the inner being: through the eyes. If one has ever looked into the eyes of a master, the brilliance of the light is unmistakable.

Methods of Meditation

There are several ways to meditate. It is possible to meditate on symbols, colors, sound, spiritual centers (of the body, called chakras), invocations, and "seed thoughts." It is advantageous to pick one type of meditation that seems most comfortable and stick with that method. After the practice of meditation becomes second nature, it is possible to choose a different type of meditation for a specific purpose or to practice more than one method on a daily basis.

First, it is important to sit in a comfortable position, but with a straight back. This way the energy can flow straight down through the crown chakra at the top of the head into the system. If it is possible to sit in a lotus position, with ankles placed on top of opposite thighs, do so. A half lotus position will do nicely, however, if you cannot achieve the full position. (Half position is achieved by sitting erect on a flat surface with the left leg bent and the left heel pulled tightly into the groin. The right leg is bent and the right heel is placed on top of the left thigh. If you simply cannot lift the right leg on top of the left, the closest approximation is still beneficial.) Open hands and legs allow energy to dissipate outside of the body; the lotus and half lotus positions close off the electrical circuits of the body, allowing the energy and vibrations to cycle through the body, thereby facilitating the continual buildup of vibrations within. You may continue to close off the circuits by placing each thumb and forefinger together and then placing the hands on the knees. Tibetan lamas teach another method of rechanneling energy throughout the system: loosely place slightly curved hands in front of the body, with thumbs together, at the solar plexus. The elbows are slightly extended at the side of the body.

In the Indian technique, the eyes are closed. The Tibetans, however, meditate with downcast eyes that are slightly open. The gaze is directed at a point on the floor in front of you, a comfortable distance away. This open-eye method accomplishes two things: it inhibits any tendency to fall asleep and it facilitates a constant state of meditation, even when one is walking around. If you can meditate with your eyes slightly open, you can meditate anytime, anywhere. If you are meditating on symbols or the chakras, however, you may find it easier to close your eyes.

A mantra is a word or phrase that carries high vibratory energy through its meaning. It can be a "seed thought" that invokes a noble purpose or feeling, for instance. The sound, repeated over and over again, focuses attention on its esoteric meaning. One mantra that is universal and extremely powerful is "ohm mani padme hum" [Ohm mah´nee pad´me hoom]. This is the short form of a longer Sanskrit mantra that invokes a feeling of compassion for mankind in general and each sentient being in particular. This mantra works on the heart center to develop a feeling of universal love. It is a beautiful phrase to repeat over and over again, opening the heart chakra to new energy. It is particularly important to say when the heart feels constricted. Another very powerful mantra is "Ohm nama Shivaya," which says "Honor thyself within." Sanskrit words carry special energy, moreover.

The period of time just before the full moon is noticeably very high in energy. Universal energy begins to build with the new moon phase, reaching its fullness with the full moon, only to slack off in the moon's waning phase. If a person can attune himself to the same rhythm in his scheduled activities, he operates on the same cycle as nature and can achieve greater harmony within his system. It is a good idea to start new activities with the advent of the new moon and allow them to develop until the full moon. It is possible to invoke and breathe in greater physical energy from new moon to full moon. Meditation, especially on the night just before the full moon, is especially potent. It is necessary to consciously open the system to take in a new level of energy, however. Otherwise, the energy bounces around throughout the unbalanced system, causing havoc with emotional reactions. There are groups of people that meet just prior to the full moon for the purpose of invoking energy, which can then be dispensed individually toward all sentient beings in the following waning period. It is not uncommon to hear snoring from many in these groups, as people often fall into deep sleep when surrounded by very high energy. If the system cannot handle the level of vibration that is generated, the protective device of sleep shuts them away from excess electrical energy they may not be able to take in.

Another very powerful meditation is called the Great Invocation. The Great Invocation was given to Alice Bailey by the Master D.K.

THE GREAT INVOCATION

From the point of light within the mind of God
Let light stream forth into the minds of men.
Let light descend on earth.

From the point of love within the heart of God
Let Love stream forth into the hearts of men.
May Christ return to Earth.

From the center where the will of God is known
Let purpose guide the little wills of men.
The purpose which the Masters know and serve.

And from the center which we call the race of men
Let the plan of Love and Light work out
And may it seal the door where evil dwells.

Let Light and Love and Power restore the Plan on earth.

It is very beneficial to repeat this mantra at least once or twice a day in combination with other methods of meditation you might choose.

Another powerful mantra is the Twenty-third Psalm from the Old Testament in the Bible. Each phrase of this psalm actually stimulates a specific chakra as it is repeated. The benefits from the stimulation of the chakras can be increased by mentally focusing on the correct chakra with each phrase. (See illustration on p. 254.)

> The Lord is my shepherd; I shall not want (root chakra). He maketh me to lie down in green pastures (sacral); he leadeth me beside still waters; He restoreth my soul (solar plexus); he leadeth me in the paths of righteousness for his name's sake (heart chakra). Yea, though I walk through the valley of the shadow of death, I will fear no evil; for thou art with me; thy rod and thy staff they comfort me (throat chakra). Thou preparest a table before me in the presence of mine enemies (crown chakra); thou anointest my head with oil; my cup runneth over (brow chakra). Surely goodness and mercy shall follow me all the days of my life: and I will dwell in the house of the Lord forever (brow chakra).

Notice that the attention goes from the throat chakra straight up to the crown chakra, bypassing the ajna or brow chakra until the last. This directs energy through the entire chakra system and then sends forth energy to mankind through the center between the eyes.

Meditation on symbols representing the physical, mental, and emotional bodies helps to align the three major vehicles

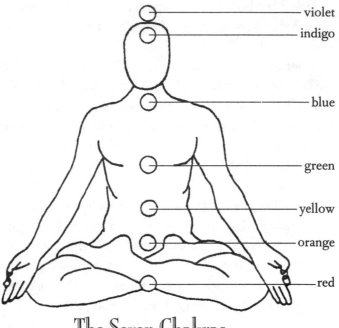

The Seven Chakras

through which we operate on the earth plane. First visualize a circle and mentally place a dot inside (this relates to the physical level of being). See the circle as a continually moving line going *clockwise* and then once again, place a dot inside each time the circle rotates. Continue to see the circle moving clockwise with a dot in the middle. Do this for five minutes. Next visualize an equal-sided cross (this represents the emotional level of being). Do this for five minutes. Finally, see an equilateral triangle for five minutes (this relates to the combination of physical, emotional, and mental levels of being). You may have difficulty making one or more of these symbols clear in your mind. Be patient and continue trying to see them clearly. You can see white symbols on a dark background or black symbols on a white background. Either way is effective. If one or more of the symbols presents some difficulty, you can be sure that symbol represents one of the vehicles that needs balancing the most. Keep focusing your attention on all three symbols. Eventually, you will find a greater synchronization among all three vehicles, and you will feel new energy as a result of alignment and balance.

To facilitate new energy's moving throughout the system, some motion can be useful, as can sound and the visualization of color. Tibetan monks sway slightly during meditation. That helps to free the body mechanism, allowing energy to pour through all the vehicles. You can aid this process by imagining the spirit's finding its perfect balance within the physical vehicle. Chanting utilizes sound, vibration, and breath to lift the level of consciousness.

By meditating on each chakra as you visualize filling it with its corresponding color (see illustration on p. 254), it is possible to augment the strength of the aura, for color in the system is important for a vital constitution. Sound is also very important for maintenance of high energy. Playing spiritual music, such as the Gregorian chants, or listening to temple bells during meditation is a way of raising the vibrational level in the the surrounding atmosphere, as well as allowing the resounding vibrations to hit responsive chords within the body. Another recent release is "Adiemus" by Songs of Sanctuary.

Lastly, a focus of attention on the third eye, or brow chakra, helps to balance the right and left halves of the brain. It is through this chakra center that energy is sent forth into the world. The visualization of a cross of light, universal, equal sided—not confined to Christian symbolism—pouring down through the crown chakra and released outwardly through the brow represents the symbolic release from the cross of the material and the uplifting onto the level of soul awareness. This is the way to cleanse all the vehicles of impurities, whether they have their origin in past lives, in present circumstances, or on a physical, mental, or spiritual level. The new inpouring of etheric energy purifies and balances the system, allowing new vitality and health to become part of life.

After choosing the method of meditation, an important consideration when going about one's daily tasks is to periodically focus on a seed thought that will facilitate new motivation in life. This focuses the mind onto one intention that is repeated and repeated until it becomes an automatic part of the consciousness. That seed thought might be one connected to service toward mankind, for example. A simple thought such as "Send me, use me" can be all-powerful in changing mental attitudes from a self-serving approach toward principles that begin to uplift consciousness and attention onto higher levels.

The transmutation of the personal will onto the level of universal will is the greatest challenge for every living being on earth. Meditation is the way in which the struggle between the little will and the higher will can take place. That struggle, which cannot be avoided and is the major initiation in life, can be likened to Moses struggling with the angel on the mountaintop.

It is the struggle to turn oneself over to the will of the spirit or the higher self. The little self may have difficulty letting go of the games it has cleverly devised, but eventually this struggle leads to enlightenment, for the transference of energy onto the soul level allows each individual to live without fear and in greater joy.

Most important of all, be sure you are ready to change your level of consciousness, and therefore your life, before you begin the daily practice of meditation. Once begun, you will never be the same again.

• • •

It is my sincere desire that each person will be able to look at his past, either through formal regression sessions or by learning to direct himself to the answers he has within. With that reexamination, he can clear away all the knots that have prevented the golden thread of consciousness from shining within. Eventually recognizing the soul inside the body and finding the atomic point in the ethers will help each person make contact with his or her true self. The particular quality of brilliance that resides within each person is the light that can heal first the self, and then relationships, and eventually the world from past tragedy and inhumanity. If everyone would dedicate some part of each day to that end, mankind could certainly prevent evil from ever taking hold on a wide scale, for evil cannot live in the light.

Bibliography

Avery, Jeanne. *Astrology and Your Health*. New York: Plutoh Publications, 1996.

Avery, Jeanne. *Astrology and Your Past Lives*. New York: Simon & Schuster, 1987.

Bailey, Alice. *A Treatise on Cosmic Fire, Esoteric Healing, Ponder On This*. New York: Lucis Publishing Company, 1925, 1953, 1971.

Bauer, Yehuda. *A History of the Holocaust*. New York: Franklin Watts, 1982.

Burrows, Millar. *The Dead Sea Scrolls*. New York: Gramercy Publishing Company, 1989.

Cayce, Hugh Lynn. *Edgar Cayce's Story of Karma*. New York: Berkley Publishing Group, 1972.

Chopra, Deepak. *The Seven Spiritual Laws of Success.* San Rafael, California: Amber-Allen Publishing & New World Library, 1993.

Gershom, Rabbi Yonassan. *Beyond the Ashes.* Virginia Beach, Virginia: A.R.E. Press, 1992.

Goldhagen, Daniel Jonah. *Hitler's Willing Executioners, Ordinary Germans and the Holocaust.* New York: Alfred A. Knopf, 1996.

Grun, Bernard. *The Timetables of History.* New York: Simon & Schuster/Touchstone, 1975.

Hale, John. *The Civilization of Europe in the Renaissance.* New York: Atheneum, 1994.

Harrer, Heinrich. *Seven Years in Tibet.* New York: Jeremy P. Tarcher, 1982.

Heich, Elizabeth, *Initiation.* Palo Alto, California: Seed Center, 1974.

Howe, Ellic. *Astrology: A Recent History, Including the Untold Story of Its Role in World War II.*

Lagnado, Lucette Matalon and Sheila Cohn Dekel. *Children of the Flames: Dr. Josef Mengele and the Untold Story of the Twins of Auschwitz.* New York: William Morrow & Co., 1991; New York: Penguin Books, 1992.

Montgomery, Ruth. *The World Before*. New York: Fawcett Crest, 1976.

Netanyahu, Benzion. *The Origins of the Inquisition*. New York: Random House, 1995.

Phylos. *Dweller on Two Planets*. Borden Publishing Company, 1952.

Sugrue, Thomas. *There Is a River*. New York: Holt, Rinehart and Winston, 1942; Virginia Beach, Virginia; A.R.E. Press, 1972.

Trager, James. *The People's Chronology: A Year-by-Year Record of Human Events from Prehistory to the Present*. New York: Holt, Rinehart and Winston, 1979.

Wiesel, Elie. *Night*. New York: Hill and Wong, 1960; New York: Bamtam Books, 1982.

Wulff, Wilhelm. *Zodiac and Swastika, How Astrology Guided Hitler's Germany*. New York: Coward, McCann, and Geoghegan, 1973.

I am currently publishing a monthly newsletter to relate information, activities, and healing techniques (or developments) around the globe. Reports from light centers and treatment clinics springing up around the world will enable you to participate and share from a distance or will instruct you as to their whereabouts when you wish to visit them.

Discussion of current cycles, described by astrology, will keep you abreast of current trends and help you understand the significance of these major changes in your own life. You will be advised of patterns that relate to finance, land and real estate, and that indicate personal hot times to take action and to lay low. Articles by experts in the variety of fields connected to the healing profession—psychologists, psychiatrists, nutritionists, and financial analysts—will keep you in touch on many levels. Major changes are due that have not occurred in the last eighty-four years.

Each issue will be designed to keep you afloat, and in balance, in all areas of life. Fore-informed is fore-armed. It will be my joy to be in touch with you on a continuing basis.

Yours truly,
Jeanne Avery

--- DETACH AND RETURN THIS PORTION WITH YOUR PAYMENT ---

Please send check or money order in the amount of
☐ $49.95 for a one year, or
☐ $99.00 for a two year subscription to
Kaleidoscope, New Age Newsletter,
payable to Jupiter Pluto Communications,
1317 Third Avenue, Suite 100, New York, NY 10021.

Name

Address

City   State   Zip

Birth date   Time   Place

☐ Please send gift subscription in my name.
☐ Please send price list of services.

OTHER BOOKS BY JEANNE AVERY:

The Rising Sign, Your Astrological Mask

Astrological Aspects, Your Inner Dialogues

Astrology and Your Past Lives

Astrology and Your Health: A Practical Guide to Physical,

Mental and Spiritual Well-being

For information about individual appointments,
lectures, and workshops for your group, or about
Jeanne Avery's annual conference, "Healing in the New Age"
held in Ibiza, Spain, please contact
Jeanne Avery at
1317 Third Avenue, Suite 100, New York, NY 10021.
Telephone: (212) 371-4063.
Books can be ordered through the same address.

Jeanne Avery
Jupiter Pluto Communications
or Plutoh Publications
1317 Third Avenue, Suite 100
New York, NY 10021